Policing Domestic Violen

Policing Domestic Violence

Laura Richards
Criminal Behavioural Psychologist, Consultant Violence Adviser to ACPO

Simon Letchford
Detective Superintendent in the Metropolitan Police and Deputy Chair
of ACPO's Domestic Violence Steering Group, 2004–6

and

Sharon Stratton
Detective Sergeant in the Metropolitan Police

OXFORD
UNIVERSITY PRESS

OXFORD
UNIVERSITY PRESS

Great Clarendon Street, Oxford OX2 6DP

Oxford University Press is a department of the University of Oxford.
It furthers the University's objective of excellence in research, scholarship,
and education by publishing worldwide in

Oxford New York

Auckland Cape Town Dar es Salaam Hong Kong Karachi
Kuala Lumpur Madrid Melbourne Mexico City Nairobi
New Delhi Shanghai Taipei Toronto

With offices in

Argentina Austria Brazil Chile Czech Republic France Greece
Guatemala Hungary Italy Japan Poland Portugal Singapore
South Korea Switzerland Thailand Turkey Ukraine Vietnam

Oxford is a registered trademark of Oxford University Press
in the UK and in certain other countries

Published in the United States
by Oxford University Press Inc., New York

British Library Cataloguing in Publication Data

Data available

Library of Congress Cataloging in Publication Data
Richards, Laura.
    Policing domestic violence / Laura Richards, Simon Letchford, and Sharon Stratton.
        p. cm.
    Includes index.
    ISBN 978-0-19-923674-9
1. Family violence–United States. 2. Police–United States.
3. Arrest–United States. I. Letchford, Simon. II. Stratton, Sharon. III. Title.
    HV6626.2.R53 2008
    363.25'9555–dc22

                                                                        2008042634

Typeset by Laserwords Private Limited, Chennai, India
Printed in Great Britain by the MPG Books Group, Bodmin and King's Lynn

ISBN 978–0–19–923674–9

10 9 8 7 6 5 4 3 2

Foreword

This fascinating book cannot set out the political recipe for the elimination of domestic abuse worldwide, but it is surely right to consider the question, 'Why *are* people violent?', before you read much further. If we are to be better at preventing domestic abuse we have to understand cause as well as effect.

Whilst there is debate about whether we are violent simply *because we are*, it is by no means clear that people are inherently violent, and even those who are violent are not violent all of the time. So what is the cause? There are no simple ways in which to express the complexities of this otherwise straightforward question, but people become violent when they feel deprived of respect they consider they deserve. This absence of respect causes a sense of shame. Humiliation, rejection and frustration associated with shame inspire anger and, when ultimately there are no other means of restoring their pride, some people resort to violence. Violence, after all, gains attention.

According to this view, in societies like ours where power and respect are socially, economically, and politically construed but unequally held, violence is inevitable. It follows that when economically 'times are hard', violence, including domestic violence, will increase.

When we think about causes further, the stereotype of masculinity in many societies includes the *expectation* of the resort to violence by men in some circumstances which are socially approved (boys playing with toy guns and as soldiers, the 'stronger sex' concept, only male soldiers fight in wars, and so forth). That expectation is implicit, but in some households generations of people have copied violent behaviours which renders the expectation explicit, even routine. Some men only know violence as the means by which to express themselves and achieve their wants and needs.

So part of the big answers to the 'Why?' question lie in social and economic solutions to the imbalance of power in our society and to re-defining what it means to learn to be a man—a 'primary prevention' approach expressed in health terms.

Yet the majority of men are not violent and the general population even less so, so how do we spot the violent individual before he or she does harm? The simple answer is we can't with any precision, but we can use our available knowledge to help 'filter' the individuals and situations in which the risk of violence is likely to be higher—a 'secondary prevention' approach.

Some observers suggest that law enforcement and criminal justice are irrelevant, even worthless, in preventing violence because the big 'Why?' answers remain unaddressed by successive governments. I don't agree. There is much to commend the 'tertiary approach'—criminal justice engagement in the management of domestic violence—whilst we improve our knowledge of and approach to the primary and secondary prevention approaches. Indeed, if the broad range of crime statistics produced over the last decade is to be believed, then concerted effort by the State has had a positive effect in reducing the incidence and severity of violence in the home. Lives are saved daily through the personal and collective efforts of public servants of whom we should be proud and protective. This should be the expectation even when they are accused of failure based upon the 'science of hindsight' after tragedy strikes, provided they did their best to protect and safeguard those in harm's way.

This book is directed towards helping the operational practitioner and concerned observer to understand the epistemology of domestic abuse, especially in trying to discern from amongst the sheer volume of incidents an appropriate response that is right each and every time.

But what does 'right' mean and who needs to think it is 'right'? I remember feeling shocked when I first heard the views of some medical professionals about their obligation to a victim of domestic abuse. If that victim was 'competent' to understand their situation and chose to continue with it, then that was a matter for them and for them alone. Contrast that appreciation of obligation with the perception of the police officer whose first duty is to protect life. There is no time constraint put on the officer's obligation; so is it just during the period of the immediate police attendance or indefinitely? Opinion rapidly diverges even amongst experts around the necessity of a continuous commitment, especially if the victim does not welcome the engagement of the State. The strict legal view is that the police (along with many agencies) have a broad moral duty to protect all human life but a narrower and more specific duty of care to protect a *specific* life in circumstances defined in law. Not everyone knows or appreciates this.

Occasionally, members of the police service and other public authorities confuse their moral and legal duties, especially when driven by the hurt of anguished families and the media. The police are not under a duty of care to each and every citizen in all circumstances all of the time. If they were, they would have to consider putting the 'at risk' victim in some form of protective custody, possibly in spite of her wishes to the contrary. Unpalatable as this is, it is a logical extension of the argument that all people must be protected all of the time. Nevertheless, every domestic abuse fatality following police contact damages trust and confidence in the police and other agencies because it preys upon our sense of vulnerability and our primal understanding that those we love and who profess to love us can do us no harm.

In this complex mix of moral and legal duties, it is essential that the police and their partners have a rigorous and robust process that helps them to identify where and when the risk of future harm is greatest. Whilst good professional risk management is vital, it must be stressed that homicide cannot be predicted and, regrettably, mistakes will be made. Agencies must not allow the routine inference to take root that a tragedy means someone (other than the criminal) is to blame. Our approach must be driven by the overriding objective to allow people to live a normal, violence-free life. Professionals must take risks to ensure that good things happen as well as preventing bad outcomes.

I sincerely hope this book will help critics, concerned professionals and interested observers to consider the positive obligations of risk management rather than just ascribing blame to tragic outcomes.

I contribute this foreword with great pleasure, not least because the subject has occupied my waking thoughts throughout my career and also because of my admiration for the authors whom I have worked with for almost a decade. I have found their commitment, knowledge and wisdom an inspiration. They know what works in domestic abuse but recognize the realities of the crowded agenda, the scarce resource, where politics and egos intrude and the 'interest' of figures with the potential to do some good is all too short. Yet, they remain steadfast to do more to save lives and I truly admire them for what they have given of themselves and their experiences to public service. They are too modest even to consider it but I have no doubt that their efforts have saved many, many lives and will continue to do so.

We are privileged to have this artefact of their experience; to be able to challenge them and ourselves but ultimately to develop our understanding of a phenomenon that will affect thousands of people throughout this country and beyond, even during the time it will take to read this book. When you put the book down and have taken from it all that you can, have the confidence and resolve that you can do more now to keep people safe when those who should love them turn to abuse and violence. How many books have you read that will save lives? This is one of them so read on.

Brian Moore
Chief Constable
Association of Chief Police Officers
Lead for Domestic Abuse
August 2008

Acknowledgements

The authors would like to express their appreciation to colleagues in a number of organizations, statutory and voluntary, who helped inspire and inform this book and who have commented on early drafts. There are many voluntary women's organizations that make a difference every day to the lives of victims and survivors and who have helped us to better understand the complexities of DV.

In particular we would like to thank: Davina James Hanman for all her help in both keeping the focus on victims safety and holding offenders to account, as well as commenting on early draft chapters; Jim Gamble, and latterly, Brian Moore for their ACPO leadership in driving the work forward, leading to a significant improvement in recent years in how the police deal with domestic violence; and last but not least, John Grieve for giving us the inspiration to try something different and for his support and encouragement to write this book in the first place.

Organizations, as well as individuals, have provided practical assistance and access to information: National Police Improvement Agency (NPIA); the Home Office; Coordinated Action against Domestic Abuse (CAADA); and Women's Aid. At Oxford University Press we are grateful to Lindsey Davis for help and guidance during the writing of this book.

We would also like to thank our partners and families who have supported us in writing this book. In particular, Sharon would like to pay tribute to her mother, who was so proud that she was involved in writing the book but unfortunately did not live to see the end result.

Contents

Abbreviations

ABE	Achieving Best Evidence
ABH	Actual Bodily Harm
ACPC	Area Child Protection Committee
ACPO	Association of Chief Police Officers
AGG	Attorney General's Guidelines
APACS	Assessments of Policing and Community Safety
ASBOs	Antisocial Behaviour Orders
BCS	British Crime Survey
BCU	Basic Command Unit
CAADA	Coordinated Action Against Domestic Abuse
CAF	Common Assessment Framework
CAFCASS	Children and Family Court Advisory and Support Service
CAIU	Child Abuse Investigation Unit
CCTV	Closed-Circuit Television
CDRP	Crime and Disorder Reduction Partnership
CHIS	Covert Human Intelligence Source
CJA	Criminal Justice Act (2003)
CJPU	Criminal Justice Protection Unit
CJS	Criminal Justice System
CPIA	Criminal Procedure and Investigations Act (1996)
CPP	Child Protection Plan
CPROs	Community and Punishment Rehabilitation Orders
CPS	Crown Prosecution Service
CROs	Community Rehabilitation Orders
CTN	Child to Notice
DAC	Deputy Assistant Commissioner
DASH	Domestic Abuse, Stalking and Harassment, and Honour-Based Violence Risk Model (2008)
DCA	Department for Constitutional Affairs
DHSS	Department of Health and Social Security
DNA	Deoxyribonucleic acid
DOB	Date of Birth
DPA	Data Protection Act 1998
DV	Domestic Violence
DVCAVA	Domestic Violence Crimes and Victims Act (2007)
DVLA	Driver and Vehicle Licensing Agency
ECHR	European Convention on Human Rights
ECM	Every Child Matters

EPO	Emergency Protection Order
F&CO	Foreign and Commonwealth Office
FCP	Family Court Proceedings
FGM	Female Genital Mutilation
FLINTS II	West Midlands Police Crime Reporting System
FLO	Family Liaison Officer
FM	Forced Marriage
FME	Forensic Medical Examiner
FME	Force Medical Examiner
FMU	Forced Marriage Unit
FOIA	Freedom of Information Act (2000)
FTO	Foreign Travel Order
GBH	Grievous Bodily Harm
GP	General Practitioner
HBV	Honour-Based Violence
HMCPSI	Her Majesty's Crown Prosecution Service Inspectorate
HRA	Human Rights Act (1998)
IDAP	Integrated Domestic Abuse Programme
IDVA	Independent Domestic Violence Adviser
IKWRO	Iranian and Kurdish Women's Rights Organizations
INI	Impact Nominal Index
IO	Investigating Officer
IPCC	Independent Police Complaints Commission
ISPs	Information Sharing Protocols
IT	Information Technology
LGBT	Lesbian, Gay, Bisexual, and Transgender
LSCB	Local Safeguarding Children Board
MAPPA	Multi-Agency Public Protection Arrangements
MAPPP	Multi-Agency Public Protection Panel
MARAC	Multi-Agency Risk Assessment Conference
MO	Modus Operandi
MoPI	Management of Police Information
MPS	Metropolitan Police Service
NAWP	Newham Asian Women's Project
NCRS	National Crime Reporting Standards
NFA	No Further Action
NGO	Non-Government Organization
NHS	National Health Service
NIM	National Intelligence Model
NO	Notification Order
NPIA	National Police Improvement Agency
NRPSI	National Register of Public Service Interpreters
NSPCC	National Society for the Prevention of Cruelty to Children
OASys	Offender Assessment System

OBTJ	Offender Brought to Justice
OIC	Officer in the Case or Officer in Charge
PACE	Police and Criminal Evidence Act (1984)
PATP	Proactive Assessment and Tasking Proforma
PCT	Primary Care Trust
PHA	Protection from Harassment Act
PII	Public Interest Immunity
PLANBI	Proportionate, Legal, Accountable, Necessary, based on Best Information/Intelligence
PNC	Police National Computer
PPAF	Policing Performance Assessment Framework
PPOs	Prolific and Priority Offenders
RAMP	Risk Assessment Management Panel
RIPE	Reassurance, Intelligence, Prevention, and Enforcement
RMP	Risk Management Panels
RoSHOs	Risk of Sexual Harm Orders
RV	Repeat Victimization
SBS	Southall Black Sisters
SDVC	Specialist Domestic Violence Court
SHA	Strategic Health Authority
SIO	Senior Investigating Officer
SOA	Sexual Offences Act (2003)
SOCPA	Serious Organised Crime and Police Act (2005)
SOPs	Standard Operating Procedures
SOPOs	Sexual Offences Prevention Orders
ST&CG	Strategic Tasking and Coordinating Group
TDA	Taking and Driving Away
TT&CG	Tactical Tasking and Coordinating Group
USI	Unlawful Sexual Intercourse
VISOR	Violent and Sex Offenders Register
VIVID	Vulnerable and Intimidated Victims Database
VPS	Victim Personal Statement
VSS	Victim Support Services
WNC	Women's National Commission
WSW	Women's Safety Worker
YO/AT	Youth Offending/Action Teams
YOI	Young Offenders Institute

Table of Cases

Table of Legislation

(References to articles in the ECHR have been tabled under Schedule 1 of the Human Rights Act)

Tables and Figures

1

Introduction

1.1 **Introduction**

This is the book that the authors have wanted to write for some time. We have all been involved, for many years, in advising both government and the Association of Chief Police Officers (ACPO) on domestic-violence policy and guidance, as well as delivering training to practitioners nationally and internationally. We are often asked for the material presented; we hope that this book meets the challenge of bringing all the material together so that it is readily accessible for practitioners to dip in and out of it as required. Market research would also appear to support the need for a practical book of this kind.

It is essential that we do not forget the many areas of good practice and learning that have been developed over the years if we are to continue to make a difference for the many victims and survivors of domestic violence. The intention is to provide those working in the field of domestic violence with easy-to-use guidance about new developments and techniques regarding the investigation and prosecution of cases, intelligence-led activity in terms of targeting offenders, risk identification, assessment, and management, how to conduct homicide reviews, the use of civil law and other protective measures, as well as issues relating to so-called honour-based violence.

1.2 **The Domestic Violence, Crime and Victims Act 2004**

Too often the crime of domestic violence is hidden away, but we are determined to bring it out into the open and show that much more can be done proactively in this area. The Domestic Violence, Crime and Victims Act 2004 introduced new powers for the police and courts to deal with offenders, while bolstering the support and protection that victims receive. Key highlights from this Act are:

- making common assault an arrestable offence (superseded by SOCPA 2005)
- significant new police powers to deal with domestic violence including making it an arrestable offence to breach a non-molestation order, punishable by up to five years in prison
- strengthening the civil law on domestic violence to ensure cohabiting same-sex couples have the same access to non-molestation and occupation orders as opposite-sex couples, and extending the availability of these orders to couples who have never lived together or been married
- stronger legal protection for victims of domestic violence by enabling courts to impose restraining orders when sentencing for any offence (until now, such orders could only be imposed on offenders convicted of harassment or causing fear of violence)
- enabling courts to impose restraining orders on acquittal for any offence—or if a conviction has been overturned on appeal—if they consider it necessary to protect the victim from harassment (this will deal with cases where the

conviction has failed but it is still clear from the evidence that the victims need protecting)
- putting in place a system to review domestic-violence homicide incidents, drawing in the key agencies, to find out what can be done to put the system right and prevent future deaths
- providing a code of practice, binding on all criminal justice agencies, so that all victims receive the support, protection, information, and advice they need
- allowing victims to take their case to the Parliamentary Ombudsman if they feel the code has not been adhered to by the criminal justice agencies
- setting up an independent Commissioner for Victims to give victims a powerful voice at the heart of government and to safeguard and promote the interests of victims and witnesses, encouraging the spread of good practice and reviewing the statutory code
- giving victims of mentally disordered offenders the same rights to information as other victims of serious violent and sexual offences
- giving the Criminal Injuries Compensation Authority the right to recover from offenders the money it has paid to their victims in compensation
- a surcharge to be payable on criminal convictions and fixed-penalty notices which will contribute to the Victims Fund—for motoring offenders the surcharge will only apply to serious and persistent offenders
- closing a legal loophole by creating a new offence of causing or allowing the death of a child or vulnerable adult (the offence establishes a new criminal responsibility for members of a household where they know that a child or vulnerable adult is at significant risk of serious harm)
- bringing in the Law Commission recommendation for a two-stage court trial to ensure that high-volume crimes like fraud and internet child pornography can be punished in full.

However, intervention and prevention must occur at a much earlier stage in order to address its root causes. Whatever form it takes, domestic violence is rarely a one-off incident. More usually it is a pattern of abusive and controlling behaviour through which the perpetrator seeks power over their victim. Domestic violence occurs across society, regardless of age, gender, race, sexuality, wealth, or geography. The figures show, however, that it consists mainly of violence by men against women.

1.3 **Multi-Agency Response**

Victims of domestic violence suffer on many levels—health, housing, education—and lose the freedom to live their lives how they want and without fear. We aim to support victims of domestic violence with a range of new measures, as well as target repeat, prolific, and violent offenders and hold them to account. To be most effective a multi-agency response is required.

Domestic violence is not a new type of crime and will always require a multi-agency response. It is pervasive and pernicious and destroys the fabric of society. The costs run high: domestic violence costs the lives of more than two women every week and the estimated total cost of domestic violence to society in monetary terms is **£23 billion per annum**. This figure includes an estimated **£3.1 billion** as the cost to the state, **£1.3 billion** as the cost to employers, and human suffering costs of **£17 billion** (Walby, 2004). The estimated total cost is based on the following:

- The cost to the criminal justice system is **£1 billion per annum**. (This represents one quarter of the criminal justice budget for violent crime including the cost of homicide to adult women annually of £112 million.)
- The cost of physical healthcare treatment resulting from domestic violence, (including hospital, GP, ambulance, prescriptions) is £1,220,247,000, ie **3 per cent of total NHS budget**.
- The cost of treating mental illness and distress due to domestic violence is **£176,000,000**.
- The cost to the social services is **£0.25 billion**.
- Housing costs are estimated at **£0.16 billion**.
- The cost of civil legal services due to domestic violence is **£0.3 billion**.

The statistics collated by Walby above are recognized as an **underestimate** because public services do not collect information on the extent to which their services are used as a result of domestic violence. The research does not include costs to those areas for which it was difficult to collect any baseline information—for example the cost to social services for work with vulnerable adults, the cost to education services, the human cost to children (including moving schools and the impact this has on their education), and it excludes the cost of therapeutic and other support within the voluntary sector.

Equally, domestic violence cannot be separated from domestic homicide. The cost of domestic homicide is estimated by the Home Office at over £1 million: a total of £1,097,330 for each death, or £112 million per year.

1.4 Aims of this Book

Many have believed for a long time that nothing proactive can be done when dealing with domestic violence. Therefore much of the policing response, historically, has been reactive. The objective of this book is to illustrate that, using different techniques, it is possible to reduce the prevalence of domestic violence whilst increasing the rate that domestic violence is reported, reduce the number of homicides as well as increase the number of offenders brought to justice, and ensure that domestic-violence victims are supported and protected across the UK. These objectives are also in keeping with the government's national plan on domestic violence. This book aims to provide practical advice and support to those who are charged with the responsibility of acting on this plan and 'police' the area of domestic violence.

It is important to note that the meaning and practice of 'policing' are changing in the light of the challenges faced by the public police and other criminal justice agencies. The term 'policing' has now been extended to include the activities of other agencies. Policing can no longer simply be understood solely as the activity of the public police institution (Wright, 2002). It is now the output of a variety of agencies with multiple objectives and lines of accountability and as a consequence it is no longer acceptable to speak of policing as though it relates to the activities of a single organization.

1.4.1 **Risk**

Equally, like the insurance industry, the police service is now in the risk business and 'risk society'. However, the police aim to prevent harm rather than offer compensation after the event. How far can prevention be taken? Consider the threat to life. The service has an obligation to protect the life of someone who faces known danger. The police service cannot guarantee life, but may be required to show that it took reasonable measures to guard a known individual against a known threat and did not carelessly or callously neglect its duty to do so. The main issue revolves around what is meant by 'reasonable'. The judgement about what degree of protection to provide an individual or group must be a matter of judgement that changes in the light of changing circumstances, including acting on confidential intelligence. The process of risk identification, assessment, and management assumes huge significance and it is imperative that officers are using robust and evidence-based processes that have been tried and tested to inform their decision-making.

The failure to consider risks and apply an appropriate strategy constitutes negligence. Court interpretations of Article 2 ECHR, such as in *Osman* v *UK* (1998) 29 EHRR 245, illustrates this point. A positive obligation was held to exist where the authorities:

> knew or ought to have known at the time of the existence of a real and immediate risk to life of an identified individual or individuals from the criminal acts of a third party and that they failed to take measures within the scope of their powers which, judged reasonably, might have been expected to avoid that risk.

Investigators and managers should take reasonable measures to manage foreseeable risks. The advent of the public inquiry, Article 2 hearings, or Independent Police Complaints Commission (IPCC) investigation are all too familiar, particularly regarding domestic-violence homicides whereby it has been deemed more could have been done to prevent a homicide.

Since 1 April 2004, the IPCC have investigated 17 domestic-violence cases (IPCC personal communication, April 2008). Ten of those IPCC cases highlighted in the Learning the Lesson Bulletin 1 on domestic violence (June 2007) which focused on the response of the police to the victim. Historically, this was an area that gave rise to serious failures in policing. Equally, Richards' (2003) report entitled *Findings from the Multi-Agency Domestic Homicide Reviews*, prepared for ACPO, also highlighted many of the same issues in terms of the police response. Great progress has been made in recent years, following the introduction by ACPO in 2004 of detailed guidance on investigating domestic violence and its statutory reinforcement by the Domestic Violence, Crime and Victims Act 2004. These cases suggest, however, that there may be some way to go before good practice is embedded throughout the police service. Findings from the thematic review by the IPCC on domestic-violence investigations highlight the need for a coordinated overview of all relevant incidents and intelligence by staff with specialist training in domestic violence. Domestic violence requires an inclusive and co-ordinated response—coherent control of the investigation on the one hand and effective communication with the victim on the other coupled with robust risk assessments made on the basis of the full picture and information shared with other forces and agencies as relevant.

1.5 **Summary**

ACPO and Home Office guidance aims to improve how the police investigate domestic violence, but serving officers are not compelled to undergo training in this field. It is therefore essential that all officers have access to guidance on effective police responses to domestic violence. The principal audience of this book are police investigators, domestic-violence specialists, those who work in the intelligence arena, along with statutory agencies such as Health, Education, Social Care, the Crown Prosecution Service (CPS), and voluntary agencies such as non-government organizations (NGOs) working in domestic violence such as Refuge and Women's Aid. The book has been structured with this wide audience in mind: plain English explanations cross-referenced against original texts; case-law citation and explanation; operational considerations; case studies; extracts of relevant legislation; and good-practice examples—all between two covers. Trainee investigators, students, and an academic audience (in the fields of law, criminology, psychology, sociology, police studies, politics, and social administration, for instance) will also find this a useful introduction to policing domestic violence. With this audience in mind, further information references have been included to guide readers towards detailed academic argument that practitioners may want to follow up. It is not the intention of the book to place too much focus on the academic debate on aspects of domestic violence, but rather provide practical guidance to practitioners.

The chapter structure throughout the book is thematic. It begins with putting domestic violence into context, the intelligence approach, and the effective investigation. Following on from that, risk identification, assessment, and management is discussed and good-practice models are provided. This is an area often overlooked by investigators, along with children as victims and witnesses, and so-called honour-based violence. The last couple of chapters discuss s 9 domestic-homicide reviews, the much-debated topic of information-sharing, ending on civil law and other protective measures. Chapters are structured around questions that have been frequently debated by practitioners. Each chapter is intended to be a self-sufficient reference guide. Readers of the entire book will notice a few areas of repetition of some points. This has been preferred to cross-referencing and is in keeping with the style of the publishers. Various features such as definition boxes, bullet-point lists, key points, checklists, and flow charts have been included in the chapters to ensure it is easy to follow and digest. Case studies have been used and most of these are scenarios encountered by the authors and other colleagues.

It is hoped that this book will be an important contribution and increase awareness for investigators and other practitioners working in the field. At the time of writing the book, ACPO, in association with the National Police Improvement Agency (NPIA), have been reviewing the original Investigative Guidance from 2004, the Guidance on Identifying, Assessing and Managing Risks in the Context of Policing Domestic Violence (2005), and developing the Domestic Abuse, Stalking and Harassment, and Honour-Based Violence (DASH, 2008) risk tool kit through the ACPO Domestic Abuse Risk Expert Panel. DASH (2008) is consolidated good practice from both the SPECSS+ and South Wales risk models. Further questions have been incorporated into the model from cutting-edge research on stalking and harassment and honour-based violence. The outcome will be a common risk tool across police and partner agencies for referral to multi-agency risk-management panels such as the multi-agency risk assessment conference (MARAC) and multi-agency public protection panels (MAPPP). Hence, this book is very timely in terms of highlighting recognized good practice.

The authors hope that this book will make a difference to the many victims and survivors of domestic violence. This is the book that we all wish we could have read when starting out on our careers. It is no longer appropriate for us to say 'we did not know or understand' or to use the excuse 'we will learn the lessons from this tragic case' when yet another enquiry has found professional agencies wanting in their response to a domestic incident. The lessons do not change. We know what they are. We just have to make sure that we put into practice the guidance and learning captured within this book if we are to truly make a difference.

Putting Domestic Violence into Context

2.1 **Introduction**

This chapter provides an overview of what is meant by domestic violence and the different terminology used. It provides some key facts on the impact of domestic violence, highlights ten of the most common myths and stereotypes, and clearly identifies what victims want the police to do.

KEY POINT

In order to provide a more responsive and effective approach to domestic violence, it is essential that those who have a duty to investigate and prosecute cases have a clear understanding of the impact and consequences of a failure to respond appropriately.

2.2 **'Just a Domestic'?**

For many years the police response to allegations of domestic violence was insensitive, ineffective, and unprofessional. There was a significant under-reporting of incidents and a failure by police to recognize and understand the issues. It is fair to say that the attitude of police officers was a reflection of society in general, where domestic-violence victims were not seen as real victims of crime. 'Domestics' were seen as just arguments and disagreements between couples, something that went on behind closed doors and did not really affect the general public. The term 'just a domestic' was a well-used one in policing and led to the minimizing of the seriousness of domestic-violence incidents. It is worth remembering that it was only in 1992 that the House of Lords ruled that there was no longer a rule of law that a wife was deemed to have consented permanently to sexual intercourse with her husband; therefore, a husband could be convicted of rape or attempted rape of his wife where she had withdrawn her consent to sexual intercourse (*R v K* [1992] 1 AC 599 (HL)).

Historically, the police response would be to downgrade calls as a low priority, advise people on the phone, mediate between parties, and very often divert them out of the criminal justice system into civil courts dealing with the matter as a private affair. Very rarely would the offender be arrested. Officers would base their decision to arrest and charge on their own evaluation of the victim's willingness to support a prosecution. Victims were seen as reluctant and unfairly perceived as unreliable witnesses. This lack of effective police response exacerbated the problem further as officers felt even more frustrated when they were continually called back to the same address. This failure by police to correctly investigate and record such crimes meant that a true picture of the level, extent, and seriousness of domestic violence remained hidden.

The work of the women's movement in the UK and elsewhere over a significant number of years, campaigning for social change and legal reform, led to a challenging of attitudes both within society and more specifically the police and wider criminal justice system. Home Office circulars to chief constables in 1995 and 2000 highlighting the need to treat domestic assaults as seriously as other forms of assault, the introduction of the Crime and Disorder Act 1998, and more recently the Domestic Violence, Crime and Victims Act 2004 have further raised the importance of both the seriousness of domestic violence and the need for the police to work in partnership and consult with the local population and other agencies to improve the police response.

2.3 What is Domestic Violence?

Domestic violence is a broad term used to describe a range of behaviour, not all of which is violent or even criminal, that takes place within an intimate or family-type relationship. It can take place in lesbian, gay, bisexual, and transgender (LGBT) relationships, and can involve other family members, including children. It can include physical, sexual, emotional, psychological, or financial abuse, forced marriage or honour-based violence. It transcends all boundaries regardless of race, religion, age, or social background.

KEY POINT—DOMESTIC VIOLENCE IS USUALLY A PATTERN

Domestic violence is rarely a one-off incident; more usually it is a pattern of abusive and controlling behaviour through which the abuser seeks power over family members or intimate partners.

2.3.1 Defining domestic violence

There are and have been many different definitions for what is often referred to as domestic violence or abuse. Each agency has its own different role and set of responsibilities in tackling domestic violence and as such has its own definition. For example, within the criminal justice system (CJS), the role of the Crown Prosecution Service (CPS) means that it only responds to criminal offences, whereas the police are required to deal with all incidents of domestic violence.

Women's Aid defines domestic violence as physical, sexual, psychological, or financial violence that takes place within an intimate or family-type relationship and that forms a pattern of coercive and controlling behaviour. This can include forced marriage and 'honour crimes' and may include a range of abusive behaviours, not all of which are in themselves inherently 'violent'.

Other agencies use more gender-specific definitions to reflect the nature of the services they provide. It is also important to note that not all forms of domestic violence or abuse are in themselves criminal acts; for example, emotional abuse. However, irrespective of gender, sexuality, or race, every person has a right to live free of abuse and violence.

2.3.2 Terminology: Domestic violence or domestic abuse?

Although the term 'domestic violence' is used widely by a significant number of agencies, within the criminal justice system particularly you will also encounter the term 'domestic abuse'. Within this book both terms are interchangeable and for commonality the term 'violence' will be used. However, there is a move for all agencies to adopt the term 'abuse' as it reflects a pattern of behaviour which is both criminal and non-criminal in nature and better reflects the true nature of this type of incident.

There is a choice of term for those adversely affected by domestic violence, namely 'victim' or 'survivor'. The term most commonly used by the police and others working in the criminal justice system is victim. However, many of the agencies that work with women who experience domestic violence find the term victim demeaning and prefer to use the term 'survivor' as they feel it better reflects the experiences of these individuals.

2.3.3 The police definition of domestic violence

All police forces in England and Wales have now adopted the following Association of Chief Police Officers (ACPO) definition:

ACPO definition of domestic violence

'Any incident of threatening behaviour, violence or abuse (psychological, physical, sexual, financial or emotional) between adults, aged 18 or over, who are or have been intimate partners or family members regardless of gender or sexuality.'

(ACPO, 2004)

Family members are defined as mother, father, son, daughter, brother, sister, grandparents, in-laws, and step-family.

The scenarios below offer some insight into what constitutes a domestic-violence incident.

Scenario

A 25-year-old female has contacted police after receiving threats to kill her from her 30-year-old ex-boyfriend. They have been separated for 18 months and have never lived together.

This is a domestic-violence incident and should be dealt with by specialist domestic-violence officers. Although the relationship ended some time before the allegation, there may be other underlying issues or previous incidents which could raise the risk of future harm: for example, stalking or harassment which if not dealt with effectively and sensitively could lead to repeat offences or escalation in risk and harm.

Scenario

An 18-year-old girl has informed her teacher that her uncle assaulted her the previous night as she was refusing to marry a male chosen by her family.

This is not a domestic-violence incident. However, it may be an allegation of forced marriage and should be handled by an officer with experience of such matters. We know from experience that these incidents can lead to honour-based violence and need a sensitive police response if we are not to increase risks further. All domestic-violence officers should be trained to deal with forced marriages and other honour-based violence offences.

Scenario

Police are called to an address where the mother reports that her 22-year-old son has assaulted his 16-year-old brother.

This is not a domestic-violence incident and should be dealt with as an assault. The ACPO definition states 'between adults, aged 18 or over'; although both parties are family members, by reason of their ages this does not constitute a domestic incident. However, depending on individual circumstances such as repeat victimization or the vulnerabilities of either party, this may be suitable for a specialist police response, and allocated to a domestic-violence-trained officer to investigate.

Scenario

Police are called to an address where it is alleged that a father has beaten his 14-year-old son. There is previous history of domestic violence against a previous partner.

This is not a domestic-violence incident but is clearly a child-abuse matter and should be dealt with by the police child protection team. There are very often links between child and domestic abuse. We know that often men who beat their children also beat their partners. It is therefore essential that police domestic-violence units and child protection teams work closely to ensure that information is shared and a joint, coordinated response put in place where there are domestic-violence and child-protection concerns.

2.4 Who Commits Domestic Violence?

There is no typical abuser. They come from all walks of life and every cultural, religious, or social group. In many cases they display to the outside world a different kind of behaviour to that at home and some people find it difficult to believe that someone they know in public can be a domestic-violence abuser. This can make it even more difficult for the victim when seeking help and officers should not make judgements based on a person's position within society.

2.4.1 Can men be victims of domestic violence?

Although domestic violence can affect both men and women at some point in their lives, domestic violence and the fear of domestic violence disproportionately affects women. One in four women will be affected within their lifetime. However, men can also be affected and research shows that men are less often injured than women, considerably less frightened, and less likely to seek medical help or report to police. They are more often than not subjected to psychological abuse rather than physical violence. Women are considerably more likely to experience repeated and severe forms of violence including sexual violence and are more likely to be killed. This does not mean that the police response to male victims should be any less effective or responsive and all of the guidance within this book applies equally to male or female victims.

2.5 Different Forms of Domestic Abuse

Although every situation is unique it is helpful for police officers to understand and recognize many of the key indicators or common factors, not all of which amount to a criminal offence, that identify and link an abusive relationship. These can include:

Table 2.1 Key indicators and common factors of domestic abuse

Behaviour	Key indicators and common factors
Physical violence	Punching; slapping; hitting; biting; punching; kicking; pulling hair out; pushing; shoving; burning; strangling.
Sexual violence	Using force, threats, or intimidation to perform sexual acts; having sex when the victim does not want to; any degrading physical/verbal treatment based on sexual orientation.
Threats	Making angry gestures; using physical size to intimidate; shouting the victim down; destroying the victim's personal possessions; breaking things; punching walls; wielding a knife or a gun; threatening to harm them or the children.
Harassment	Unwanted attention such as following the victim; checking up; turning up uninvited; opening postal mail; repeatedly checking to see who has telephoned them; sending unwanted gifts such as flowers or chocolates; embarrassing them in public.
Denial	Saying the abuse does not happen; trivializing or downplaying what has happened; refusing to accept they have behaved inappropriately; if any of it is accepted, saying that the victim brought it upon themselves and caused the abusive behaviour or crying, begging for forgiveness, and saying it will never happen again.
Isolation	Monitoring or blocking the victim's telephone calls; monitoring or blocking of emails; restricting where they can or cannot go; preventing them from seeing their friends and relatives; making them ask for money.
Destructive criticism and verbal abuse	Shouting; mocking; accusing; name calling; verbally threatening; belittling; degrading; undermining.
Disrespect	Persistently putting the victim down in front of other people; not listening or responding when they talk; interrupting telephone calls; taking money from them without asking; refusing to help with childcare or housework.
Breaking trust	Lying to the victim; withholding information from them; being jealous; having other relationships; breaking promises and shared agreements.
Pressure tactics	Sulking; threats to withhold money from the victim; disconnecting the telephone; taking the car away; threats to commit suicide; taking the children away; threats to report them to welfare agencies unless they comply with demands regarding the children; lying to family and friends about them; telling them they have no choice in any decisions.

2.6 How Serious is the Problem of Domestic Violence?

Domestic violence is a serious, under-reported problem that generates other crime and violence and contributes to a variety of costly issues affecting families, children, communities, schools, and employers. For police officers it is also one of the most common calls and often the most common violence-related call. There are many statistics concerning domestic violence but listed below are just some of those that have a direct impact on policing.

KEY POINTS—DOMESTIC VIOLENCE AND POLICE

- Domestic violence accounts for 17% of reported crime (Nicholas, Povey, Walker and Kershaw, 2005).
- Domestic violence accounts for 16% of all violent crime (Home Office, 2008a).
- On average two women a week are killed by a male partner or former partner (Home Office, 2008a).
- 40% of all female homicide victims are killed by their current or ex-partner compared with about 5% of male homicide victims (Povey, 2005).
- Domestic violence is the largest cause of morbidity in women aged 19–44, greater than war, cancer, and motor vehicle accidents (Krug et al, 2002).
- About 1 in 4 women and 1 in 6 men have been a victim of domestic violence since the age of 16, though women are likely to suffer greater injury and be classed as chronic victims (Walby and Allen, 2004).
- 89% of those suffering four or more attacks are women (Walby and Allen, 2004).
- One incident is reported to the police every minute (Stanko, 2000).
- Domestic violence is most likely to result in repeat victimization and more likely to result in injury than any other type of crime (Home Office, 2008a).
- In monetary terms it costs society £23 billion per annum (Walby, 2004). The cost to the criminal justice system is £1 billion.
- Abused women are at least four times more likely to attempt suicide than women who are not at risk, particularly if recently abused (Golding, 1999).
- Children witness about three-quarters of abusive incidents. About half the children in such families have themselves been badly hit or beaten. Sexual and emotional abuse are also more likely to happen in these families (Royal College of Psychiatrists, 2004).

2.7 Why Do Victims Call the Police?

The main reason is because they are looking for immediate protection and help from the police. Equally, they may have had enough of the violence and threats and want someone to make it stop. There may have been an escalation or life-threatening incident and they are in genuine fear of their own and their children's safety. The offender may well have left the address for a short time or be in another room giving them an opportunity to call for help. Sometimes these calls will be from friends, neighbours, or members of the public, usually at a point of crisis, and often in response to either a request from the victim or something they have witnessed or heard. In all cases the police response should be immediate to establish the nature of the incident.

2.7.1 Victims' experiences

In 2003 the Women's National Commission (WNC) published a report, entitled *Unlocking the Secret*, which highlighted many of the experiences of victims of domestic violence and in particular their contact with the police. Some examples of these experiences are given below:

> I had to jump out of a bathroom window. He smashed down the door; he had a carving knife. I was hysterical. But he told the police I was having mental problems and they wished him luck! I was desperate but there was no point calling them again and he loved it; they played right into his hands. (WNC, 2003: 12)

KEY POINT—INVESTIGATE ALL ALLEGATIONS

Very often victims are panic stricken and are in crisis, which is not surprising in this set of circumstances where she has escaped with her life. Offenders will use this to cover their own actions portraying the victim as suffering mental illness and that this is the cause of the problem. Officers must investigate all allegations to corroborate or refute each person's account—in this case was there damage to the door? Where is the bathroom window? Where is the knife? Would a forensic examination support the victim's account?

Doing nothing is not an option.

> My experience is that the first few times I called the police for help I did not get much sympathy from them. I put up with the domestic violence for a few years and the police were saying 'if you put up with it for so long, why are you now reporting it?' (WNC, 2003: 12)

KEY POINT—POLICE RESPONSE

Many victims suffer years of abuse before they report to police. There are many reasons why. When they do finally contact police, an unsympathetic response can have a significant impact on future reporting and lead to increased risks to the victim. Officers must investigate each case thoroughly, deal with the facts presented, and not pre-judge any likely outcome or the motives for making an allegation.

2.7.2 **What do victims want the police to do?**

The initial police response can have a significant impact on both the victim and the outcome of the contact. Most victims found that being believed, taken seriously, and being put in touch with local support agencies was key to enabling them to remove themselves from the violence and ensure the protection of themselves and their children.

Victims want the police to:

- provide a fast response when they are in danger and need help
- believe them and not judge or ask them questions (such as 'what did you do?')
- speak to them away from the offender
- assist them to find or access other support agencies that can help them either with physical changes such as accommodation or emotional support
- collect evidence at the scene including speaking with family and neighbours as long as this is done thoughtfully and they are kept up to date with developments
- stay in touch for a sufficient time to enable them to access these services
- take the decision to prosecute out of their hands, as long as appropriate support is provided
- be trained in domestic-violence issues so they understand it properly

2.8 **Positive Action and Arrest**

In cases where a power of arrest exists it will normally need to be exercised to allow the investigation to be completed and/or to prevent further offences.

KEY POINT—PURSUE ALL LINES OF ENQUIRY

When reporting or attending domestic incidents you have a duty to pursue all lines of enquiry. You will need to gather and preserve the widest range of evidence and not focus solely on the willingness of the victim to give evidence. Victims should never be asked if they want the offender arrested. The decision to arrest remains with the officer, not the victim; any decision to charge remains the responsibility of the CPS.

In *Osman v UK* (1998) 29 EHRR 245, it was held that the police could be liable for breach of Art 2 (Right to Life) Human Rights Act 1988 if they had not taken 'reasonable preventative operational measures' to avoid a 'real immediate' risk to life which they ought to have known about. Any questions to the victim along the lines of 'what do you want us to do?' are NOT appropriate.

Questions should relate to the offence in terms of what happened, the history of domestic violence and the victim's view of his/her situation, NOT his/her opinion on the appropriate action for the officer to take.

Positive action by police will enable the best evidence to be collected and offenders challenged about their behaviour. Many offenders will only stop offending when a power greater than them gets involved. Within an abusive relationship they very often have the power and control. By positive police interventions we take back that power and show the victim that they do not have to suffer, and the offender that their actions will not be accepted. Any failure to arrest where a power exists or to take positive action will result in increased risks to the victim and a perception by the offender that they are untouchable.

2.9 **Ten Myths and Stereotypes about Domestic Violence**

There are many myths and stereotypes surrounding domestic violence and many of these are perpetuated by police officers. It is essential that all officers fully understand these issues and the impact on victims if they are to be in a position to provide a professional response which makes victims and their children safer and holds abusers accountable for their actions.

TEN MYTHS AND STEREOTYPES ABOUT DOMESTIC VIOLENCE
MYTH 1. THEY MUST LIKE IT OTHERWISE WHY DON'T THEY JUST LEAVE?

FACT

Many victims often make repeated attempts to leave violent relationships but are prevented from doing so by increased violence and controlling and coercive tactics on the part of the abuser. Other factors which inhibit a victim's ability to leave include:

- **Fear of further violence:** Leaving may end the relationship but it does not always end the violence and abuse. Many victims are tracked down and further abused when they leave, often for weeks and months afterwards.
- **Lack of knowledge and access to help:** Despite increased awareness about domestic violence, many victims do not know how to use their legal and housing rights. Even if they are aware of these services, some may experience problems due to language difficulties, inappropriate responses from service providers, living in isolated areas, or a lack of funds.

- **Economic dependence:** The victim might be financially dependent on the perpetrator. If a victim is working, they may lose their job due to needing time off work, moving too far away, or staying off work so they cannot be found there. For others, becoming a single parent may mean working is no longer possible; others may face months of legal wrangling over property and other financial matters.
- **Staying because of the children:** Many victims think they should stay in their relationship for the sake of their children.
- **Social dependence:** Victims may like the rest of their lifestyle (social group, house, etc) and do not want to lose it. It is the abuse that they do not like and want to stop. They do not want to admit to others that the relationship has failed or they fear stigma, embarrassment, and the judgement of others if they knew about the abuse/violence.
- **Social isolation:** Most victims experiencing domestic violence are extremely isolated either because their partners have deliberately tried to isolate them from sources of support including family and friends or because they are too ashamed or afraid to tell anyone; or if they have, the responses have been unhelpful and judgemental.
- **Emotional dependence:** Conflicting feelings of fear, shame, bewilderment, feelings for the abuser, hope that things will improve, and a commitment to the relationship (but not the violence), often contribute to a victim staying in an abusive situation.
- **Lack of confidence:** After living with an abusive partner, the self-esteem of most victims has been eroded to the point where they no longer have confidence in themselves, including their ability to survive alone, and many believe that there are no other options.
- **Cultural reasons:** Many victims have been brought up to believe that real fulfilment comes from being a wife and mother or that divorce is wrong and may even be encouraged to stay in the relationship by family members or religious leaders.

MYTH 2. DRUG AND ALCOHOL ABUSE CAUSES DOMESTIC VIOLENCE

FACT

Abusers frequently make excuses for their violence, claiming loss of control due to alcohol or drug use, or extreme stress. Although drug and alcohol abuse may intensify existing violent behaviour, it does not cause domestic violence. In fact many abusers are not drunk when they assault their partner. Drugs, alcohol, and stress merely act as catalysts for the behaviour that already exists.

MYTH 3. VICTIMS PROVOKE THEIR PARTNER'S VIOLENCE

FACT

Victims are not to blame nor do they ever deserve such abuse. Victim provocation is no more common in domestic violence than in any other crime. Whatever problems exist in a relationship, the use of violence is never justified or acceptable.

MYTH 4. MOST ASSAULTS ARE REALLY JUST A COUPLE OF SLAPS AND THEY ARE NOT REALLY SERIOUS

FACT

Domestic violence accounts for more than a quarter of all violent crime (Home Office, 2008). It is the largest cause of morbidity in women aged 19–44, greater than war, cancer, and motor vehicle accidents (Krug et al, 2002). It is rarely a one-time occurrence and usually escalates in frequency and severity over time, causing more serious injury than any other type of crime. Any act of domestic violence should be taken seriously.

MYTH 5. SOME WOMEN GO FROM ABUSER TO ABUSER—IT MUST BE SOMETHING ABOUT THEM

FACT

Women who find that their second or third partner is an abuser will often be blamed by others for the violence—'it must be something about her' or she will blame herself—'I always seem to pick abusers'. Some men intentionally target vulnerable people and those that have previously been abused. The abuser may use the tactic of charm early in the relationship to find out that she was previously abused. He uses this information to blame her for the violence—'see, it must be something that you are doing wrong, or there would not have been two of us'—or to silence her—'you are not going to tell anyone, because if you do they will never believe you because you said that before'.

MYTH 6. IT MAINLY HAPPENS TO POOR WOMEN ON COUNCIL ESTATES

FACT

Women from poor and wealthy backgrounds experience domestic violence. However, although income levels do not affect whether you are abused, they do affect how you respond. Women on lower incomes are more likely to come to the notice of and/or use the police whereas middle-class women may be less likely to seek assistance because they fear personal embarrassment, shame, stigma, or the possible damage to their partner's career if the violence was disclosed.

MYTH 7. ABUSERS ARE MENTALLY ILL

FACT

Abuse tends to be a learned behaviour, not a mental illness. Abusers' experiences as children and the messages they get from society in general tell them that violence is an effective means to achieve power and control over their partners. It is also reinforced if it works and they get what they want. Abusers are accountable for their actions.

MYTH 8. DOMESTIC VIOLENCE IS ABOUT 'LOSS OF CONTROL'

FACT

Violent behaviour is a choice. Abusers use it to control their victims. Domestic violence is about perpetrators *using* their control, not *losing* their control. Their actions are very deliberate, such as directing their assaults to parts of the body where the bruises are less likely to show. Some can control their behaviour outside the home and mask it to other people. Others are violent inside and outside the home as it is their life-view and how they tend to behave in general or normally to women.

MYTH 9. MEN WHO ABUSE THEIR PARTNERS ARE OFTEN GOOD FATHERS

FACT

Men who abuse their partners are more likely to abuse the children in the home. Domestic violence is the number one predictor for child abuse. Even when children are not directly abused, they suffer as a result of witnessing one parent assault another. Abusers often display an increased interest in their children at the time of separation, as a means of maintaining contact with, and thus control over, their partners.

MYTH 10. VICTIMS EXAGGERATE THE ABUSE TO GET RE-HOUSED OR FOR CUSTODY OF THE CHILDREN

FACT

Victims are more likely to deny or minimize the abuse than to exaggerate it. The majority of victims have suffered many incidents of abuse before contacting police.

2.10 **Use of Advertising to Raise Awareness**

The role of the criminal justice system and specifically the police is to hold offenders accountable for their actions, enforce the rule of law, and to make victims and their children safer. The use of advertising to reinforce these messages has been found to have significant value in raising awareness, increasing reporting, and challenging behaviour.

In 2003 the Metropolitan Police Service (MPS) ran an advertising campaign: 'Your partners silence no longer protects you'. This was a direct change from the traditional campaigns run by police that encouraged victims to report abuse. This one specifically targeted the offenders of domestic violence in an attempt to confront offenders, as well as indicating that the police would seek out men who abused their partners even where the victim was unwilling to support a prosecution.

Figure 2.1 Your partner's silence no longer protects you

(MPS, 2003)

This campaign was followed during Christmas 2005, a time of high reporting, with: 'There are no longer any safe houses for men who commit domestic violence'. This campaign specifically targeted male offenders who made up 85 per cent of all offenders of domestic violence reported to police.

Figure 2.2 There are no longer any safe houses for men who commit domestic violence

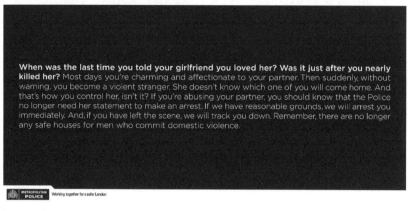

(MPS, 2005)

The campaigns featured posters on transport systems, in male washrooms, sporting venues, licensed premises, and—for the first time—a series of radio adverts. The idea was to challenge men when they least expected it.

Figure 2.3 Beer mats domestic violence campaign

(MPS, 2005)

2.11 **Effective Implementation—Measuring Success**

It is important that both police and non-police agencies implement a range of performance measure to monitor the impact of polices and procedures.

> **KEY POINT—POLICE PERFORMANCE ASSESSMENTS FRAMEWORK**
>
> The only national performance indicator at this time relevant to domestic violence is the Police Performance Assessments Framework (PPAF) Indicator 8a, which is: 'of Domestic Violence incidents, the percentage where an arrest was made related to the incident'.

PPAF will shortly be replaced with Assessments of Policing and Community Safety (APACS). This will enable the Home Office and partners with the capability to monitor and assess performance in relation to policing and community safety.

Other measures or themes for performance review that might be implemented include:

- domestic-violence incident statistics
- domestic-homicide statistics
- domestic-violence arrest and charge statistics
- domestic-violence-related crime statistics and detections
- repeat-victimization statistics (relevant to victims and repeat offending)
- case tracking and attrition rates
- policy compliance information
- service-user feedback on service provision
- feedback from other domestic-abuse providers
- successful outcomes as a result of multi-agency risk-assessment conferences (MARACs)
- performance information resulting from Crime and Disorder Reduction Partnership (CDRP) working, such as crime audits

All staff should be aware of domestic-violence performance measures and should be actively involved in maintaining and improving upon performance levels.

> **Further information and reading**
>
> Stanko, E (2000), 'The Day to Count: A snapshot of the impact of domestic violence in the UK', *Criminal Justice*, 1(2).
> Women's National Commission (2003), *Unlocking the Secret: Women open the door on domestic violence. Findings from consultations with survivors* (Women's National Commission).

3

An Intelligence-Led Approach

3.1 **Introduction**

This chapter will assist analysts and police to identify and target the most dangerous offenders and vulnerable victims within a National Intelligence Model (NIM)
compliant structure. It will also identify and highlight the links to other areas
of criminality including child abuse, sexual violence, stalking and harassment,
dangerous people/offenders, and the wider issues of public protection illustrated
by case studies. This effective use of intelligence across a range of offending will
allow for proactive targeting of perpetrators using an evidence-based approach.
Domestic violence provides lots of intelligence which is rarely analysed or used
effectively. The approach outlined in this chapter will help manage the volume
to identify and deal with the 'critical few'.

Police information on domestic violence can provide a grounded, evidence-
based approach to challenging understanding and agency responses in this area.
The information offered by those who contact the police for help, and recorded
by the police as criminal incidents, is an invaluable source of knowledge. The demand placed on key service providers by domestic-violence cases—one incident
of domestic violence is reported to police every minute (Home Office, 2008b)—
means that it is important to find ways to respond appropriately to the different
typologies of cases, nature of need, and levels of risk. These calls about domestic
violence include a wide range of incidents—from criminal damage to sexual assault. A joined-up, victim-oriented, intelligence-led approach to policing, which
holds the perpetrator accountable for their actions, can make a very specific contribution to the safety of victims of domestic violence.

The ideal model should be detectives working with the analysts and with academics. Academics can provide the framework for sound methodology when
analysing routinely collected data. Using methods of routinely collected information can not only provide a useful means to target resources more effectively
and provide officers with the tools to do their job, but the products of the research can also be used as an evidence base to change legislation.

Former Deputy Assistant Commissioner (DAC) John Grieve of New Scotland
Yard's Racial and Violent Crime Task Force put this into practice with a group of
experienced crime consultants who formed the Understanding and Responding
to Hate Crime Team. This Home-Office-funded team worked within an intelligence cell at New Scotland Yard, alongside dedicated and innovative analysts
and detectives. This model of operational intelligence was the interaction of academic research, data analysis, and practitioner tactical innovation that proved
to be one of the most successful Home-Office-funded targeted policing initiatives, resulting not only in organizational change implementing risk models and
homicide reviews (Chapter 9), but also contributed to a change in legislation.

Rigorous analysis undertaken by the Understanding and Responding to Hate
Crime Team (2001) evidenced that it is 'ordinary' crime, not the extraordinary,
that makes the bulk of the workload in the Police Service and has the greatest impact on people's lives in reality. To continue labouring under the misapprehension

that targeted violence is committed by the dangerous stranger is to lose context and the understanding that hatred and violence is more often found closer to home and too often directed at the intimate partner or neighbour, friend or acquaintance, as argued by Stanko (1990). The fact that the offender often knows, or knows of, the victim provides the offender with additional resources and makes the victim additionally vulnerable. The way in which anxiety about safety is publicly expressed serves to separate the fear of crime from private knowledge about danger. A common misconception is that a significant proportion of sexual offences are committed by strangers when, in fact, research suggests that the majority of such offences are perpetrated by someone known to the victim, such as a partner, family member, or acquaintance.

Another misconception is that offenders generally practise particular types of offence, such as sexual offences, violent offences, or property offences. In reality there is a considerable overlap between types of offence committed. It is crucial these links are made through intelligence and analysis across the field of public protection to avoid a repeat of lessons learnt from the Bichard Inquiry (2004), which highlighted an inability to identify the offender's pattern of behaviour over time, as well as failures in the gathering and use of intelligence and sharing information.

3.2 **What is Crime Analysis?**

There are six core types of crime analysis, detailed in the table below:

Table 3.1 Types of analysis

Type of analysis	Explanation
Strategic	Focuses on longer-term problems
Tactical	Involves analysing current crime problems
Administrative	Provides summary information and data on trends and patterns
Investigative	Profiles victims, suspects, networks, and associations
Intelligence	Focuses on organized crime where problems are already known
Operations	Examines the use of resources

Analysis is defined by both its function and its outcome, such as strategic analysis where the aim is to support strategy and by the type of information used, such as intelligence analysis.

This chapter briefly introduces six approaches to analysis. These approaches are interdependent:

3.2.1 Strategic analysis

This reviews the trends and patterns in context to support planning and policy decisions. It allows the police service to anticipate future developments and long-term planning around the nature of allegations, as well as the appropriateness of the police response.

3.2.2 Tactical analysis

This reviews current crime problems to support proactive operational activity. This can include crime-series identification, as well as profiling victims and suspects.

3.2.3 Behavioural analysis

This provides behavioural profiling of the victims and the perpetrator's offending behaviour. By profiling the offenders you can learn lessons about dangerousness, lethality, prevention, protection, and enforcement.

3.2.4 Investigative analysis

This reviews information and intelligence in line with an investigation.

3.2.5 Performance analysis

This reviews performance data.

3.2.6 Operational analysis

This provides analysis of the use of resources in the organization.

3.3 Understanding the Context of Domestic Violence

Domestic violence has always posed a special problem and difficulty to police. Domestic violence accounts for 18% of all violent crime in England and Wales (Home Office, 2008a). On average **two women a week are killed** by their current or ex partner: this constitutes around one-third of all female homicide victims (Povey, 2005).

Domestic violence is a persistent and consistent call on law-enforcement resources. Knowing how the incidents have similar patterns, overlap, and also how they differ will help direct crime prevention. Before starting any analysis, it makes sense to think about the questions which need to be answered, outlined in the checklist below.

Checklist: Key questions before starting any analysis

- When do the problems tend to peak: day of the week, time of day, any seasonal patterns, and what are long-term reporting trends?

- Is the problem an emerging problem, increasing, or has it been constant for some time?

- What is it about the areas where the problem is persistent?

- What do we know about the victims?

- Who are the repeat victims?

- What do we know about offenders?

- Who are the repeat offenders?

- Who are the most violent offenders?

- Who are the most violent repeat offenders?

- Do the offenders commit other crimes?

- Who are the sexual domestic-violence offenders?

- Are they committing offences outside the home?

- Has their forensic profile been taken? Is it currently stored on the national DNA database?

- What other sources of data can we use that will help us better to understand the problem? For example, what data is kept by the local probation, prisons, social care and health providers? Can we access that data?

- How many murders are domestic-violence-related?

- How many victims had previously reported domestic violence prior to the murder?

- Was the police/agency response appropriate?

- Could more have been done in terms of intervention and prevention?

- What risk model are you using?

- What tactical intervention options are available?

3.4 **Domestic Violence and the National Intelligence Model (NIM)**

In the UK the NIM is being promoted as a tool for improving the collection and use of intelligence. It was released to the police service, law enforcement agencies, and relevant public authorities in May 2000 and is the subject of UK-wide police implementation mandated by the Home Office (ACPO, 2005d).

The NIM introduces a doctrine and framework to normalize practices and eradicate inconsistencies. It sets out an operational structure for the organization of intelligence processes across police services. Principally, the model advocates a systematic procedure of gathering, storing, and analysing intelligence to support a tasking meeting that reviews problems and allocates police resources accordingly. The model recommends a specific meeting structure to develop fast time and slow time responses. As well as outlining specific analytical products, it also highlights a distinction between the three NIM levels as set out in Table 3.2.

Table 3.2 NIM levels

NIM Level	Explanation
Level 1	Defined as a crime that has a local impact which can be tackled by the local command unit.
Level 2	Defined as cross-border crime.
Level 3	Defined as national and international crime.

The NIM sets out how gaps in strategic and tactical knowledge can be filled by issuing intelligence requirements. The intelligence requirement is a series of questions about the available intelligence on the subject. Analysis is crucial to the theory of intelligence-led policing. The overarching strategic response drives the operational response, in terms of the problem and target profiles. The overall strategic position should determine which issues become subject to problem profiles which should give a more detailed understanding of the threat/problem. Each product informs what should happen next in terms of intelligence collection, dissemination, and enforcement. The conclusion of a problem profile should inform the selection of suspects to target. The intelligence requirements adopted in a target profile should reflect the intelligence gaps from the problem profile. This means that the intelligence effort becomes geared in part to addressing strategic gaps in knowledge.

Crime analysis has developed alongside the reliance on criminal intelligence to direct police activity, the growth of information, and the requirement to monitor police performance. The process of intelligence-led policing exemplifies concerns with identifying, prioritizing, and intervening to minimize risk.

3.4.1 **Domestic violence and the NIM structure**

All intelligence products inform the Tactical Tasking and Coordination Group (TT&CG), which is responsible for prioritizing, actioning, and disseminating the outcome of crime analysis.

Table 3.3 Summary of NIM products

NIM products	Description
Strategic assessment	An overview of domestic-violence performance, trends, patterns, and policing problems in context of strategic forecasts to inform planning and policy development. Informs the development of a control strategy.
Tactical assessment	A short-term review of domestic-violence crime problems with recommendations for policing-based activity.
Problem profile	A detailed analysis of a domestic-violence-related problem to inform the targeting process.
Subject profile	A detailed analysis and profile of an offender, to inform targeting decisions. For domestic violence, this could be in terms of proactive targeting, as well as problem-solving opportunities.

3.4.1.1 Tactical Tasking and Coordination Group

Previously domestic violence was not the subject of analysis or proactive targeting. Now practitioners and intelligence professionals MUST ensure, given the volume of the calls and the dangerousness of some of the offenders, that products are submitted to the TT&CG, which operates at both a strategic and tactical level.

The strategic meetings take place every three or six months, informed by the strategic assessment. They focus on developing the priorities in line with local and national objectives. The outcome of the meetings are the control strategies, which act as a plan to capture policing activities in relation to intelligence, prevention, and enforcement.

The tactical tasking meeting is every two weeks and is informed by the tactical assessment. Recommendations should be made in relation to **Reassurance, Intelligence, Prevention, and Enforcement (RIPE)**. The key aim is to target offenders proactively, manage hot spots, prioritize crime series, focus resources, and apply preventative measures. A new addition to this is structuring the presentations around:

- the intelligence picture in terms of patterns
- statistics and trends
- proactive subjects
- problem solving, if proactivity is not appropriate.

The problem-solving element around certain domestic-violence offenders should occur at the weekly operations meetings, when other specialist practitioners (field intelligence officers (FIOs), domestic-violence officers, sexual offences officers, missing persons officers, and members from the dangerous offenders unit, for example) are around the table. Options are discussed and a plan submitted to be sanctioned at the tasking meeting. This has proved an effective way of doing business, given that not every domestic-violence offender is suitable for proactivity. Where possible, all opportunities for proactive intervention should be exploited. There are other methods of detection and we can catch the offender in different ways that would not identify the victim or person reporting it. We should be asking, 'What has he got in his garage? Is he a drug trafficker? Is he a burglar? What does his intelligence profile show?' From thinking about the offender holistically, we can then start investigating that person.

3.5 Domestic-Violence Analysis

There is a need to be knowledge-based and understand patterns, particularly in terms of escalation of violence leading to lethality. The NIM works better for traditional volume crime, rather than serious crime. Therefore, it is necessary to develop further models and products for the purposes of intelligence-led police- and multi-agency-directed activity to tackle domestic violence. For instance, domestic homicide cannot be separated from domestic-violence incidents. Victims have often been in contact with key agencies for assistance prior to their death. The speed and/or quality of service providers' responses to abused individuals' emergency requests may have a direct bearing on whether or not a serious assault becomes a homicide. Research suggests certain characteristics could be more predictive of homicide than others. Hence the murder event should be 'mapped' in conjunction with domestic-violence incidents.

3.5.1 Identifying high-risk and repeat victims

There is also a need to identify high-risk and repeat victims, as well as high-risk and repeat offenders. Once identified, there is a need to respond and shape intervention strategies according to the needs of the victim, as well as target offenders. It is possible to identify people, locations, or situations associated with an exceptionally high risk of serious violence and target these individuals in terms of preventative interventions.

By viewing victims of domestic violence as the same as victims of other crimes, it is possible that service providers may inadvertently expose them to increased risks of repeated victimization and possible support options might be missed. Conversely, by viewing perpetrators of domestic violence as separate from perpetrators of other types of crime, it is possible that crucial intelligence is lost and possible tactics to disrupt the patterns of abuse are overlooked.

3.5.2 **Victim analysis and profiles**

Domestic abuse affects victims from all socio-economic backgrounds, occupations, religions, and races. It is crucial to understand the victimology. The victim is part of the crime that has been committed, just as the crime scene, particular words used by the offender, the offender, and other factors all are of paramount importance in understanding the context and profile of the offence. However, the victim profile does not tend to be looked at in real detail with regards to domestic violence. Information should be collected on:

- victim ages
- gender
- sexual orientation
- disability
- ethnicity
- employment status
- whether the victim is pregnant or has recently given birth
- if there are children in the household who are/have been victimized or subjected to abuse—they are normally secondary victims.

The victim profile should be analysed in conjunction with the population profile, to ascertain whether the victim profile reflects the population, or whether certain age groups or ethnic groups are disproportionately represented. For example, if immigrant communities are identified as under-reporting domestic abuse and sexual offences, a neighbourhood problem-solving plan might be required. Neighbourhood policing teams should work with the domestic-abuse coordinator to assist information-gathering and enforcement issues, as appropriate to their role profiles.

Aggregated information relating to the prevalence of reporting of domestic-abuse cases and the number of identified high-risk cases should also be considered for inclusion in neighbourhood profiles. The purpose of this profile is to record information about the neighbourhood and to assist the community engagement and collaborative process. Information relating to specific cases will not, however, be appropriate to include in any publicly available document.

3.5.3 **The importance of listening to what victims tell us**

It is important to listen to what victims are saying about offenders. It is crucial to understand how victims are targeted and victimized, and who else they think might be suffering at the hands of an abuser. This is to understand behaviour and equally to inform any risk assessment, management, and intervention opportunities to reduce the likelihood of future victimization.

The victim's perception of the level of risk is an important element that should be included in risk assessment as the victim has the most detailed knowledge of the suspect (Weisz et al, 2000). When victims are very frightened, when they report being afraid of further injury or violence, when they are afraid of being killed, and when they are afraid of their children being harmed, they are significantly more likely to experience additional violence, threats, and emotional abuse (Robinson, 2006a). Thus, victim perception cannot be ignored. Officers also should be aware that victims frequently underestimate their risk of harm from domestic abusers. Whilst not every assessment on the victim's part will be accurate, their fears for their own safety are integral in assessing the risks to them.

Many domestic-violence offenders are serial offenders, who go from one abusive relationship to the next. Once a violent man leaves his partner, it does not mean the violence ends. Evidence suggests that many find new partners to abuse (Richards, 2003). Hence, there are three victims involved in domestic violence: the primary victim; the secondary, who are the children; and the future victim whom the offender goes on to abuse. Furthermore, research into offending behaviour and studies of groups of offenders, their previous convictions, and offending history demonstrates that often offenders do not restrict their criminal activity to a single offence type (eg, sexual offences or violent offences) or to a single category of victim (eg, partner, child, adult, male, female, individuals in a particular age group, or with a particular appearance). Many offenders are not convicted for domestic violence, therefore the intelligence profile is crucial. Perpetrators that have a conviction for domestic violence-related offences are the exception rather than the norm (Hester, 2006; Hester and Westmarland, 2005, 2006). This has been evidenced by a number of high-profile cases, one of which is the case of Ian Huntley, found guilty of murdering Holly Wells and Jessica Chapman. In the days following Huntley's conviction, there was widespread public disquiet when it became clear that he had been known to the authorities over a period of years. In fact, he had come to the attention of Humberside police in relation to allegations of eight separate sexual offences from 1995 to 1999 (and had been investigated in yet another). This information had not emerged during the vetting check, carried out by Cambridgeshire Constabulary at the time of Huntley's appointment to Soham Village College late in 2001.

The Bichard Inquiry was set up by the Home Secretary to:

> Urgently enquire into child protection procedures in Humberside Police and Cambridgeshire Constabulary in the light of the recent trial and conviction of Ian Huntley for the murder of Jessica Chapman and Holly Wells. In particular to assess the effectiveness of the relevant intelligence-based record keeping, the vetting practices in those forces since 1995 and information-sharing with other agencies, and to report to the Home Secretary on matters of local and national relevance and make recommendations as appropriate.

Huntley had offended inside and outside the home, was known for forming relationships with young girls, had been reported for unlawful sexual intercourse, and was violent to his girlfriends. Many links were not made and the victims and their families were not listened to.

The Serious Case Review conducted by Sir Christopher Kelly (2004) highlighted the key issues:

> Huntley's history of serial sexual exploitation should have rung significant warning bells. . . Some connections that could have been made to identify a pattern in Huntley's behaviour were missed.

> There were significant shortcomings and inconsistencies in the way information was shared between some of the agencies, particularly Social Services and Police.

A number of case studies show similar issues; namely few offenders get convicted for domestic violence or rape offences. However, a lot of intelligence exists about what they are doing. If the intelligence and other databases had been searched, and the links made, a very different picture of the offender's level of dangerousness would have emerged. Many regions have previously not used this untapped reservoir to make the links across offending behaviour and criminality, identify patterns of repeat and serial behaviour, and risk-assess offenders. It is also of vital importance to officer safety when attending an address to know who they might be coming into contact with and what sort of weapons they may have at the address, for example.

Case study

The victim met the suspect five years ago when she was working as a nurse in Rampton. He was visiting a friend there. In this incident the suspect had been drinking and returned to home address. He **forced anal intercourse**. He also **forced an object up her anus** but the victim would not specify what. **He has a history of violence and has recently been released from prison for GBH on his ex-partner.** She was in intensive care for six months as a result of the assault. He is currently on licence for this offence. This is the **third time he has raped** the victim. On the last occasion, he said he would bring other men back to rape the victim as well. Suspect has a drink problem.

Previous crime reports:

The victim went to put the bins out. Suspect came out, kicked her over, accused her of spying on him, and threatened to break her legs. He then pulled out a knife and said he was going to kill her. The victim would not tell police who suspect was. She had been beaten all over body and face. In another incident he wielded a knife at victim and threw it at her. He had been waiting outside the house for the victim to come home.

A search of the intelligence database revealed several 'hits' on the named suspect:

Entry 1   Suspect was recently released from prison for GBH on ex-partner in Nottingham. Served 20 months. He is extremely violent. Has martial-arts background.

A search of the Police National Computer (PNC) also showed that the suspect had warnings for offending on bail. He also had other offences recorded against his name: nine offences against person; **1 sexual offence (USI)**; 10 offences against property; 10 theft; 1 public disorder; 1 offence courts/police; 3 firearms; and 2 miscellaneous.

Checklist—Victim analysis

- Analysis of the main victim groups can help ensure that resources are targeted at the right people.

- Are there any gaps or under-reporting issues within particular communities?

- Are there children in the household? Do not forget that children in the home address may also be victims of the domestic violence.

- Are patterns of abuse similar for female and male victims?

- Are any same-sex incidents recorded? What are the patterns of abuse?

- Are the victim and offender separated? This is a heightened risk factor.

- The victim profile should concentrate on factors that have been shown to be risk factors for domestic violence—as outlined in the ACPO Domestic Abuse, Stalking and Harassment and Honour Based Violence (DASH 2008) Risk Identification, Assessment and Management Model.

- Are there any mental health issues or drug/alcohol dependencies?

- Is there evidence of repeat victimization? Just because it has not been recorded, it does not mean that the victim is not a repeat victim.

- Do you have a Risk Management Panel such as a Multi-Agency Risk Assessment Conference (MARAC) or Domestic Violence Action Group? If so, the high-risk, vulnerable, repeat victims and high-risk offenders should be flagged to this risk forum.

3.5.4 **Analysis of repeat victimization (RV)**

The British Crime Survey (BCS) shows that domestic violence is also more likely to involve repeat victimization than any other 'criminalized' behaviours. Additionally, domestic violence is more likely to result in injury than other offences against the person. Whilst there are some one-off incidents of domestic violence, invariably by the time the victim contacts the police, they have been exposed to a repeated pattern of abuse. This is particularly true where the offences are more serious. Approximately 42 per cent of victims are victimized more than once (Nicholas, Kershaw and Walker, 2007).

3.5.5 **Defining repeat victimization (RV)**

Violence also often increases in frequency and severity over time (Walby and Myhill, 2000b) and a common feature in most domestic abuse cases is repeat victimization. This is usually defined as more than one incident reported to the police in a given period, for example, 12 months (ACPO, 2008a). However, the victim-profile analysis should look back longer than a period of 12 months, or things will be missed.

Focusing police resources on repeat incidents is seen as effective in terms of both policing and cost (Hanmer and Griffiths, 2000). Previous victimization is a significant factor in risk assessment, and should be considered when allocating the level of priority in dealing with the problem. It should also be an integral part of any domestic-violence campaign. Repeat victimization is a crucial feature of domestic violence and it is the change in the rate of repeat victimization in relation to individual victims that needs to be monitored following interventions and in relation to change over time.

Domestic violence, in common with other hate crimes, tends to be poorly reported and in an ideal situation reporting rates should be *increasing* in successful areas with repeat victimization rates decreasing. This is a vitally important point. It must be measured and monitored and included in any analytical product. It is 'hot people' rather than 'hot spots' that need to be mapped, measured and monitored following intervention.

3.5.6 **Can domestic violence be mapped in the same way as other crimes?**

In short—no. Currently forces appear to be monitoring, mapping, and dealing with domestic violence (and other hate crimes) as they would deal with other traditional volume crime, such as burglary or car theft: ie they map it geographically into 'hot spots' and see reductions in rates as a sign of success. There needs to be a radical rethink of this approach in relation to violent crimes of this type.

The geographical spread of domestic violence is not an important consideration for analysis. The focus must be at the individual level. **It is the individuals who are repeatedly victimized that should be mapped and monitored.** This approach looks very different and implies the need for effective interventions at the individual level and a performance indicator which related to reducing repeat attacks. **A flagging system must of course be introduced to enable monitoring and analysis.** Interestingly, what may also happen is a decrease in the rate of repeat victimization, but also an increase in the rate of reporting, given that victims will realize that effective action is possible.

Case study

The suspect and victim were being evicted because of their constant screaming and arguing. He 'lost' it, dragged her off the sofa, punched and slapped her. He held her on the floor and held a deflated plastic baby toy over her nose and mouth. She fought free and crawled to the baby's room and grabbed the cot, which the baby was in. He then dragged her to the kitchen and tried to strangle her three separate times with a plastic bag. Suspect is 19 years old but has been offending from a very young age.

A search of the intelligence database revealed several 'hits' on the named suspect:

Entry 1	Mother rang with information that her son is driving a car illegally. Vehicle is also known for drugs.
Entry 2	Arrested for taking without consent (TDA) as he had also stolen a bike with two others. He was arrested after a police chase and gave a false identification and date of birth. He became violent when he was told he was going to be cuffed. He had to be restrained.
Entry 3	Suspect was arrested for theft of a moped. A DNA hit came back matching him as the suspect. Warning for officers that if/when stopped in the future gives false identification.
Entry 4	Suspect's cousin was allegedly hit by a bus conductor. The suspect's gang swarmed around him. The suspect said he wanted revenge. The conductor was fearful for his life.
Entry 5	Information that suspect was bragging that he has a tool for removing ignition barrels. Suspect has been stealing bikes/mopeds and cars, stripping them and selling them for profit. He is looking for new place to stash the stolen goods.
Entry 6	Suspect was arrested for theft of a moped. He is now serving six months in Feltham Young Offenders Institute (YOI) for a GBH at Wimbledon station. He beat male up as would not give him cigarette. The suspect and three others fractured his skull.

Entry 7	Suspect is in custody at Feltham YOI for a GBH and for breaching bail twice. There has also been a decrease in moped thefts since suspect in custody.
Entry 8	Suspect is dealing drugs to kids on estate.
Entry 9	Ex-girlfriend visited the suspect and an argument ensued. He poured a jug of boiling water over her back. She was taken to hospital and he was arrested for Grievous Bodily Harm (GBH).
Entry 10	Beginning of 2000 the suspect stated he had drugs at home address to get him out of house.
Entry 11	Beginning of 2000 the suspect burgled his ex-girlfriend's home address. He covered the flat in bleach and ripped up her clothing. He threatened to shoot her if she called the police. The suspect is very violent and capable of carrying out threats. He previously poured boiling water over her.
Entry 12	Emergency call by suspect's mother stating he was smashing her house up after argument with estranged girlfriend. The girlfriend told him she was leaving the area with the child because of his violence and threats. He punched her in face and returned to his mother's house. The girlfriend is trying to get emergency accommodation. She is currently in temporary accommodation at moment. The victim will not substantiate the allegation at this time.
Entry 13	Police saw a Peugeot travelling at high speed. They flagged it down and the driver gave false particulars. He also had false plates on a stolen car. Took suspect's fingerprints as police unhappy with identity. He had two outstanding breaches of Probation orders and aggravated vehicle taking. Girlfriend and mother went to police station. Girlfriend staying in hostel and not living with the suspect. Suspect would not give home address.

A search of the Police National Computer (PNC) also showed that the suspect had warnings for being: Violent, two alias names and dates of birth used. He was also recorded as wanted on warrant at time of incident.

Checklist—Repeat victimization

- First decide the most appropriate analytical method to use to measure and monitor repeat victimization.

- Ensure there is a flagging system in your area for repeat victimization. If there is already a system, are incidents being reliably flagged and accurately recorded? Consider undertaking additional analysis to check RV recording and flagging rates.

- Efforts should be made to increase reporting rates, whilst decreasing repeat victimizations. Ensure there is monitoring of this and inclusion in the analytical product.

- Consider monitoring GBHs on a monthly basis and check for repeat victims.

- Repeat victimization should be considered as an integral part of the analysis, given the high rates of repeat victimization and offending for domestic violence (ACPO definition). Be clear about whether this refers to all incidents, or only those that have been recorded as a crime, as well as whether the person or an address is being used to determine levels of repeat victimization.

- Data from partner agencies, such as probation and health providers, may provide additional information on repeat victimization and should be used where possible in conjunction with police data.

- More detailed analysis on repeat victimization, and repeat offending, would be beneficial to ensure this is being recorded accurately, and that resources are therefore being targeted most effectively.

- Ensure mapping of any media campaigns against reporting rates.

3.5.7 Offender/subject profiles

The intelligence and information that can be accessed by officers and analysts during their investigation seeks to demonstrate exactly how dangerous some of these perpetrators are; the main point being that, if an intelligence-led perpetrator profile is not compiled, how can officers properly investigate the crime and the Crown Prosecution Service (CPS) make informed decisions about charge, without the full case history and risk assessment? Moreover, how can they make the links between other offences the perpetrator may be committing inside and outside the home, if these crucial parts of the jigsaw are missing?

There are proven links between those who rape in the home (domestic) and outside the home (stranger) (Richards, 2004). Many rapists 'practise' at home. Equally, given that those who are sexually assaulted are subjected to more serious injury and there is a stronger link with murder, it is recommended that the victims and offenders of domestic-violence sexual assault and rape should be profiled as a matter of priority. All opportunities should be exploited around proactive targeting of offenders and problem solving in terms of intervention and prevention. We have an opportunity to prevent crime and identify serial and dangerous offenders using this method.

Case study—Levi Bellfield

On 25th February 2008 Levi Bellfield, 39, was found guilty of two murders—Amelie Delagrange and Marsha McDonnell, and one attempted murder, Kate Sheedy. All his victims were targeted close to bus stops as they made their way home alone at night.

Prior to that he had been offending violently for more than a decade, both inside and outside the home—but the links had not been made. Many of those offences had been reported to police. His range of offending included ABH, GBH, kidnap, murder, indecent assault, rape, threats to kill, possession of an offensive weapon, harassment, theft, affray, blackmail, impersonating police, domestic violence, child abuse, deception and drugs.

In an interview with the media, DCI Colin Sutton, who led the murder hunt, described him in some detail: 'When we started dealing with him he came across as very jokey, like he's your best mate. But he's a cunning individual—violent. He can switch from being nice to being nasty, instantly.'

Bellfield searched for victims on streets he knew intimately. Detectives tracked down a number of ex-girlfriends, who all described a similar pattern of behaviour when they got involved with him. 'He was lovely at first, charming, then completely controlling and evil. They all said the same', said DS Brunt, who spoke to several of them.

A couple of weeks after his relationship with a woman began, Bellfield would take her mobile phone and swap it with another which contained only his number, saying it was all she needed. He would then stop her from seeing friends, parents, or going out without his permission, and would constantly phone to check what she was doing.

One former girlfriend said that following an argument he told her to sit on a stool in the kitchen and not move. He went to bed and she sat there all night. DS Brunt said: 'We asked her what she did about going to the toilet and she said she would rather wet herself than have moved from that stool. That shows how frightened they were of him.'

Another girlfriend made a statement to police about the abuse she suffered at the hands of Bellfield and gave interviews to the media after the trial stating that she had been **beaten, tortured and raped** at **knifepoint** (BBC News, 28 February 2008, and interview with the *Mail on Sunday*, 3 March 2008).

It is important to ask the right questions about an offender's behaviour and assess the victim's vulnerability. Victims tell us about the:

- threat, allegation, and injury
- time/location of above
- behaviour and dangerousness of offender
- victim's diversity, vulnerability, and risk level.

KEY POINT—ASK QUESTIONS

Remember: you don't know what you don't know and you never will know if you do not ask.

This information can be used to aid understanding of what victims tell service providers about their experiences of domestic violence. The victim's account, twinned with perpetrator intelligence-led information should be the cornerstone of the investigation. When this information is set beside data held by these agencies and the behaviour of perpetrators, it generates a comprehensive picture of the nature and extent of abuse in terms of risk, threat, and dangerousness. Information can be analysed to target persistent offenders and to prevent repeat victimization and chronic offending. It has also brought into sharp relief the need to place domestic violence in its context:

- The ongoing relationship between the perpetrators and victim may enhance vulnerability to future abuse and act as a barrier to help-seeking options.
- Perpetrators may also be abusing children within the household.
- They may have a history of abusing others in a domestic context.
- They may also be offending outside the home.

All databases should be exploited and used to glean as full a profile of the offender and their offending behaviour as possible. Databases include:

- crime reporting systems
- force intelligence systems
- firearms
- violent and sexual offenders register (VISOR)
- impact nominal index (INI)
- child protection indices
- public protection systems
- vulnerable and intimidated victims database (VIVID—West Yorkshire's innovative system)/FLINTS II (West Midlands Police's very advanced crime and intelligence data warehouse system), for example

- prolific and priority offender systems (POPOS)
- missing persons
- Police National Computer (PNC)
- Forensic Science Service (FSS).

This list is not exhaustive.

Case study

The victim answered the door thinking it was her new boyfriend. The suspect then forced the victim into the bedroom and strangled her until she passed out twice. When she came round, the suspect forced sexual intercourse. The suspect removed the victim's clothes and knickers from the scene. Her child witnessed this and was told to 'fuck off to her room'. Sex offender register also looking for the suspect as he has not registered. He takes regular medication for depression and to control his behaviour. His brother is currently in prison for murder. On arrest, suspect assaulted officer and tried to resist arrest. He previously served seven years for raping and strangling a juvenile in 1992.

A search of the intelligence database revealed a lot of 'hits' on the suspect:

Entry 1	Whilst in **prison for rape**, his wife and children left him due to history of domestic violence.
Entry 2	**He has formed a new relationship with a female who has two young children. She's been told about his conviction for unlawful sexual intercourse (USI) and is considering the relationship. There are concerns about the children. They have been put on the 'at risk' register.**
Entry 3	Suspect is the boyfriend/minder of a prostitute.
Entry 4	He has bad mood swings and is *not* taking his prescribed drugs.
Entry 5	Officer visited the suspect but felt very uneasy with him. Cockroaches and dirty home address (hostel).

A search of the Police National Computer (PNC) also showed the suspect had warning for being violent and having mental health issues, as well as several previous convictions: **Known sex offender, but not registered, sexual offences (2)**, offences against person (2) and offences against property (2).

Case study

The victim was punched in the face, head, and body by suspect. He also threatened to shoot her and demanded that she remove her clothing. He then put an aerosol can in her vagina saying 'Push it up inside you. Fucking do it or I'll keep punching you'. The suspect was drunk and threw drink into the victim's eyes. He also stole jewellery from the victim's neck. He made the victim drive him home and said that he was going to get a gun to kill her. The victim stopped when she saw a police vehicle and told the officers what happened. He was then arrested. The suspect has forced sexual intercourse in past.

A search of the intelligence database revealed several 'hits' on the named suspect:

Entry 1	Suspect is a drug dealer and a residential burglar.
Entry 2	**The previous day the victim reported an assault and kidnap as the suspect has been harassing victim and made threats to kill her.**
Entry 3	Suspect is a drugs dealer and has been threatening a 'punter'.
Entry 4	Suspect was caught smuggling cocaine with girlfriend through customs.
Entry 5	Suspect arrested for blackmail.
Entry 6	Failed to stop when flagged down by police in his car. When he was arrested a small crowd gathered around the police van and **called him 'RAPIST'.**
Entry 7	He is very anti-police.
Entry 8	On a police stop the suspect did 'V' sign at police, flashed genitals to a passer-by and was very abusive. He was arrested under the Public Order Act. He was very aggressive.
Entry 9	Going to Jamaica.
Entry 10	Suspect is selling drugs.
Entry 11	Suspect rented a car with a stolen credit card.
Entry 12	Suspect was stopped but refused to give his details to the police. He had his hands in his pocket as if getting a weapon out.

A search of the Police National Computer (PNC) showed that the suspect has warnings for weapons, violence, and drugs. He also had several previous convictions: threats of firearms, possession of knife, violent, GBH, drugs importation of cocaine, fraud (1), theft (2), and offensive weapons (2).

From the research and analysis, create a list of 10–20 prominent nominals. Are they high risk on the risk indicator checklist? Consider flagging these individuals for tasking or problem solving. Consider whether they should be referred to any Risk management panels such as the MAPP or MARAC. Are there any other public protection issues? Create a bulletin of over night high risk cases. This should form part of a public protection daily bulletin with all high risk public protection jobs detailed for the SMT and local and central investigative teams. Early intervention and prevention can then be wrapped around those jobs.

Checklist—Offender analysis

- Consider whether the offender is a serial offender. Many are recidivists and evidence suggests that once a violent offender leaves the partner, the abuse escalates. It does not mean the violence ends. Many find new partners to abuse.

- Identify 10–20 prominent/high risk (serious and serial) offenders for targeting or problem solving.

- Does the offender have any previous convictions? Consider what previous intelligence there is about the victim or offender. The intelligence picture is likely to be different from the conviction rates, given that the national conviction rate for domestic violence previously at 11.7% (Her Majesty's Inspectorate of Constabulary (HMIC)/Her Majesty's Crown Prosecution Service Inspectorate (HMCPSI), 2004). The conviction rate for rape is even lower at 6%. This means the most dangerous offenders can slip through the net. The domestic violence conviction rate is starting to improve with the advent of Specialist DV court.

- Consider creating an over night briefing bulletin of high risk cases for your SMT and the Public Protection Unit.

- Consider the links between domestic and stranger rape, particularly when looking at offender profiles, their modus operandi (MO), and what outstanding stranger rapes/assaults and other violent offences you may have.

- Links MUST be made between domestic violence and other crimes when presenting profiles of prolific offenders, through the use of intelligence and other information sources. It should also be made clear whether the offender is tagged as a prolific and priority offender (PPO), is an NIM target, or is linked to more than one victim for domestic violence.

- Check whether their DNA has been taken? Is their DNA profile on the National DNA Database? It is vital that their DNA is taken as they could be committing other offences outside the home.

- Consider behavioural analysis. For example did the offender use a weapon? If so, specify what it was. Was it threatened or physically used? Compare injury level with allegation code. Are there mental health issues? Drug or substance abuse? If it is sexual assault, what is the MO?

3.5.8 **Analysis of trends over time**

It is important to look at trends over time to establish the volume of offences, as well as patterns of reporting. If patterns of reporting are established, this could inform where resources are targeted. Analyse longer-term trends, preferably looking at how the frequency of incidents has changed over the past four or five years. This gives ample data to identify seasonal changes and distinguish real changes from random fluctuations. Using a moving average can help remove the effects of random variations. In relation to domestic violence it is possible that increases in reporting could be seen as a sign of success. This needs to be thought through at Borough Command Unit (BCU) level.

Equally, it is useful to compare time periods over previous years when analysing the changes over time. The offences included within the analysis should be in line with current definitions and recorded crime and incident counting rules. Any variation from this within the problem profile needs to be explained clearly. Providing a breakdown of domestic violence by offence type is useful in understanding more about the nature of the problem.

The analysis should consider *all* crimes that result from domestic incidents, including non-violent crimes. This may be particularly relevant when looking at repeat incidents, as incidents that are non-violent may escalate later to more serious violent offences. Strategies and tactics for dealing with domestic incidents that follow on from the analysis should be inclusive of *all* types of offence.

More detailed analysis of high-risk homes may help identify other incidents that might be a trigger for a violent offence, and help plan for this in collaboration with other agencies. Map media campaigns and sporting events specifically against reporting rates. This will ensure that the right places are being targeted at the right time along with resources, such as specialist domestic-violence officers being made available to respond when the risk increases.

Checklist—Analysis of trends over time

- How many incidents happen on a yearly basis? Compare several years to understand seasonal trends.

- What media campaigns have been run that may have influenced reporting rates?

- What sporting activities/events occurred such as football or rugby?

- What are the offending rates across bank holidays and the Christmas /New Year period?

- What proportion is serious violence?

- What are the high-risk homes?

- Who are the repeat victims?

- Who are the repeat offenders?

- Are there opportunities for proactive targeting or problem solving?

- Create a fact sheet detailing this information. This a quick reference document which can be easily and quickly understood as well as reproduced when required, at conferences, tasking meetings, and domestic-violence fora, for example.

Figure 3.1 Domestic abuse fact sheet
Metropolitan Police Service

UNDERSTANDING & RESPONDING TO HATE CRIME FACTSHEETS

domestic violence

The Metropolitan Police Service (MPS) follows the Association Of Chief Officers Of Police definition of domestic violence:

any incident of threatening behaviour, violence, or abuse (psychological, physical, sexual, financial or emotional) between adults who are or have been intimate partners or family members, regardless of gender

Not all these behaviours currently constitute criminal offences. In addition, in some incidents of domestic violence recorded by the police no criminal allegation is made. In these non crime book cases, police may still diffuse frightening and potentially violent situations.

Recorded allegations 2001: base A

During the first six months of 2001, there were **44,476** allegations of domestic violence recorded by the police. This is equivalent to one contact every six minutes, and represents a consistent and persistent call on police time.

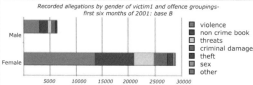
Recorded allegations by gender of victim1 and offence groupings-first six months of 2001: base B

- violence
- non crime book
- threats
- criminal damage
- theft
- sex
- other

The majority of allegations of domestic abuse that come to police attention relate to offences of violence.

Domestic assaults also account for a notable proportion of violent crime: they comprise one third of all common assaults, over a quarter of offences of Actual Bodily Harm (ABH) and one in eight of Grievous Bodily Harm (GBH).

Although the numbers vary, the patterns of the nature of abuse reported are similar for female and male victims, as well as for those in same sex relationships.

The intimate nature of the current or previous relationship between the victim and the perpetrator in cases of domestic violence can mean that supporting a prosecution is not always a viable option. The safety of the victim and their children must always be the paramount consideration. A number of boroughs within the MPS have introduced or are piloting advocacy projects that offer other help and assistance to victims, and - where appropriate – quide them through the court process.

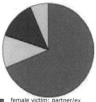
Gender and Relationship - Crime Allegations for Jan-Jun 2001: base B

- female victim: partner/ex
- male victim: partner/ex
- female victim: other relationship
- male victim: other relationship

(92% of these cases involved only one victim)

The MPS use a broad definition of domestic violence, but the majority of incidents involve partners or ex-partners. Abuse by other family members or within other relationships accounted for over a third crime allegations from male victims - much greater than for female victims.

Non crime book cases, where the relationship was known, followed a similar pattern.

PLEASE NOTE:
Non crime book cases do not necessarily involve a suspect, and as such relationships between suspects and victims can not always be recorded.

Research has found that:

❖ only roughly half of those subjected to domestic violence will tell someone about their experiences

❖ HOWEVER, the police are one of the agencies that they are most likely to contact.

Of those getting in touch with the police in relation to an incident of domestic violence, three fifths call 999. The use of third party reporting systems is currently limited, but it is hoped this will become more common over time.

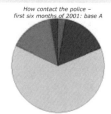
How contact the police – first six months of 2001: base A

- away from station
- 999
- other
- in person at station
- call police station

Over half of contacts are within the hour of the incident taking place, with three quarters being reported within 24 hours. However, two thirds of those reporting in person to the station did so more a day or more later.

METROPOLITAN POLICE   *Working for a safer London.*

A JOINT PROJECT FUNDED BY THE HOME OFFICE TARGETED POLICING INITIATIVE

The time when incidents of domestic violence occur follows a fairly fixed pattern. Only a small proportion of cases progress on to the later stages of the criminal justice process. That an individual has experienced harm does not in itself mean that they are more likely to support a prosecution of their assailant.

Studies have shown that:

❖ in comparison to other types of assault those subjected to domestic violence, and women in particular, are more likely to be upset & frightened by the incident, both in the shorter & longer term
❖ domestic violence is more likely to result in injury than other types of assault
❖ the levels of fear, shock & difficulty sleeping reported are equivalent to those of people whose have experienced a burglary
❖ victims of domestic violence are more likely to become repeat victims than for any other type of crime.

Analysis of MPS crime reports shows that people contact police for different reasons: to stop violence/for protection; to prevent future victimisation/escalation; to access other means of support. Data contained in routine monitoring forms can help to both understand and show ways to meet these & other needs.

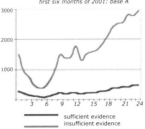

Whether there was sufficient evidence to proceed by time when incident committed - first six months of 2001: base A

sufficient evidence
insufficient evidence

The MPS domestic violence strategy emphasises a commitment to tackling domestic violence by working in partnership with all key agencies. Two strands are at the heart of this approach:

❖ victim and children's safety
❖ perpetrators' accountability.

An analysis of January – March 2001 sexual assaults between partners and ex-partners suggests that the women reporting such incidents have experienced other domestic abuse from their assailant. In addition many of these attacks result in injury. Such domestic violence sexual offences should be considered as very serious events requiring creative interventions.

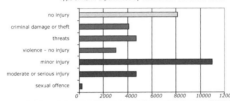

Type of harm experienced by victims: Jan–Jun 2001: base B

no injury
criminal damage or theft
threats
violence – no injury
minor injury
moderate or serious injury
sexual offence

0 2000 4000 6000 8000 10000 12000

An in-depth analysis of a day count of all allegations recorded by the MPS revealed that:

❖ more than one in eight cases recorded issues around child contact or disputes over custody
❖ more than one in twenty incidents involved a victim who was pregnant; in several other cases the victim had recently given birth
❖ in more than one in fifteen incidents the perpetrator made use of an object or a weapon to threaten and/or hurt the victim: these objects included a chisel, a knife, a pair of scissors, a golf club, some keys, a can of soft drink, a metal table lamp, a shoe, a door, a ball point pen, a gun
❖ the types of injuries sustained included: bite marks, bruising, a broken foot, chunk of hair, cuts, split lip, puncture wound, slash wound, stab wound, swollen pelvis
❖ many of the victims reported that they were shocked, distressed and/or afraid
❖ property was damaged in one in twelve cases, including toys, a telephone, furniture and a car windscreen.

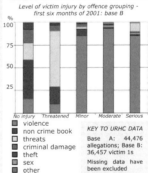

Level of victim injury by offence grouping - first six months of 2001: base B

No injury   Threatened   Minor   Moderate   Serious

■ violence
■ non crime book
□ threats
■ criminal damage
□ theft
■ sex
■ other

KEY TO URHC DATA

Base A: 44,476 allegations; Base B: 36,457 victim 1s

Missing data have been excluded

FURTHER INFORMATION - the following websites may be of interest:
The Metropolitan Police Service (www.met.police.uk), Women's Aid Federation of England (www.womensaid.org.uk), Domestic Violence Data Source (www.domesticviolencedata.org), Home Office (www.homeoffice.gov.uk)

Every London borough has a Community Safety Unit (CSU) with officers specially trained to investigate domestic, racial & homophobic incidents. You can contact your nearest CSU through your local police station - details should be set out in your telephone directory.

IN CASES OF EMERGENCY RING 999

Figure 3.2 Sexual assault fact sheet
Metropolitan Police Service

UNDERSTANDING & RESPONDING TO HATE CRIME FACTSHEETS

sexual assaults

Rape is perhaps the most devastating of all acts conducted by one human on another. Woman or man, the damage to the victim is life changing. The term rape includes all serious sexual offences defined as rape, buggery, indecent assault involving oral sex, the use of instruments or the exercise of violence (including attempts) and other circumstances deemed to be especially serious by an investigating officer.

The Metropolitan Police Service (MPS) is committed to doing more to target rapists and to protect Londoners from sexually motivated crime. The Project Sapphire Strategy has been set up to achieve this.

The Project Sapphire Strategy aims to focus on improving the MPS's performance on rape investigation and aims to significantly enhance the care given to victims across London.

Recorded allegations for the first six months of 2001 by gender of victims:

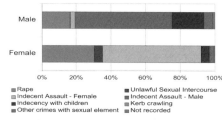

- Rape
- Indecent Assault - Female
- Indecency with children
- Other crimes with sexual element
- Unlawful Sexual Intercourse
- Indecent Assault - Male
- Kerb crawling
- Not recorded

An in depth analysis of sexual assault allegations recorded on one day in the MPS in March 2001 revealed that:

❖ 29 allegations for sexual assault were recorded including rape (7), indecent assault - female (15), indecent assault - male (1), indecent exposure (2), indecency against children (2), USI (1) and gross indecency (1)
❖ 2 were male victims, 26 female and 1 report did not state gender of victim
❖ 16 offenders were known (5 family), 9 were strangers, 4 reports did not state relationship
❖ the majority of victims were under 20 (13 were > 16yrs)
❖ 1 offence involved drug rape
❖ in 9 cases no offender description was given in the report
❖ 3 offenders had previous convictions for sexual assault
❖ Levels of violence: in 6 offences the victims were physically hit and punched in face, and threats to kill were made in one offence.

The **Understanding and Responding to Hate Crime** project is developing a strategic overview of hate crime information recorded by the MPS. Using a victim-oriented approach, the URHC team has developed a methodology for interrogating routinely collected information.

In the main, the data presented on this factsheet are based on the 4796 sexual assaults recorded on the Crime Report Information System (CRIS) from January to June 2001 as supplied by PIB; missing data have been excluded in all cases.

Analysis has also been conducted on all domestic violence flagged sexual assaults recorded on CRIS from January to June 2001.

Number of incidents recorded as Sexual Assaults by the MPS Jan-Jun 2001

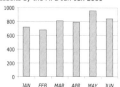

During the first six months of 2001, there were 4796 allegations of sexual assault recorded by the police. Of these:
❖ almost half were indecent assaults against females
❖ over 1 in 4 were rapes
❖ 1 in 15 were indecent assaults against males
❖ 1 in 16 involved indecency with children.

Time incident was committed:

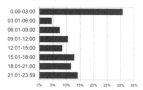

Approximately 1 in 3 sexual assaults take place between midnight and 3:00 a.m. They occur across all days of the week and just under 1 in 3 assaults are reported by dialling 999.

3% of all rapes and sexual assaults reported between 1st April 2000 and 31st March 2001 were committed by male minicab drivers. The majority of these offences were committed at night.

Age of victim and suspect:

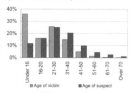

■ Age of victim   ■ Age of suspect

One third of victims reporting sexual assaults to the police are under 16.

METROPOLITAN POLICE   *Working for a safer London.*

A JOINT PROJECT FUNDED BY THE HOME OFFICE TARGETED POLICING INITIATIVE

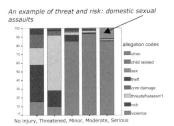

An example of threat and risk: domestic sexual assaults

allegation codes

other
child related
sex
theft
crim damage
threats/harassm't
ncb
violence

No injury, Threatened, Minor, Moderate, Serious

A risk assessment tool has been developed for domestic violence incidents. The risk assessment process has been informed by in depth analysis of domestic violence sexual assaults.

Given that those who are sexually assaulted are subjected to more serious an injury, it has been included as a strong indicator on the risk assessment.

Further, it is recommended that any report of domestic sexual assault be regarded as an incident of serial domestic abuse requiring a thorough investigation and development of a support package.

Detailed analysis was conducted of the 175 domestic sexual assault incidents that took place between January and March 2001.

An offender profile was established:
* 1 in 2 offenders had a criminal record
* 1 in 12 offenders flagged as "high risk" due to dangerousness in terms of re-offending and exhibiting disturbing behaviour
* 1 in 25 offenders had previous convictions for sexual assault.

Other findings included:
* 1 in 2 partners were separated/ing at time of offence
* children were present during the assault in 1 in 4 situations
* 3 in 4 victims had made previous reports of domestic violence to the police
* 6 victims were pregnant at the time of assault
* 1 in 4 victims wanted to pursue the allegation
* 3 in 4 victims did not want to pursue, citing: concern for children; fear of not being believed; vulnerability; fear of retaliation; fear of court process; amongst other reasons.
* of 175 domestic sexual assaults, only 4 perpetrators received a sentence, the maximum for which was 14 months.

Age of victims (comparison of Haven self-referrals and MPS data):

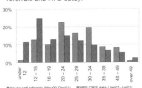

Haven self-referrals (May00-Dec01)   MPS CRIS data (Jan01-Jun01)

under 12, 12 – 15, 16 – 19, 20 – 24, 25 – 29, 30 – 34, 35 – 39, 40 – 49, over 49

The establishment of 'The Haven' (a sexual assault referral centre) based at Kings College Hospital, Camberwell has provided victims in parts of South London with a standard of care never seen before in London. From May 2000 until December 2001, the Haven saw 1073 clients.

Relationship codes used in MPS (Jan–Jun 2001)

no relationship code (44.7%)
acquaintance (6.0%)
ex-partner (3.7%)
partner (0.2%)
family member (33.8%)
colleague (3.5%)
neighbour (6.0%)
other relationship (12.4%)
other specified code (3.7%)

Relationship codes used in the Haven (May 2000–Dec 2001):

stranger (32.0%)
hardly known (19.4%)
acquaintance (30.4%)
ex-partner (9.1%)
partner (4.9%)
family member (1.3%)
colleague (0.1%)
not known (2.0%)
not documented (0.9%)

Between January and March 2001, there were 1428 sexual offences recorded in the MPS. 175 were domestic (although 187 were recorded 12 were not relevant), 90 stranger rapes, 441 stranger indecent assaults on females, 29 stranger assaults on males, 27 indecent assaults committed on children and 19 child abductions.

Of the 441 stranger indecent assaults, only 24 were of a 'serious nature'. 364 were deemed 'low level'. Of the 90 rapes, 26 offences involved the victim initially trusting the suspect, 16 involved victims being approached outdoors, 10 involved drugs, 9 were committed by minicab drivers, 8 involved prostitutes, 4 were car abductions, and 2 were aggravated burglaries. 15 did not fit into any of the above categories.

If the victim does not want contact with Police they can receive full medical care from the Haven. Victims may also complete anonymous forms detailing the offence and/or be invited to submit forensic samples.

From May 2000 until December 2001, the Haven treated 92 multiple assailant sexual assaults. Of those, 41 were on victims aged under 17 (9 assaults were on 16–17 year olds).

FURTHER INFORMATION:
1. MPS (2001) Project Sapphire Strategy: Improving rape investigation and victim care
2. MPS (2001) Service Intelligence Unit: Sexual Offences Committed by Minicab Drivers in the MPD
3. MPS (2001) Sexual Offences Strategic Report (Jan-March 2001)

Contacts
The Haven, King's College Hospital, NHS Trust, The Caldecot Centre, 15–22 Caldecot Road, London SE5 9RS Tel: 0207 346 1599
Project Sapphire Team TPHQ Cannon Row, Westminster: 0207 321 (4)7224.

IN CASES OF EMERGENCY RING **999**

3.5.9 **Alcohol, drugs, and mental-health-related incidents**

More often than not alcohol, drugs, and mental health are factors in domestic-violence incidents. This could be either the victim or the offender, and sometimes both. This should be included in any detailed analysis to understand the extent of the problem, the risks, and inform planning. The nature and severity of the risks posed and the factors that may trigger further offending (stopping medication, drug/alcohol abuse, loss of job, and separation, for example) are important in determining which risk-management options are appropriate. You will need to be aware that some offenders may disclose that victims are 'mad' or that they are drunk or taking drugs to minimize victim credibility, as well as dilute police action taken towards them. This is a common tactic used.

Checklist—Alcohol, drugs, and mental-health-related incident analysis

- Ensure robust data collection. Does your force have a system for flagging alcohol, drugs, and mental health? If you do have flags, dip sample domestic-violence offences to detect whether there are flagging or recording issues, ie that flags are being used appropriately and offences are being accurately recorded.

- Clearly indicate whether the involvement of alcohol, drugs, or mental health issues relate to the victims and/or the offender. You will need to ascertain whether this was disclosed by the offender, the victim, someone else, or whether it was a judgement made by the reporting officer.

Case study

The victim and suspect had been drinking at his home address. He said he was 'going to fuck her'. He got a knife and some scissors and threatened to cut her throat and kill her. He put his hand over her mouth and forced sexual intercourse, fellatio and sexual intercourse again. He cut her top with the knife. The victim is terrified of him.

Other crime reports: actual bodily harm on partner.

A search of the intelligence database revealed several 'hits' on the named suspect:

Entry 1	Suspect arrested for shoplifting (**previous conviction for buggery in 1992. He served an eight-year sentence).**
Entry 2	Suspect armed with knife, drove victim to isolated area, repeatedly hit her about the head and forced her to remove her jeans. He ripped her blouse open, forced sexual intercourse several times over 2–3-hour periods in Peterborough.
Entry 3	**In mid 1989, the suspect indecently assaulted his neighbour.**

A search of the Police National Computer (PNC) showed that the suspect has warnings for: being violent and for weapons, using two aliases and a number of previous convictions: **sex offences**, offence of buggery, and one indecent assault of neighbour (2), fraud (4), theft (3), dishonesty (1), offences relating to police/court/prison (1), drug offence (1), offensive weapon, knife (1), and miscellaneous offences (2).

3.5.10 Risk assessments and referral to agencies

The argument for the requirement of a risk-assessment process is based on the need to enhance victim safety, manage lethal situations, to make better use of intelligence and to increase the standard of the investigation and supervision. Risk models should be grounded in prevention rather than prediction. It ensures that a risk-management plan aimed at specific risk variables is put into place. When properly applied, risk assessment can serve as a paradigm for effective case management.

The importance of partnership in terms of risk assessment and multi-agency risk-management strategies should not be overlooked. Information-sharing must be enabled with common-sense principles underpinning it in order to have an impact in reducing domestic violence and domestic-related murders. Too often murders could have been prevented if information had been shared with the right agency at the right time. Decision-making must improve and confidence between the agencies must increase if we are to make a difference and effectively begin to save lives.

The analyst should identify whether an ACPO-compliant risk model is being used. If one is being used, this must be included in the analytical product. An increased understanding of risk will enable service providers to plan those resources better.

Early identification of risk and gaining a full and holistic picture of the offending behaviour is crucial to pick up patterns in escalating violent behaviour. Offences should not be treated as isolated one-off incidents and intelligence logs should be created in each serious incident in particular.

Case study—Risk assessment

The victim was sitting in a stationary van when the suspect asked her to go with him because it was his birthday. She said no and he punched her through the open window and cut her head open. Her left eye required five stitches. There is ongoing violence and harassment of the victim and others. The suspect carries a can of ammonia. He is known to be violent and uses drugs. There is a long history of domestic violence and harassment. They are ex-partners and suspect was on bail at time of incident. The officer conducted a risk assessment at time of the incident. It was believed to be 'non-critical'. **However, the victim was murdered by the suspect three months later.**

A search of the intelligence database revealed several 'hits' on the named suspect:

Entry 1	**Child at risk.** Suspect's child with previous partner. Suspect tearful and stated he wanted to see the child.
Entry 2	Suspect was stopped in mid-2000.
Entry 3	**In 2002 the suspect was convicted and sentenced for murder of new partner.**
	There were NO intelligence logs completed for 33 incidents before the murder, or for the murder itself.

A search of the Police National Computer (PNC) showed that the suspect has seven different PNC records from: 1979, 1984, 1987, 1988, 1990, 1991, and 1992, warnings for being violent (assault with intent to rob), weapons (pocket knife), suicidal, drugs (attempt to sell cannabis and Class A drugs), and for offending on bail and breaching bail conditions. He has used an alias, has one impending prosecution, offences against person (1), and numerous previous convictions: theft and kindred offences (7), drug offences (1), firearms/weapons (2), and miscellaneous offences (1).

Checklist—Risk assessment

- Is intelligence being inputted about offending behaviour?

- Is an ACPO-compliant risk model being used across force?

- How are you measuring its impact? Is it proving successful?

- Has the arrest rate increased?

- Have repeat victimization rates decreased? Measure and monitor this to see whether interventions are successful.

- Is there a flagging system for standard, medium, and high cases? How many standard-risk offences have been identified?

- How many cases have been referred to either DV action groups, MARACs, risk-management panels (RMPs) or multi-agency public protection panel arrangements (MAPPA)?

- How many domestic-violence murders have you had in force? Keep a spreadsheet of them, detailing the victim, offenders, MO, previous reported incidents, established risk factors, for example.

- Were there previous reports to police prior to the murder?

- How many of those were cases that were risk assessed and/or referred to a risk management panel?

3.5.11 Results analysis

Results analysis evaluates the effectiveness of intervention activity. If new tactics, interventions, operations, campaigns, or risk-management panels are being introduced, it is crucial to measure the impact and effect of them. This should be planned for at the very start of the new initiative. Data should also be identified for capture prior to the commencement of any operation. There are two evaluation initiatives:

- **process evaluation**—is concerned with how the initiative was implemented
- **outcome evaluation**—identifies the impact on crime and determines whether the outcome is attributable to the interventions.

Checklist—Results analysis

- What are the aims and objectives of the initiative/campaign/operation?

- Consider at the outset, not at the end, of the operation how you are going to measure its impact. Is it proving successful?

- What data can you collect to measure impact? For example, you could consider: the reporting rate; compliancy rate with risk model; levels of repeat victimization; levels of GBHs reported to police; performance and arrest rate; number of referrals to other agencies; and number of murders.

- How many high-, medium-, and standard-risk offences have been identified?

- How many high-risk cases have been referred to MARAC?

- Results analysis should inform future decision-making and should be given careful consideration. Lack of monitoring, assessing, and evaluating the impact of any new initiative, operation, or model renders the exercise worthless. You must ascertain what worked well and what did not. This also informs the corporate knowledge bank on 'what works and what doesn't'-approach to policing domestic violence.

Checklist for analysts and officers involved in domestic violence work

- What definitions are you using in terms of domestic violence and repeat victimization? For example, for repeat victimization, are you using the victim's name or their address?

- Are you using calendar years or financial years for analysis of trends?

- Are you using crime or incident data?

- When do these problems tend to peak (day of the week, time of day, any seasonal patterns, and what are long-term reporting trends)?

- Is the problem an emerging problem, increasing, or has it been constant for some time?

- What is it about the areas where the problem is persistent?

- What do we know about the victims?

- Who are the repeat victims? Analysis should look at 'mapping' individuals who are repeatedly victimized to ensure interventions are focused on the individuals who experience repeat offences and reduce repeat victimization.

- What do we know about the offenders? Analysis should identify repeat and prolific offenders. Who are the repeat offenders? Who are the most violent offenders?

- Who are the most violent repeat offenders? The police should look to problem-solve repeat offenders, either as a single agency, using specialist officers (such as field intelligence, domestic violence, child protection, dangerous offenders, sexual offences, and missing persons, for example). These offenders should be flagged by the analysts to be discussed at the weekly operations meetings.

- Do the offenders commit other crimes?

- Consider the links between stranger and domestic rape. Has their forensic profile been taken? Who are the sexual domestic-violence offenders? Are they committing offences outside the home?

- What other sources of data can we use that will help us better to understand the problem? Consider the use of non-police data to provide a more complete picture of the problem, where time constraints permit. Other statutory and voluntary agencies, such as the Probation Service, and health service providers may have data relating to this problem, and the individuals involved, particularly in relation to repeat victimization.

- How many murders are domestic-violence-related? Analysis should map serious domestic violence incidents and murders together to better understand the problem.

- How many victims had previously reported domestic violence prior to the murder?

- Is there a flagging system for DV incidents, repeat victimization, and for standard, medium, and high offences? This enables more meaningful analysis.

- Was the police/agency response appropriate?

- Could more have been done in terms of intervention and prevention?

- What tactical intervention options are available?

- Ensure that you carry out results analysis if any new tactics, operations, campaigns, or risk-management panels are brought into force.

- Consider producing fact sheets to easily show trends and patterns over time.

Further information and reading

ACPO (2005d), *Guidance on the National Intelligence Model*, available at <http://www.acpo.police.uk/asp/policies/Data/nim2005.pdf>.

Clarke, RV, and Eck, J (2003), *Becoming a Problem-Solving Crime Analyst in 55 Small Steps* (London: UCL Jill Dando Institute).

Richards, L (2004), 'Getting away with it: A profile of the domestic violence sexual and serious offenders' (London: Metropolitan Police Service), available at <http://www.met.police.uk/csu/index.htm>.

Stanko, EA, Kielinger, V, Paterson, S, Richards, L, Crisp, D, and Marsland, L (2003), 'Grounded crime prevention: Responding to and understanding hate crime', in Helmut Kury and Joachim Obergell-Fuchs (eds), *Crime Prevention: New approaches* (Germany: Weiser Rings), 123–53.

Effective Investigation

4.1 **Introduction**

This chapter provides practical guidance and advice to improve the investigation at all stages of the police response. It also highlights the need to ensure that the safety and protection of victims and their families is central to the investigation, along with holding abusers to account through the criminal justice system.

KEY POINTS—PRIORITIES

The Association of Chief Police Officers (ACPO) state that the priorities of the police service in responding to domestic violence are as follows:

- to protect the lives of both adults and children who are at risk as a result of domestic violence
- to investigate all reports of domestic violence
- to facilitate effective action against offenders so that they can be held accountable through the criminal justice system
- to adopt a proactive multi-agency approach in preventing and reducing domestic violence.

In theory, domestic violence should be one of the easiest crimes to investigate as both the victim and the offender are known to each other and the scene of the crime is easily identifiable. Yet historically the number of cases which had been successfully prosecuted was poor. This previous lack of successful prosecutions was generally due to poor investigation both at the scene and subsequently by police officers who placed too much reliance on the victim's readiness to give a statement and their willingness to pursue a complaint through to court. When a victim later withdrew their allegation or was reluctant to assist with enquiries, then without any other supporting evidence prosecuting lawyers would often take the view that the case was unlikely to succeed at court and it was dropped.

There has, however, been a noticeable improvement in the last few years with successful prosecutions by the Crown Prosecution Service (CPS) rising from 46 per cent in 2003 to 66 per cent in 2006, as well as a doubling of the amount of cases prosecuted (CPS, 2006).

4.1.1 **Positive action**

The need for positive action at all stages of the police response from initial call through to subsequent investigation cannot be overemphasized. ACPO Guidance on Investigating Domestic Abuse (2008) provides a positive obligation on all officers responding to domestic incidents to safeguard the lives of the victim and any children, thereby protecting them from any further harm. The guidance states that: 'Where an offence has been committed in a domestic-violence case, arrest will normally be "necessary" within the terms of PACE to protect a child or vulnerable person, prevent the suspect causing injury, and/or allow for the prompt and effective investigation of the offence.'

Officers reporting or attending domestic-violence incidents have a duty to pursue all lines of enquiry. They need to gather and preserve the widest range of evidence and not focus solely on the willingness of the victim to give evidence. Victims should never be asked if they want the offender arrested. The decision to arrest remains with the officer, not the victim; any decision to charge remains the responsibility of the CPS. Where an arrest is not carried out, an officer must document and be able to account for their decision.

Case study

The victim was assaulted by her boyfriend who had also damaged her flat. She refused to provide a statement and he was interviewed without one. He admitted the offences and was charged with common assault and criminal damage, even without a statement from the victim. He was convicted at court and given a community punishment and rehabilitation order for 12 months and ordered to pay £200 costs and compensation within a month.

4.2 Putting the Offender at the Centre of the Investigation

Police training tends to focus the initial responses around the victim. This can sometimes lead to an over-reliance on the victim in terms of the investigation and the victim needing to provide the evidence. Where the victim is either reluctant or unwilling to assist, officers become frustrated that they are unable to take positive action. It is important at this stage to recognize why victims of domestic violence are reluctant to provide statements or assist the criminal justice system (CJS) in prosecuting their attacker. Victims may be reluctant to proceed for many reasons (Richards, 2004):

- fear of retaliation and reprisal from the abuser
- concern about the distress and upset it would cause the children
- fear that they would not be believed
- fear of the legal system and court process itself
- victim has been sexually assaulted before and does not want to go through 'horrific' court ordeal again
- not wanting to give evidence
- too distressing and in too fragile a state of mind to give evidence
- not wanting to anger the abuser further when he came out of prison

- not wanting the abuser's wife/girlfriend and children to find out about affair, and/or
- fear of repercussion between the two families.

It is therefore essential that police officers and staff identify and pursue all available avenues of enquiry. By building a case around the suspect, should one part of that evidence be withdrawn, ie the victim's statement, it may still be possible to proceed with the case on other admissible evidence.

Figure 4.1 Effective evidence-gathering in domestic-violence cases

The following diagram demonstrates a range of evidence that can be collected by officers that can assist in supporting a prosecution. By placing your suspect at the centre of your investigation, you can build a case, which does not solely rely upon the willingness of the victim to give evidence.

Effective investigation and evidence-gathering is therefore critical. The use of 999 calls, photographs taken at the scene, the gathering of medical evidence immediately, together with an interview of the defendant under caution would all provide valuable evidence which could enable the prosecution to proceed even where the victim subsequently wishes to withdraw. The subsequent presentation of these cases, ideally within Specialist Domestic Violence Courts (SDVC), will lead to lower levels of attrition at court and consequently higher numbers of offenders being brought to justice.

4.3 **Initial Reporting—'First Time, Right Time'**

First contact with police can be through a number of different channels such as emergency calls for help, contact via neighbours or friends, or directly at the police station or to officers on the street. In all cases, staff must be proactive in their approach. A professional initial response will lead to a higher number of incidents being correctly classified as crimes with a consequential higher level of evidence-gathering and arrest.

> **KEY POINT**
>
> 'You do not get a second chance to make a good first impression'

This is the beginning of the investigation and all staff have a crucial role to play in maximizing any evidential opportunities that may be vital in any subsequent trial. It is important to remember that victims may be reluctant to disclose what is actually happening to them at this time particularly if the offender is still present, or they may well minimize what has taken place.

At this stage callers may be distressed, under the influence of drink, or in genuine fear of their life. They would not be calling for police if they were not in crisis or in need of help. It is essential that you remain professional, sensitive, and supportive to the caller, providing reassurance whilst ensuring that information regarding the incident is established quickly and effectively and that officers are dispatched to the scene immediately.

Police supervisors and managers should ensure that all staff who are likely to be the first point of contact for victims such as those employed within force control rooms or front offices are trained in how to respond to reports of domestic violence and that incidents are correctly recorded in line with force policy and National Crime Recording Standards (NCRS). ACPO in conjunction with the National Police Improvement Agency (NPIA) have developed a comprehensive training package to support this: Module 2—NPIA Responses to Domestic Violence Modular Training Programme.

4.3.1 **Call-takers and information-gathering**

Full details of the incident and of all parties involved should be recorded and flagged appropriately on the incident log, in line with local policy.

> **GOOD PRACTICE—CALL-TAKERS**
>
> Call-takers should have ready access to a suitable set of prompts to enable them to support the victim and gather evidence. This must not delay deployment of officers to the scene where the offender is still present or the victim is still at risk.

The following call-taker's checklist has been identified as good practice by *Lessons Learned from the Domestic Violence Enforcement Campaigns* (Home Office, 2006a). It should be used by call-takers to seek, record, and disseminate the following information:

GOOD PRACTICE—PRIMARY QUESTIONS BEFORE DEPLOYMENT OF OFFICERS

What is happening?	
Is the caller able to speak freely?	If not consider tapping on the phone for yes/no answers.
	Keep the line open if possible.
Where is the caller?	
What is the caller's name?	
What is location of the incident?	
What time did the incident happen?	Is the incident still taking place?
Is anyone injured?	How severely?
	Do they need an ambulance?
Where is the suspect now?	Inside/outside the house?
What are the personal details of the suspect?	Name, address, telephone number, DOB, gender.
If suspect has left the scene, where are they likely to be found?	Does the suspect have access to a vehicle?
	What is the description and registration of vehicle?
What is the description of the suspect? (Include clothing)	
Where is the victim?	
Are there any children present?	Are they safe?
	Did they witness the incident?
Are any weapons involved?	If so, what type?
	Where are the weapons now?
	Who has access to them?
Can access be gained to the premises?	If not, what are the key considerations for access?
	Barricade? Dog? High-rise flat?

What is the relationship between the caller, suspect, and victim?	
Is any person present under the influence of drink or drugs?	
What is the demeanour of the caller, victim, suspect?	What background noise can be heard? (Record shouting, words spoken, etc.)
Is there a history of domestic violence, reported or otherwise?	
Is there a court order or injunction relating to the suspect?	If so, what are the conditions? Does the court order have a power of arrest?
Are there any special needs to consider?	Any communication difficulties, which require an interpreter? Any cultural issues to be aware of? Any hearing difficulties? Any speech difficulties? Any mobility/other disabilities?
What are the personal details of all parties involved.	Name, address, DOB, telephone number, gender.
Record the first account of what the caller says has occurred.	Record details verbatim.
When the victim's safety has been established, give basic advice about crime scene until police arrive.	This should include: not moving anything (or allowing others to do so); not cleaning up or tidying the house; not washing or taking a shower; not changing clothing; not allowing children, relatives, neighbours, or animals to enter areas where the incident took place (where possible).

Once initial information has been obtained, you should ensure that officers are dispatched to the incident as soon as possible. It is vital that you provide these officers with sufficient information to ensure their own personal safety on arrival, and details of both the caller and other persons present or involved.

GOOD PRACTICE—INFORMATION TO BE PASSED TO ATTENDING OFFICERS

Location and description of the
suspect, where necessary.

Whether any weapons used or at
the scene, or suspect known to
carry weapons.

If any persons present are under
influence of drink or drugs.

Any other factors that may affect
the police response.

Those relating to same sex, disability,
mental health, if the person reporting is
able to speak freely.

Any communication difficulties.

For example, language, hearing, speech.

Any difficulties gaining access to
scene.

For example, dogs, lifts.

Any relevant history, injunctions
with or without power of arrest,
and child protection issues.

Details of any children present.

Having ensured the prompt attendance of officers you should seek the following additional information and where appropriate pass this to officers at the scene:

GOOD PRACTICE—ACTIONS FOLLOWING DEPLOYMENT OF AN OFFICER TO THE SCENE

Prioritize the safety of officers and others.

Ensure medical assistance is en route, where
appropriate.

Ensure support (back-up) is available for
the officer(s) attending the incident, where
appropriate.

Inform the caller that an officer has been
dispatched.

Inform the caller when a police
officer(s) has arrived at the
scene so that the officer can be
safely admitted to the premises.

Make appropriate checks of IT and/or paper-based systems for previous reported domestic-violence history.	Crime reports Intelligence database PNC Bail conditions Civil injunctions Previous harassment warnings Court Orders (powers of arrest) Child contact orders Child protection intelligence systems Child protection register VISOR Offender has access to firearms?
Is there a court order or injunction relating to the suspect?	If so, what are the conditions? Does the court order have a power of arrest?

GOOD PRACTICE—DOMESTIC-VIOLENCE RESPONSE/INVES-TIGATION CARS

A number of forces operate a dedicated DV car, staffed by specialist officers, during peak times. In some areas they will undertake an investigative role at the scene, whereas in other areas their role is to advise and direct investigations carried out by other front-line staff. Both uses are considered to be beneficial in enhancing the investigation.

4.3.2 Evidential use of 999 recordings

All police control rooms and call centres record emergency calls to police. The use of these recordings should not be overlooked. Evidence of first complaint made by the victim to a third party may be presented to the court to show consistency in the victim's account. Additionally background noise may reveal comments made by the accused, which may support the prosecution case. These recordings may also prove useful during interviews with offenders and to assist CPS decision-making when reviewing cases for charge. Early consultation with the CPS should be sought, particularly when considering the evidential use of 999 calls.

GOOD PRACTICE—999 CALLS

Immediate access to 999 calls should be made available to investigators. West Midlands Police employ a system that enables the force control room to play the content of the 999 recording down the phone to an officer at the BCU. A number of other forces are able to send digital recordings to investigators via email, which can then be used, in subsequent interviews.

4.4 **Attending the Scene**

4.4.1 **Officer safety**

Officer safety is paramount when attending scenes of domestic violence. Easy access to knives and other weapons makes it particularly dangerous for officers. Domestic incidents present unique risks to attending officers and account for a significant number of injuries on duty. Before arrival at the scene any known risks on the premises or occupants should have been sought from control room staff. A dynamic risk assessment should be conducted when entering premises, particularly where there is an immediate threat to life and officers need to use powers to force enter. Where firearms are intimated or known to be present, officers should seek specialist support. Where possible all persons in the premises should be identified and parties separated, ideally to rooms where people do not have ready access to knives or other weapons.

It is important that officers remain vigilant and identify any potential risks to themselves and other parties present.

4.4.2 **Identifying the primary aggressor**

Very often you will be presented with conflicting accounts from those present with both parties making counter-allegations against each other. Often the victim may have less obvious injuries than the aggressor, particularly if they have acted in self-defence or where injuries have been inflicted on concealed parts of the body. It is therefore essential that you try to establish who the primary aggressor is. The primary aggressor is the person determined to be the most significant, rather than the first aggressor.

It is important at this stage that officers identify the primary aggressor. This is to ensure that victims are afforded protection from further abuse and that offenders are held accountable. Many repeat offenders know that by 'getting in' their story first or blaming the other party they will create confusion and make it difficult for officers to arrest and prosecute the right person. Quite often offenders present themselves as calm and collected whilst victims are often distraught. They will attempt to control events by blaming the incident on the actual victim or stating they acted in self-defence.

KEY POINT

Remember that domestic violence is about power and control. Some offenders are very manipulative and learn the police systems and processes, using them to try and manipulate officers and professionals.

The following table will assist you in trying to establish the primary aggressor and should form part of your initial investigation.

GOOD PRACTICE—IDENTIFYING THE PRIMARY AGGRESSOR

Is there a previous history of domestic violence between the parties involved?	Check police crime and intelligence records. Who is shown as victim/offender?
Seriousness of injuries—does this corroborate what each party is saying?	Remember bruises may not always be visible, particularly on darker skin. If weapons alleged, where are they?
Are injuries offensive or defensive injuries?	Check for marks around arms where they have been held up for protection (defensive) or marks/scuffs on knuckles (offensive).
Is there evidence to suggest either party acted in self-defence including pre-emptive strikes?	Scratches to offender's face may be consistent with victims who are being strangled. Was force used reasonable?
Consider the age, height, and weight of the parties	Is the person physically capable of doing what is alleged?
Is there any other evidence to corroborate accounts?	Witnesses, damage to property etc. If victim says suspect forced entry, is there damage to show this?
Is there any criminal history of propensity to violence?	Check previous offending history.
Is either party in genuine fear of their safety?	Listen to what is said. DV victims tend to minimize the threat; if they say they are in fear take it seriously.
Does either party have a motive to lie?	If guilty, suspect may go to prison or lose job.
Is there evidence of use of alcohol or drugs?	Establish use and time of consumption—does it support accounts?
Who called 999 and what was the nature of the call?	Ask someone to listen to recording whilst still at scene if possible. If not, what is recorded on initial call log?
Are there any existing court protection orders?	Who issued to, on what evidence?

This list is not exhaustive and officers will need to use their knowledge and experience according to each individual set of circumstances.

KEY POINT

Remember whatever action you take you may need to justify your rationale at a later time. Your decisions must be clearly documented and auditable.

4.5 Dealing with the Victim

Most victims minimize what has happened to them, particularly when the police are involved. It is therefore important to be patient and sensitive to their needs, recognizing that they are likely to be distressed and, at a time when they are in crisis, you will be asking lots of questions of them. In all cases officers should:

- see the victim on their own in a secure and private place
- reassure the victim about confidentiality
- administer first aid to the victim and note if medical treatment will be sought
- describe the victim's location upon arrival
- note time dispatched, arrived, and when victim initially spoken to
- record any spontaneous statements made by the victim
- describe the victim's emotional condition
- describe the victim's physical condition, including size in relation to the suspect
- note victim's relationship with suspect
- note if victim is pregnant
- describe any visible injuries in detail (size, location, and colouration—use full body maps)
- record any defensive injuries and either party's claims of self-defence
- describe other suspected injuries
- record history of abuse and history of court orders
- record contact number/address for victim where she/he can be safely contacted
- consider deploying an accredited Family Liaison Officer (FLO).

GOOD PRACTICE—INVESTIGATION PACKS

Investigating officers must undertake prompt and thorough investigations by obtaining all available evidence from the scene, witnesses, and other sources to effectively protect the victim and any children. The use of a suitable investigation pack, to standardize and quality-assure the process involved in domestic-violence investigations, should be seen as good practice.

4.5.1 **Conducting risk assessments**

By conducting a professional and thorough investigation you will be able to identify specific risks relevant to each incident. It is essential that you not only document these risks and the necessary risk-management plan but also review it at all stages of the investigation, including on release from custody through to any court appearances.

In all cases you should:

- document a clear and effective risk identification, assessment, and management plan (your decisions need to be clearly recorded and auditable)
- use an ACPO-approved identification/assessment model
- complete a risk assessment of the threat including risks to the victim and anyone else involved
- refer it on for action
- put an appropriate intervention plan into place.

More detailed guidance on risk assessments can be found in Chapter 5 below.

4.5.2 **How can I investigate fully when the victim is reluctant to provide a statement or go to court?**

This is probably one of the most asked questions when delivering training to police officers and staff and is often used as an excuse for failing to take any action. Well, the answer is simple. In cases of homicide, do we rely on the victim telling us they want us to arrest the offender or on their willingness to provide a statement? Most definitely not—so why should it make any difference in domestic-violence cases?

KEY POINT

Paragraph 3.5 of the Codes of Practice issued under the Criminal Procedure and Investigations Act (CPIA) 1996 requires that:

officers conducting criminal investigations should pursue all reasonable lines of inquiry, whether these point towards or away from the suspect. What is reasonable in each case will depend on the particular circumstances.

It is also important to note that the CPS Policy for Prosecuting Cases of Domestic Violence (2005) points out that just because a victim asks police not to proceed any further with the case or withdraw the complaints does not necessarily mean the case will be stopped. Where this is likely, officers should seek an early consultation with CPS lawyers. For further guidance on prosecuting cases and competency and compellability of victims and spouse to give evidence see 4.11.11 below.

4.5.3 **Can a victim consent to an assault?**

A claim by the victim that they in fact 'consented' to being assaulted does not prevent you conducting a further investigation and prosecution. In *R v Brown* [1994] 1 AC 212 (a case involving sado-masochistic acts in private) the House of Lords held that as a matter of public policy, a person may be prosecuted and convicted of causing serious bodily harm even if the victim consents. In other words, it is not in the public interest to allow consensual serious assaults to take place.

4.5.4 **Dealing with allegations of attempted strangulation**

Victims often make allegations of strangulation to police but at the time of reporting there may be no visible injury. This has meant that the seriousness of this form of assault is often overlooked or not documented correctly. Bruises take time to show and equally the darker the victim's skin pigmentation, the less likely it is to see visible markings. The lack of visible evidence does not mean that it has not happened.

In some cases the offender may be the only one with visible injuries where the victim has scratched them in an attempt to breathe and/or escape. It is therefore vital that officers should look for and document injuries around the eyes, nose, behind the ears, inside the mouth, neck, shoulders, and upper chest area. Changes in the voice may also be apparent. Where present these should be photographed and a medical examination by the force medical examiner conducted.

Officers should also look for the following symptoms, which in some cases may necessitate the need for an urgent medical examination or referral:

- petechia—burst blood capillaries in eyes
- hoarse or raspy voice
- loss of voice
- pain and/or difficulty swallowing
- coughing
- nausea and/or vomiting
- internal neck injury
- difficulty in breathing or inability to breathe
- light-headedness
- involuntary urination or defecation.

4.5.5 **Taking a statement from the victim**

Try to obtain a statement from the victim as soon as practicable to support the alleged offence. In allegations of serious sexual assault an officer who is trained in sexual offences investigation should undertake these. In some cases the use of special measures may be appropriate. See 4.11.9 below for further guidance.

Statements should be as comprehensive as possible and contain:

- the family composition
- the history of the relationship and any other previous incidents (reported or unreported)
- the actual incident
- the victim's injuries (physical and emotional) and their extent
- whether a weapon was used, the type of weapon, and where it came from
- whether any threats have been made since the attack
- whether any children were present and if so the effect on them
- the victim's view of the future of the relationship
- whether there is any damage at the location, ie broken furniture, ornaments, windows, or ceramics, whether the telephone was ripped out etc
- the victim's negative statement when they do not want to take a specific course of action—this is vital if you are looking to prosecute without the victim's support.

You should consider ABE/video interview with the victim on first report and also you should invite the victim to make a Victim Personal Statement (VPS) even if it appears the victim is/may be reluctant to support a prosecution.

4.5.6 **Statements from intoxicated victims and witnesses**

Statements must not be taken from victims or witnesses who are drunk. Officers will need to use their professional judgement with regard to each witness as to how the level of intoxication will affect the victim or witness's ability to make a statement at the time of the incident. Where possible, an initial victim statement should be obtained, even if it amounts to an outline statement.

In deciding if a victim or witness is capable of making a statement officers should consider and record in their notebook and the beginning of any statement:

- the amount of alcohol consumed
- the effect of consuming that amount of alcohol on the witness
- the witness's understanding of the terms of the s 9 certificate at the beginning of the statement, and
- whether or not the witness is able to give a coherent account of the events.

Taking statements from witnesses at this early stage will be useful for CPS decision-makers and will assist with taking forward 'victim-reluctant' prosecutions. In all cases, officers should endeavour to obtain corroborating evidence to support the victim's evidence. It is the prosecutor's role to establish what is and what is not admissible or useful in court. Officers should assist the CPS by gathering as much information as possible in the first instance.

4.5.7 **Victim personal statements (VPS)**

VPSs seek to give victims more of a voice in how cases are dealt with. In general, a VPS will be taken in every case when an MG11 statement is taken from a victim of crime. A second statement may be taken later, so that the victim can explain the longer-term effects of the crime.

4.5.7.1 When an MG11 statement is taken

Draw a line under the evidential section of the MG11 witness statement form. (When a victim statement is taken on video, the VPS should be on video as well.) Write along the following lines:

> I have read the victim personal statement (VPS) leaflet and the VPS scheme has been explained to me. What follows is what I wish to say in connection with this matter. I understand that what I say may be used in various ways and that it may be disclosed to the defence.

Take the victim's statement in his or her own words, using the following checklist:

- **Effects**—what has been the effect of the crime on them (eg medical/psychological damage or social effects)?
- **Bail**—do they have concerns about any suspect being bailed?
- **Information**—would the victim like to receive information about the progress of the case?
- **Concerns**—do they have any particular concerns about being a witness at court or feeling vulnerable as a victim?
- **Victimization**—do they feel victimized regarding the crime on account of their gender, sexuality, faith, cultural background, or disability? If so, do they wish to add anything about their feelings or about the effect of the crime?
- **Compensation**—are they seeking compensation?
- **Other comments**—is there anything else that they wish to add?

4.5.7.2 Things to tell the victim

The VPS is entirely optional—the statement can say as much, or as little, as the victim wishes to say. Once made, a VPS cannot be altered or withdrawn. However, it is possible to make a further VPS, clarifying or correcting anything previously said. It will form part of the case papers and is disclosable to the defence. It will be taken into account by all criminal justice agencies (ie police, CPS, etc) where it is in the public interest to do so. While the court can take into account the effect that the crime has had on the victim, it will not take into account the victim's opinion about how the offender should be punished. Do not raise the victim's hopes that the scheme will deliver more than this.

4.5.7.3 If the victim chooses not to make a VPS

Record this fact on the witness statement form. Give them a copy of the VPS leaflet and explain that the victim can make a VPS later, if they wish. Put details of the police point of contact on the back of the leaflet.

4.5.7.4 Longer-term effects of the crime

Should a further statement be necessary detailing the longer-term effects of this crime then it should be taken on a further MG11. This can be done even where an initial VPS has not been completed. Before completing this statement you will need to check if there are any 'case handling' issues with the CPS. Once completed it should be linked to the original case papers.

4.5.8 **Use of interpreters**

The use of family members, particularly children, to interpret at the scene should be avoided, unless it is necessary to prevent an immediate threat to life. You have no way of knowing that what you are saying to the victim is being interpreted in the way you wish or that the answers you get back are a true record of what the victim is saying. This may be particularly relevant in cases of so-called honour-based violence. The victim may also feel embarrassed disclosing certain things in front of a family friend or relative.

Where available, the use of telephone interpreting services should be used for brief and straightforward communications, for example, establishing initial details of incident and persons involved. This service is not appropriate for use in evidential procedures.

To ensure an effective investigation you should obtain, through your own police service procedures, a registered interpreter who should be registered with the National Register of Public Service Interpreters (NRPSI).

GOOD PRACTICE—INTERPRETERS

The Metropolitan Police Service (MPS) has produced a number of translated information sheets, which can be provided to domestic-violence victims explaining the role of the interpreter and how to stop the interview if they are unhappy with how it is being translated. They have also trained a number of interpreters in dealing with victims of domestic violence.

4.5.9 **Victim Support—Independent Domestic Violence Adviser (IDVA)**

The need for ongoing support to victims cannot be overstated. Although police can provide initial victim support, police officers are neither trained nor resourced to provide professional support to victims. There are, however, many independent and non-governmental organizations that have the experience and professional knowledge to provide this support. Most police services now have well-established links with these agencies and their details should be made available as early as possible to victims and witnesses.

4.5.9.1 Independent Domestic Violence Adviser (IDVA) Service

Where they are in existence independent domestic-violence advisers working alongside police officers, CPS and other support agencies have been shown to make a real difference in dealing with these cases.

An independent domestic-violence advisory service involves the professional provision of advice, information, and support to survivors of intimate-partner violence living in the community about the range, effectiveness, and suitability of options to improve their safety and that of their children. This advice must be based on a thorough understanding and assessment of risk and its management, where possible as part of a multi-agency risk-management strategy or multi-agency risk assessment conference (MARAC) process.

While IDVA services may accept all referrals, their focus is on providing a premium service to victims at high risk of harm, to address their safety needs, and help manage the risks that they face. IDVAs typically provide short- to medium-term casework, focusing on safety advice covering improved physical security as well as remedies available from the civil and criminal justice systems.

An IDVA provides this service both at the point of crisis and in relation to medium- and long-term safety and support. The work of such IDVAs has clear and measurable outcomes in terms of improved safety and a reduction in repeat offences. The service should be provided in such a way as to be sensitive to all cultural and other differences and needs. The IDVA also helps to ensure that all agencies involved in an individual case fulfil their obligations.

4.6 Dealing with Witnesses

Although domestic violence frequently takes place in private, events are often witnessed by other parties. This could, for example, include friends, family, neighbours, and work colleagues. Their evidence may be crucial in assisting you to identify the primary aggressor and also in supporting a later prosecution.

The following real-life example demonstrates how independent witnesses may be vital in securing convictions where victims decline to assist police.

Case study

The victim was assaulted by her boyfriend whilst at hospital which was **witnessed** by a security guard and captured on CCTV. The victim **refused** to provide a statement, however the security guard did. The suspect was charged with ABH and at court was **convicted** of assault and received a four-month sentence despite the victim trying to deny the incident happened when she gave evidence.

Consider:

- identifying all witnesses/potential witnesses and speaking with them separately
- recording all witnesses' addresses and phone numbers
- obtaining statements from witnesses, neighbours, family members, ambulance staff, doctors, FMEs, midwives, previous partner(s), etc
- listing names and ages of all children present
- separately interviewing the children (The Guidance for Vulnerable or Intimidated Witnesses should be complied with at all times).

4.7 **Dealing with the Suspect**

Previous sections have provided guidance on identifying the primary aggressor or suspect. However, it is essential that having done so you document your interaction with the offender and try to substantiate or disprove what they tell you has happened. In particular you should:

- administer first aid to the suspect and note if medical treatment will be sought
- describe suspect's location upon arrival
- record any spontaneous statements made by the suspect at any point during the encounter/interaction
- describe the suspect's emotional condition
- describe the suspect's physical condition
- photograph/describe any evidential marks on the suspect inflicted in self-defence by the victim
- document where no injuries present
- document evidence of the use of drugs or alcohol by the suspect
- ask the suspect if he/she is aware of the terms of applicable court orders
- identify who is the primary aggressor.

KEY POINT

Domestic-violence offenders often present themselves as calm and collected. Some are very manipulative and learn the police systems and processes, using them to try and manipulate officers and professionals.

4.8 **Powers of Arrest**

Section 110 of the Serious Organised Crime and Police Act 2005 amended the powers of arrest available to a constable under s 24 of the Police and Criminal Evidence Act 1984. Officers should consider whether the action of arrest is proportionate given the balance between the need to prevent further offences and protect the victim and any children present and the interests of the alleged offender. Arrest will usually be necessary to allow an investigation to be completed and prevent further offences. Officers need time with the victim during the period of arrest to ascertain the risk, evidence of violence, past and current threat, the precise nature of the offence committed, and the wider context of the relationship. Do not lose sight of the fact that victims can, and do, often minimize the threat/danger to themselves and/or to others.

Ultimately, it is the officer's decision whether or not to arrest, NOT the victim's. In *Osman v UK* (1998) 29 EHRR 245 it was held that the police could be liable for breach of Art 2 (Right to Life, HRA 1998) if they had not taken 'reasonable' 'preventive operational measures' to avoid a 'real immediate' risk to life which they ought to have known about.

The question to the victim 'What do you want us to do?' is NOT appropriate first off. Questions should relate to the offence in terms of what happened, the history of domestic violence, and the victim's view of their situation—NOT his/her opinion on the appropriate action for a police officer to take. If there is serious injury or threat to the victim sufficient for a charge, an arrest is clearly an appropriate response.

KEY POINT—RESPONSIBILITIES

Do not lose sight of the fact that the basic tenets of your responsibilities as an officer are:

- the preservation of life and
- the prevention and detection of crime.

A useful mnemonic to use is **PLANBI:**

- Is the arrest Proportionate to the allegation and offence under investigation?
- Do I have a power to Legally arrest?
- Can I Account for my actions if challenged?
- Is it Necessary in the circumstances?
- Is it based on Best Intelligence/Information available to me at the time?

4.8.1 Possible offences

Domestic violence can cover a wide variety of behaviour which can constitute a number of different criminal offences. The following Table 4.1 provides a number of examples of behaviour and possible offences.

Table 4.1 Examples of possible types of offences

Examples of behaviour	Possible offences
Pressurising a victim/witness to 'drop the case', or not to give evidence	**Witness intimidation, obstructing the course of justice, conspiracy to pervert the course of justice**
Physical violence, with or without a weapon, including punching, slapping, pushing, kicking, head butting, and hair-pulling	**Common assault, actual/grievous bodily harm, wounding, attempted murder**
Violence resulting in death	**Murder, manslaughter**
Violence resulting in miscarriage	**Child destruction, procuring a miscarriage or abortion**
Choking, strangling, suffocating	**Common assault, actual/grievous bodily harm, attempting to choke, strangle or suffocate**
Spitting at a person	**Common assault**
Threatening with an article used as a weapon, eg a knife, tool, telephone, or chair	**Threats to kill, common assault, affray, threatening behaviour**
Throwing articles, eg crockery, even if they miss their target	**Common assault, actual/grievous bodily harm, criminal damage, affray, threatening behaviour**
Tying someone up	**Common assault, actual bodily harm, false imprisonment**
Threatening to kill someone	**Threats to kill, harassment**
Threats to cause injury	**Common assault, affray, threatening behaviour***
Threats seriously to damage or undermine social status	**Harassment, blackmail**
Damaging or destroying property or threatening to damage or destroy property	**Criminal damage, threatening to cause criminal damage, harassment**
Harming or threatening to harm a pet	**Criminal damage, cruelty to animals, harassment**
Locking someone in a room or house or preventing them from leaving	**False imprisonment, harassment**
Preventing someone from visiting relatives or friends	**False imprisonment, kidnapping, harassment**

Table 4.1 Examples of possible types of offences

Examples of behaviour	Possible offences
Preventing someone from seeking aid, eg medical attention	**False imprisonment, actual bodily harm**
Preventing someone from dressing as they choose or forcing them to wear a particular make-up, jewellery and hairstyles	**Actual bodily harm**, harassment**
Racial abuse	**Racially aggravated threatening behaviour*, disorderly conduct*, or harassment**
'Outing', eg sexual orientation or HIV status	**Harassment, actual bodily harm**, blackmail**
Enforced financial dependence or unreasonably depriving someone of money	**Harassment**
Dowry abuse	**Blackmail, harassment, common assault, actual/grievous bodily harm**
Unreasonable financial demands	**Blackmail, harassment**
Persistent verbal abuse, eg constant unreasonable criticism	**Harassment, actual bodily harm****
Offensive/obscene/menacing telephone calls, text messages, or letters	**Improper use of public telecommunication systems, malicious communications, harassment**
Excessive contact, eg numerous phone calls to check someone's whereabouts	**Harassment**
Secret or enforced administration of drugs	**Common assault, actual/grievous bodily harm, administering poison**
Neglecting, abandoning or ill-treating a child	**Child cruelty**

* If the threatening or disorderly words/behaviour are used in a dwelling house, the offence can only be committed if the other person is not inside that or another dwelling.

** Actual physical or mental harm must be proved to have resulted from the behaviour.

4.8.2 Arrests where the victim refuses to give evidence at court or provide a statement

Just because a victim declines to support a prosecution does not preclude you from arresting the offender, provided that the arrest is necessary to obtain sufficient evidence to support a prosecution and the victim is declining to give evidence rather than stating what they first alleged did not in fact take place.

It is the role of police to pursue all lines of enquiry and not just to focus solely on the willingness of the victim to give evidence. Therefore, officers should, in the first instance, identify and pursue all available avenues of investigation to gather as much supporting evidence as possible, which may negate the need to rely solely on the evidence of the victim.

A withdrawal statement should be taken stating why the victim is withdrawing. The CPS will also ask why the victim is withdrawing, why the police think the victim is withdrawing, and the level of risk posed to the victim, children, and other persons' safety. Police and CPS should explore **ALL** options fully. In some cases where the violence is so serious, or previous history shows a real and continuing danger to the victim, children, or other person, then the public interest in going ahead with a prosecution will outweigh the victim's wishes.

In all cases the use of special measures (4.11.9 below), 'hearsay' evidence, and whether a victim/witness should be compelled to give evidence should be considered.

4.8.3 Consequences of arresting the wrong person or arresting both parties—dual arrests

Where possible officers should refrain from arresting both parties, often referred to as dual arrests, unless it is clear that a failure to arrest will seriously undermine any future investigation or subsequent prosecution. Officers should look to arrest the primary aggressor and not just arrest both parties, believing it is easier to 'sort it out at the station'. This does not prevent the subsequent arrest of the other person, subject to the evidential test, once initial arrest enquiries have been undertaken.

The consequences of arresting the wrong person should not be underestimated and may lead to:

- victims thinking twice before calling the police again, leaving them vulnerable to further harm
- child(ren) learning to distrust the police, particularly in cases where both parents are arrested as child(ren) will associate the presence of police with the breakup of the family
- offenders being rewarded for manipulating the system
- offenders not being held accountable for their actions and getting away with it.

4.8.4 Police action where there is no power of arrest

Officers make frequent mention of the 'perceived lack of powers of arrest', particularly with regard to common assaults, with many citing the Human Rights Act 1998. However, this Act should be seen as an opportunity to facilitate proactive and creative police and multi-agency responses to domestic violence, not as a barrier for effective action. Home Office circular 19/00 states that in a case of domestic violence where there is evidence that supports the power of arrest, the 'alleged offender should normally be arrested'.

Where the power of arrest does not exist, there are still a number of options available, such as referral to other agencies and taking detailed statements for use in future criminal/civil proceedings. Some form of **POSITIVE ACTION** must **ALWAYS** be taken. This is in terms of both options surrounding the offender and safety planning in terms of the victim. At the very least, the victim should feel s/he has the option for protection.

Case study

The victim was assaulted by her boyfriend, which was witnessed by her daughter. He was also on life licence from prison for a conviction for murder. The victim **refused** to substantiate the allegation. However, the officer contacted the Licence Department regarding the suspect and they decided to revoke the licence immediately in light of the information supplied to them by the police. He was also **charged** with the assault and remanded in custody despite **no statement** being provided by the victim.

In managing any risks identified the following mnemonic, **RARA**, may assist officers in making defensible decisions. Further guidance on risk assessments and risk management can be found in Chapter 5 below.

Remove the risk:	by arresting the suspect and obtaining a remand in custody.
Avoid the risk:	by re-housing victim/significant witnesses or placement in refuge/shelter in location unknown to suspect.
Reduce the risk:	by joint intervention/victim safety planning, target hardening, enforcing breaches of bail conditions, use of protective legislation and referring high-risk cases to a MARAC.
Accept the risk:	by continued reference to the Risk Assessment Model, continual multi-agency intervention planning, support, and consent of the victim, and offender targeting within proactive assessment and tasking pro forma (PATP), risk-management-panel format (such as MARAC, or multi-agency public protection panel (MAPPP)).

4.8.5 Lawful detention of suspects in police custody where victim declines to give evidence?

The questions for the custody officer to consider when a suspect arrives at the station after arrest or returns to answer police bail before charge for enquiries to be made are governed by s 37 of PACE. They are the same for any offence:

(a) Is there sufficient evidence to charge the suspect with the offence?

(b) If not, do I have reasonable grounds to believe that the suspect's detention without charge is necessary to secure or preserve evidence relating to an offence for which the suspect was arrested or to obtain such evidence by questioning?

Arresting officers and custody officers are not expected to predict the likely outcome of a case at court at this stage. The existence of a signed withdrawal statement from the victim does not, and never has, as a matter of course, prevented police from seeking evidence to support a prosecution.

The decision whether to pursue an investigation must be made on a case-by-case basis. In deciding whether it is practicable and appropriate to pursue an investigation, it is necessary to take account of all the circumstances surrounding the offence and the offender, the time and resources which would be needed, and the likely outcome.

In domestic-violence cases, the police must consider the victim's future safety and assess the likelihood of the suspect committing further assaults. The police have a duty to make every reasonable effort to protect victims identified as being 'at risk' and to ensure that violent offenders do not evade the consequences of their actions. The Risk Assessment Model is crucial in helping you to determine the risks posed to a victim and/or the child(ren).

4.9 **Obtaining Best Evidence**

4.9.1 **Crime scenes**

You may only get one opportunity to identify, gather, and document evidence from crime scenes particularly where, for example, broken furniture, damaged property, and blood may be evident. It will more than likely be cleared up after police have left. The significance of your initial actions in the first 'Golden Hour' cannot be underestimated.

KEY POINTS—CRIME SCENES

- Early identification and preservation of all crime scenes is paramount.
- Identify scenes to corroborate victim's account, for example damage to property, torn clothing, phone lines, etc.
- Consider capturing evidence through answer phone messages, threats made on answering machines, text messages, email, cards, letters, or itemized phone billing.
- Seize previous letters or cards apologizing for behaviour ('Sorry cards') as these may corroborate the victim's accounts of previous violence.

4.9.2 **Forensic opportunities**

The use of crime-scene examiners and seizure of forensic exhibits should not be overlooked and may be useful in corroborating events. A number of recent cases have used fingerprint evidence to refute how a particular object that was used as a weapon was being held at the time.

KEY POINTS—ATTENDING INCIDENTS

- Seize and secure all forensic opportunities such as victim's swabs from injuries (if bite or skin not broken).
- Use sexual offences early-evidence kits.
- Seize clothing, fingerprints, weapons, and objects used.
- Liaise with crime-scene examiner.
- Consider expert witness to interpret forensic marks on weapons, blood splatter, etc.

4.9.3 **Evidence-capture using photographs or video**

Consider the use of both photograph and video capture at the scenes of domestic incidents. This is not only to capture evidence of injuries but also to capture damage to property, clothing, etc. A visual image of injuries/damage often has more of an impact in court proceedings than a written description. These may also be vital in proceeding with a case if the victim later withdraws. Before taking any pictures of injuries, you should seek and record the victim's consent. It is also worth taking further photographs of injuries, after 24 hours and seven days, as injuries, particularly bruising, often take time to show. The use of digital cameras should be seen as best practice as this allows you to email them to the CPS when discussing charging decisions.

KEY POINTS

In all cases consider:

- using digital camera instant evidence capture
- photographing victim/suspect (with consent) scene, damage to property, etc
- videoing evidence at scene
- using specialist crime-scene photographer
- showing images during interview and in bail and charging decisions.

> **GOOD PRACTICE—USE OF DIGITAL PHOTOGRAPHS AND VIDEO CAMERAS**
>
> Digital photographic equipment and or video cameras should be made available to patrol staff to be used in domestic-violence offences, enabling images to be produced without delay to enhance the evidence available for first interview.

4.9.4 Use of body-worn cameras

Body-worn video devices are small video cameras worn primarily on the side of the head, with the ability to record video and sound. They have the potential to improve significantly the quality of evidence provided by police officers, giving them the opportunity to confront offenders with captured footage at interview. Use of these devices was piloted in Devon and Cornwall Constabulary in the five months to March 2007, focusing on domestic violence, alcohol-related violence, and violence in public places.

During this time there was an increase in converting a violent incident into a crime (71.8% to 81.7%), an increase in charge/summons (10.2% to 15.0%), an increase in sanction detections (29% to 36.8%), and a reduction of 22.4% in officer time spent on paperwork and file preparation. Following the results of this pilot study, the government has made £3 million available to encourage rapid take-up of this technology nationally.

4.10 Conducting Interviews with Suspects

All interviews should be conducted in accordance with ACPO Investigative Interviewing Strategy (ACPO, 2004) using the interview model **PEACE** and following the seven principles of investigative interviewing.

P—Preparation and Planning. You should prepare an interview plan identifying:

- the aims and objectives of the interview
- the points to prove for the offence
- what evidence is available and from where it can be obtained
- what evidence is needed and how it can be obtained.

You will also need to have a full understanding of PACE and the codes of practice and ensure that you are fully prepared before commencing the interview, eg stationery, exhibits, location, etc.

E—Engage and Explain. You should try to establish a rapport with the suspect before asking for a full account. It is also necessary at this stage to fully explain how the interview will progress and also to administer the caution, making sure the suspect understands it. The officer should also present any 'significant statements', silences, and relevant comments at this stage.

A—Account. This stage is directed at obtaining the fullest possible account from the suspect. You can do this either by using a cognitive approach or by conversation management. You should:

- clarify the suspect's account, and, where necessary challenge it
- endeavour to put all the facts alleged in the victim's statement and any other evidence collected during your initial investigation to the suspect.

Reference should also be made to any photographs of injuries sustained by the victim; it is important to note whether the suspect admits guilt rather than agrees with the victim's statement. The offender's admissions are important should a victim withdraw their statement, as any 'agreement with the statement' would then be inadmissible in court.

C—Closure. You should ensure that there is a planned closure, rather than an impromptu end, to the interview. You will need to summarize and check back as to what the suspect has said, including an opportunity for the suspect to ask any questions.

E—Evaluate. After each interview is completed, you should review whether the objectives of the interview were met and what material you have gained from it. It may be necessary to undertake further enquiries to corroborate or refute any defence given by the suspect during interview or conduct a further interview to clarify any issues.

The seven principles of investigative interviewing are:

1. The role of investigative interviewing is to obtain accurate and reliable information from suspects, witnesses, and victims in order to discover the truth about matters under police investigation.
2. Investigative interviewing should be approached with an open mind. Information obtained from the person who is being interviewed should always be tested against what the interviewing officer already knows or what can be reasonably established.
3. When questioning anyone, a police officer should act fairly in the circumstances of each individual case.
4. The police interviewer is not bound to accept the first answer given. Questioning is not unfair because it is merely persistent.
5. Even when the right to silence is exercised by a suspect, the police still have the right to put questions.
6. When conducting a suspect interview, police officers are free to ask questions in order to establish the truth.
7. Vulnerable people, whether victims, witnesses, or suspects, should be treated with particular consideration at all times.

4.10.1 Can an interview still be conducted if the victim has changed their mind?

When proposing to interview the suspect police are under no obligation to inform the suspect or their solicitor if a victim changes their mind. If asked about the witness, care must be taken not to mislead the suspect/solicitor. However, nothing prevents police from simply declining to say anything about this issue and reminding the suspect/solicitor of what the victim alleges the suspect to have done and that police have a duty to investigate that allegation. It is for the suspect to decide whether to answer the questions.

A solicitor may object if a copy of the victim's statement of complaint is not provided, but for the reasons set out above, this does not prevent police from continuing the investigation.

4.10.2 Assessment of evidence and 'no comment' interviews

If the suspect (and their solicitor) are aware of the victim's reluctance, it is important not to assume that this will lead to a 'no comment' interview and that such interviews can never have any evidential value. The need to interview must be determined by the need to ask all the relevant questions and not on the anticipated outcome.

In some cases, the victim might change their mind and wish to give evidence; in others, there may be evidence from other sources, such as photographs of injuries to the victim or injuries to the suspect about which the suspect can be legitimately questioned.

If there has been a complete 'no comment' interview and the suspect is then charged, the solicitor may try to claim that no further evidence was obtained in interview and so there must have been sufficient evidence to charge prior to interview and therefore the period of detention without charge to interview was unlawful. This is not so. In seeking to obtain sufficient evidence to provide a realistic prospect of conviction, police are entitled to test the evidence so far obtained by giving the suspect the opportunity to confirm or deny the evidence or add anything he/she wishes and thereafter to consider the results.

The suspect's response in declining to offer an innocent explanation when presented with any admissible incriminating evidence does therefore have a value when assessing the evidence.

4.10.3 Evidence of bad character

Part 11 of the Criminal Justice Act 2003 has had a radical effect on the way cases are reviewed and prosecuted. Evidence of a defendant's bad character will play a much greater part in the investigation and prosecution of cases than it did under the previous law. It is likely to form an essential part of your evidence against a defendant because bad character is now not only relevant to credit but also relevant to the issue of guilt.

It is vital to understand which gateway to use to adduce evidence of bad character and prepare for it prior to interview. It is necessary, first off, to obtain details of a defendant's bad character including previous convictions, facts of the previous convictions, the nature of any defences used in the previous cases, and whether the defendant pleaded guilty or was found guilty. A form MG16 will also need to be completed containing these details and passed to the prosecutor at the earliest opportunity and preferably at the pre-charge stage.

4.10.3.1 What is bad-character evidence?

It is evidence of or a disposition towards misconduct (s 98) which is not related to the offence charged, or misconduct related to the investigation or prosecution of that offence (eg, witness intimidation).

4.10.3.2 When is a defendant's bad character admissible?

There are seven different conditions or gateways which must be passed if evidence of bad character is to be admissible in evidence, unless it appears to the court that the admission of the evidence would have such an adverse effect on the fairness of the proceedings that the court ought not to admit it.

Section 101(1) of the Act states that, in criminal proceedings, evidence of the defendant's bad character is admissible if, but only if:

(a) all parties to the proceedings agree to the evidence being admissible,

(b) the evidence is adduced by the defendant himself or is given in answer to a question asked by him in cross-examination and intended to elicit it,

(c) it is important explanatory evidence (ie, evidence without which it would be impossible or difficult properly to understand other evidence in the case, and its value for understanding the case as a whole is substantial),

---

KEY POINT—CASE LAW

If the evidence is more than minor or more than trivial it will be admissible if it assists the court to understand the case as a whole. For example, evidence of violence by D on a different occasion than that charged, evidence that D prevailed upon V, his girlfriend, to have an abortion, and evidence about D's knowledge of the effect of violence upon his girlfriend given that she had had a stroke are all part of the important explanatory evidence to the relationship (see *R v Underwood* [1999] *Crim LR* 227).

(d) it is relevant to an important matter in issue between the defendant and the prosecution,

'matter in issue' includes:

- whether he has a propensity to commit offences like the one he is charged with, except where propensity makes it no more likely that he is in fact guilty of this offence
- whether he has a propensity to be untruthful, except where it is not suggested that his case is untruthful in any respect

> **EXAMPLE**
>
> D is charged with assaulting his wife. He has a history of violence, in relation to both his wife and others. He claims that on one occasion in issue, she received her injuries falling down the stairs. In this case, D's previous convictions for violence are admissible (subject to the discretion to exclude) to show his propensity to commit offences of the kind with which he is charged and, subject to the facts, any acquittals would also be admissible too (as the definition of bad character also includes acquittals).

  (e) it has substantial probative value in relation to an important matter in issue between the defendant and a co-defendant,

  (f) it is evidence to correct a false impression given by the defendant. . .

(The defendant gives a false impression if he is responsible for the making of an express or implied assertion which is apt to give the court or jury a false or misleading impression about the defendant. This can be made on being questioned under caution, before charge, about the offence with which he is charged, or on being charged with the offence or officially informed that he might be prosecuted for it.)

  (g) the defendant has made an attack on another person's character

another person's character is attacked if:

- evidence is adduced attacking the other person
- questions intended or likely to attack the character are asked by or on the defendant's behalf
- he attacked the person in interview before charge or when charged.

4.11 **Prosecution of Cases**

The prosecution of domestic-violence cases is the responsibility of the Crown Prosecution Service (CPS), which has published *Policy on Prosecuting Cases of Domestic Violence* (2005). The CPS will review the police evidence and decide the most appropriate charge. This may not always be the offence for which the offender was first arrested. Where they make a decision not to charge, or decide to drop or substantially amend a charge, they are responsible for informing the victim in writing of the decision and the reasons for it.

> **GOOD PRACTICE—CHARGING THE SUSPECT**
>
> Where evidence exists, good practice is to charge for offences under the Protection from Harassment Act 1997 in addition to any primary offence; this will enable protection for the victim in the form of a restraining order on conviction. **NB** The primary offence cannot be used as a course of conduct to prove the harassment.

4.11.1 Referral of cases to the CPS

The CPS will make decisions on whether or not to prosecute domestic-violence cases according to the Code for Crown Prosecutors. They will review the case in line with the code using either the 'full code test' or, in limited circumstances, the 'threshold test'. You should have an understanding of this process and assess how the evidence you have collected is sufficient for each stage.

4.11.1.1 Full code test

This test has two stages; the first is the 'evidential stage' and the second the 'public interest stage'. If the case does not pass the first stage it will not go ahead—no matter how serious or important it is.

Stage 1—The evidential stage: The CPS must be satisfied that there is enough evidence to provide a 'realistic prospect of conviction' against each defendant on each charge. This means that a jury or a bench of magistrates or a judge hearing the case alone, properly directed in accordance with the law, is more likely than not to convict the defendant of the charge alleged.

Stage 2—Public interest stage: If the case does pass the evidential test, the CPS will then decide whether a prosecution is needed in the public interest. The CPS view domestic violence as an aggravating factor and not one of mitigation. A prosecution will usually take place unless 'there are public interest factors tending against prosecution which clearly outweigh those tending in favour'. When considering the public-interest test, one of the factors they will always take into account is 'the consequences for the victim of whether or not to prosecute, and any views expressed by the victim or the victim's family'.

4.11.1.2 The threshold test

This test will be applied to those cases in which it would be inappropriate to release a suspect on bail after charge but the evidence to apply a full code test is not yet available. Where this is the case, then the CPS will decide whether there is at least a reasonable suspicion that the suspect has committed an offence and, if there is, whether it is in the public interest to charge the suspect.

4.11.2 **Completion of pre-charge case review (MG3)**

It is essential that the CPS be provided with sufficient information in order to decide on the most appropriate charge and also on the merits of proceeding with a prosecution when the victim is reluctant or unwilling to support a prosecution.

The good-practice table below does not replace the MG3 but should complement it. A completed copy of this document should be placed in the police file and a second copy attached to the MG3, once completed by the duty prosecutor. When complete this document should be marked 'Restricted'.

GOOD PRACTICE—PRE-CHARGE CASE REVIEW	
History of the relationship	Nature and length of relationship between the complainant and suspect.
	The officer's view on the future relationship.
	Likelihood of recurrence.
	Views on safety of victim and any children.
Composition of the family	Any children in the household?
	Are the children related to suspect?
	Do they live with the suspect and/or complainant?
	Did the children witness this or previous incidents?
	Effect of proceedings on any children.
Previous incidents involving any of the parties	Number of previous calls made to police by complainant or individuals in household.
	Whether any previous calls made by third parties in relation to suspect, complainant or relevant parties.
	Copies of police reports to be supplied?
Civil orders made or pending and any breaches	Whether any civil/family proceedings pending.
	Nature of any orders imposed in the court and/or whether any orders breached by suspect.
Evidential strengths, weaknesses	Does the offender admit the offence or admit one offence and deny others?
	Has the victim previously withdrawn a case and if so why?
	Any outstanding lines of inquiry?
	If previous incident resulted in No Further Action (NFA), detail the reasons.

Ability/willingness of the victim to give evidence	Does the complainant have a support network, for example, an IDVA or Victim Support?
	If complainant has made a withdrawal statement or indicated he/she wishes to retract original allegation, indicate what action has been taken following the withdrawal/retraction and whether case can still proceed.
	Provide a report or statement with your views on withdrawal or retraction including whether prosecution should apply for a witness summons.
	Undertake a further risk assessment associated with proceeding in the absence of the complainant's consent or if decision taken to discontinue the proceedings.
Special Measures	Have special measures been considered?
	Detail whether the complainant or witnesses are vulnerable or intimidated and what special measures are required (supporting evidence and information should be obtained).
Risk Factors	Document any known high-risk factors. Use ACPO-approved risk identification/assessment model.
Bail considerations	Does the suspect know where the complainant lives?
	Would knowledge of the complainant's address or whereabouts pose a risk to the complainant?
	If the suspect is granted bail, what steps will the police undertake to ensure the complainant is notified? Will a review of complainant's safety undertaken?
	Is the MG7 sufficiently comprehensive, for example, does it deal with all of the objections to bail, previous incidents, vulnerability of complainant?
	Does the custody sergeant approve the application to remand suspect in custody?
	Has the officer considered all relevant intelligence/including evidence of bad character?

	Does the suspect pose a flight risk?
	Is there evidence/information to suggest that the suspect has breached bail conditions in the past?
Any other relevant information	Information from other statutory or voluntary agencies, eg social care, local health authority, or victim support scheme.

4.11.3 Medical statements for minor assaults

All assaults that result in an injury require supportive evidence of the injuries sustained in order to afford a realistic prospect of a conviction. However, where the injury amounts to grazes, scratches, abrasions, minor bruising, swellings, reddening of the skin, superficial cuts, a 'black eye', or is likely to result in a charge of common assault under s 39 of the Criminal Justice Act, then a medical report is unlikely be necessary.

CPS prosecutors (duty prosecutors) have been instructed that in the course of providing charging advice, or continuing to review a case, they should always consider the case on its merits. Crown prosecutors should always start by assessing the available evidence against the code for crown prosecutors and the charging standard. A medical report is likely to be unnecessary where it does no more than merely record injuries and/or treatment already described by a victim or police officer, particularly if there are also photographs.

Example

The victim was bitten on the hand by suspect. However, she **refused** to provide a statement. She was willing to have **photographs** taken of her injuries by various people including a police photographer. These photos were exhibited along with a statement from the officer who spoke to her about what she had said happened during the incident. The suspect was **charged** with ABH based on the photos and the officer's statement and was remanded in custody by the court awaiting trial without a victim statement.

In all cases, the investigating officer (IO) should:

- record the victim's injuries in their notes, using body maps if available
- ensure that details of the injury are contained within the victim's and or witness statements
- photograph the injuries.

4.11.4 Cases where the victim withdraws support for the prosecution or no longer wishes to give evidence

Where a victim wishes to withdraw their complaint, a full withdrawal statement will be taken by the investigating or other appropriate officer, which will include:

- the reasons for wishing to withdraw the complaint
- establishing whether they are saying the offence did not occur or whether they are saying that they do not wish the investigation or prosecution to continue
- whether any pressure, directly or otherwise, has been placed on them
- who they discussed the case with
- whether any civil proceedings have been instigated
- the impact on their life and that of any children.

The investigating officer or the officer taking the statement of withdrawal will inform the CPS lawyer of their view on:

- the veracity of the victim's account
- whether any coercion or pressure has been brought to bear (consider investigating further offences of witness intimidation)
- whether the case should be pursued independently of the victim based on the strength of the evidence
- whether the victim is likely to respond to a witness summons or warrant
- how a victim might react to being compelled
- safety issues relating to the victim and any children.

This should be prepared on Form MG6 where time permits.

The officer taking the withdrawal statement should be in a position to make their own statement about surrounding circumstances covering, amongst other things, the issues of duress and the state of fear of victim, and should be prepared to attend court to give such evidence orally in the case of an application being made under s 23 of the Criminal Justice Act 1988 or s 116 of the Criminal Justice Act 2003.

With the most appropriate sensitivity, the victim should be told that making a withdrawal statement does not necessarily preclude them from the requirement to attend court and give evidence if necessary. In such cases the victim may be invited to make a victim personal statement to express their views as to why they do not support a prosecution and their views now on the incident/relationship/defendant.

In some cases, the CPS may determine that, notwithstanding the victim's withdrawal, it is in the public interest to proceed with the prosecution and in some instances it will not be possible to proceed without the complainant's evidence. You will still need to continue your investigation despite the fact that the victim indicates his/her unwillingness to attend court, as the CPS will consider:

- if witness summons is appropriate
- whether the procedure in s 23 of the Criminal Justice Act 1988 is appropriate to make an application to read the witness's statement in his/her absence
- whether to make an application under s 116 of the Criminal Justice Act to admit hearsay evidence
- if there is sufficient evidence to proceed without the victim
- in certain circumstances, after careful consideration, applying for a witness warrant.

Case study

The female victim was stabbed nine times by her husband. This was witnessed by the 15-year-old daughter. The victim **withdrew** her allegation and **refused** to give evidence. There was a long history of previous serious crimes where she had declined to proceed. After consultation with CPS the victim was warned to attend court and treated as a **hostile witness** when giving evidence. From evidence given by doctors, other witnesses, and the police he was **found guilty** and sentenced to 12 years' imprisonment by Blackfriars Crown Court.

4.11.5 Disclosure (MG6)

When considering the requirements under Criminal Procedure and Investigations Act 1996 in relation to retrieval, retention, and recording of material obtained during the investigation, the following procedures should be followed:

- All reasonable lines of enquiry will be followed whether they point towards, or away from, the perpetrator.
- Details of all persons spoken to (neighbours, etc) and any notes made should be disclosed.
- All items made (logs, crime reports, etc) or retrieved in the course of the investigation must be recorded on the MG6C.
- Disclosure officers must consider the contents of each item to establish whether they or any part of them should be disclosed.

- If items are to be disclosed they must be listed on the MG6E.
- Any third-party material should be identified and the person/agency holding the material should be asked to retain it in case it is required to be disclosed. It should not be retrieved by the officer.
- All crime reports, particularly details of investigation, will be edited by the officer to ensure that any information that identifies the victim, their whereabouts, or their contact details is removed.
- Officers are reminded to sign the declaration on the MG1 and the MG6 series.
- Include crime reports of all previous DV incidents in relation to the parties concerned.

4.11.6 Cautioning domestic-violence offenders

Cautioning of offenders should be seen as a last resort in the prosecution of offences and only after all avenues of investigation have been completed and the alternative would be no further action.

The ACPO Guidance on Investigating Domestic Abuse (2008) states that cautions should only be considered as an appropriate disposal when:

- there is some evidence that it is a first domestic-abuse offence and there have been no other reports or intelligence of previous abuse to the victim or previous partners/family members
- the defendant has no previous police record for violence
- the case has been reviewed by the CPS and they have taken the decision not to progress a prosecution
- the investigation has been reviewed and the IO is satisfied that there is no further potential for investigation development
- any other possible criminal justice sanctions have been examined and progressed.

Home Office Circular 30/2005 provides further guidance in relation to simple cautions as they relate to domestic violence. Simple cautions should be considered in preference to an NFA decision, as a potential disposal in the absence of a charge/summons, for the following beneficial reasons:

- an admission of guilt is necessary for a simple caution, and the knowledge that someone has made this admission may provide the victim with some resolution
- once administered, a simple caution for a recordable offence appears on a person's criminal record and can be cited in future proceedings.

A simple caution (for a recorded offence) is a sanction detection and will be recorded as an offender brought to justice (OBTJ), which reflects the effort and resources expended by police in investigating the offence, successfully identifying the perpetrator, and contributing to victim satisfaction.

4.11.7 **Use of expert witnesses**

The use of expert witnesses is fairly well established within the criminal justice system, but in the context of domestic-violence cases it is still a fairly new concept. The use of such experts should not be overlooked and may be useful in challenging stereotypes and myths often held by those who are unfamiliar with the complex dynamics of domestic violence, particularly where victims retract statements or return to a violent relationship. It is important to understand that an expert would not be called to bolster the personal credibility of a witness. Rather, the purpose would be to provide a context against which the witness account could be assessed.

Although not appropriate in all domestic-violence cases it may be beneficial in those cases where it is necessary to:

- inform fact-finders of commonly-known characteristics of abuse victims so that they can compare the behaviour of the victim with that profile
- reduce the likelihood that the jury will develop negative feelings against the victim based on myths and misunderstandings
- enable the fact-finders to examine the facts without interference of bias or emotion
- challenge the plausibility of the victim's account at trial, not to bolster the victim's own personal qualities of truth-telling or falsehood
- explain why victims retract and give the fact-finder reason to assess in-court retractions
- assist the fact-finder to evaluate credibility, not to enhance that credibility.

If you feel that the use of an expert witness may be beneficial in your case then an early case conference with the CPS should be sought. More detailed guidance is given by Dempsey (2004).

4.11.8 **Hearsay evidence**

The law on admissibility of hearsay evidence has recently been revised by Part 11 of the Criminal Justice Act 2003; the purpose was to modernize the hearsay rule in order to send 'a clear message that, subject to the necessary safeguards, relevant evidence should be admitted where that is in the interests of justice' (Michael Wills, Parliamentary Under-Secretary of State for the Home Department, House of Commons Standing Committee B, 28 January 2003, col 602). It will be a matter for the prosecuting lawyer to decide which evidence is admissible subject to s 114 of the Act. It is important that a record is made of all comments made by victims, witnesses, or suspects to the IO during the investigation, as these may be later admissible in evidence. Section 116 of the Act allows the use of hearsay evidence—where the victim is too frightened to give evidence, too ill, or cannot be traced—and has been used successfully in domestic-violence cases.

Example

At Bradford magistrates court in March 2006 the CPS made a successful application to include the evidence of more than one officer that an assaulted wife said 'Michael, he has hit me' at the time of the assault. She was too frightened to make a complaint and could not be traced at the time of her husband's trial (for common assault). The application was made to the district judge to include the hearsay evidence from the officers and the trial that followed led to a successful conviction.

Hearsay can include any statement or matter stated. A statement is any representation of fact or opinion made by a person by whatever means; and it includes a representation made in a sketch, photofit, or other pictorial form.

4.11.8.1 When is it admissable?

Hearsay evidence will be admissable under the following conditions (s 114):

(1) In criminal proceedings a statement not made in oral evidence in the proceedings is admissible as evidence of any matter stated if, but only if—

    (a) any provision of this Chapter or any other statutory provision makes it admissible,

    (b) any rule of law preserved by section 118 makes it admissible,

    (c) all parties to the proceedings agree to it being admissible, or

    (d) the court is satisfied that it is in the interests of justice for it to be admissible.

(2) In deciding whether a statement not made in oral evidence should be admitted under subsection (1)(d), the court must have regard to the following factors (and to any others it considers relevant)—

    (a) how much probative value the statement has (assuming it to be true) in relation to a matter in issue in the proceedings, or how valuable it is for the understanding of other evidence in the case;

    (b) what other evidence has been, or can be, given on the matter or evidence mentioned in paragraph (a);

    (c) how important the matter or evidence mentioned in paragraph (a) is in the context of the case as a whole;

    (d) the circumstances in which the statement was made;

    (e) how reliable the maker of the statement appears to be;

    (f) how reliable the evidence of the making of the statement appears to be;

    (g) whether oral evidence of the matter stated can be given and, if not, why it cannot;

    (h) the amount of difficulty involved in challenging the statement;

    (i) the extent to which that difficulty would be likely to prejudice the party facing it.

(3) Nothing in this Chapter affects the exclusion of evidence of a statement on grounds other than the fact that it is a statement not made in oral evidence in the proceedings.

4.11.8.2 Admissibility of hearsay evidence in cases where the witness is unavailable

Section 116 of the Criminal Justice Act sets out a series of categories under which first-hand hearsay evidence, whether oral or documentary, will be admissible, provided that the witness is unavailable to testify for a specified reason. The new provisions will be available to the prosecution and the defence.

(1) In criminal proceedings a statement not made in oral evidence in the pro-ceedings is admissible of any matter stated if:

   (a) oral evidence given in the proceedings by the person who made the statement would be admissible as evidence of that matters,

   (b) the person who made the statement (the relevant person) is identified to the court's satisfaction, and

   (c) any of the five conditions mentioned in the subsection (2) is satisfied.

(2) The conditions are:

   (a) that the relevant person is dead;

   (b) that the relevant person is unfit to be a witness because of his bodily or mental condition;

   (c) that the relevant person is outside the United Kingdom and it is not reasonably practicable to secure his attendance;

   (d) that the relevant person cannot be found although such steps as it is reasonably practicable to take to find him have been taken;

   (e) that through fear the relevant person does not give (or does not con-tinue to give) oral evidence in the proceedings, either at all or in con-junction with the subject matter of the statement, and the court gives leave for the statement to be given in evidence.

(3) For the purposes of subsection (2)(e) 'fear' is to be widely construed and (for example) includes fear of the death or injury of another person or of financial loss.

(4) Leave may be given under subsection (2)(e) only if the court considers that the statement ought to be admitted in the interests of justice, having regard:

   (a) to the statement's contents

   (b) to any risk that its admission or exclusion will result in the unfairness to any party to the proceedings (and in particular to how difficult it will be to challenge the statement if the relevant person does not give oral evidence),

   (c) in appropriate cases, to the fact that a direction under section19 of the Youth Justice and Criminal Evidence Act 1999 (special measures for giving of evidence by fearful witnesses etc) could be made in relation to the relevant person, and

   (d) to any other relevant circumstances.

4.11.9 **Special measures**

When considering or seeking the use of special measures for vulnerable or intimidated witnesses, an early discussion with the CPS is essential to ensure that the necessary applications are made to the court.

KEY POINT—VULNERABLE OR INTIMIDATED WITNESSES IN COURT

The Youth Justice and Criminal Evidence Act 1999 introduced a range of special measures available to assist vulnerable or intimidated witnesses to give evidence in court; these can include:

- screens in the courtroom—preventing the witness from seeing the defendant (s 23)
- evidence by live link—where a witness gives evidence from outside the court-room (s 24)
- evidence given in private—where the courtroom is cleared (s 25)
- removal of wigs and gowns by lawyers and judges (s 26)
- video-recorded evidence-in-chief—where the police interview is visually recorded and played at trial as the witness's main evidence (s 27)
- video-recorded cross-examination—where any further evidence is recorded in advance of the trial and played on the day (s 28)
- intermediaries—people who act as 'go-betweens' to improve the communication and understanding of the witness (s 29)
- aids to communication—devices used by the witness to assist them in understanding questions and communicating their answers (s 30)

The categories of persons eligible to apply for special measures are:

- children under the age of 17 (s 16(1))
- those who suffer from a mental or physical disorder, or who have a disability or impairment that is likely to affect their evidence; (s 16(2))
- those whose evidence is likely to be affected by their fear or distress at giving evidence in the proceedings (s 17).

Courts will determine whether a witness falls into any of these categories, although witnesses who are alleged to be the victims of a sexual offence will be considered to be eligible for help with giving evidence unless they tell the court that they do not want to be considered eligible. Courts must also determine whether making particular measures available to an eligible witness will be likely to improve the quality of the evidence given by the witness and whether it might inhibit the testing of his/her evidence.

4.11.10 **Video interviewing victims**

Video-recorded evidence is an important new measure for vulnerable or intimidated witnesses but it is not the only special measure and it will not necessarily be appropriate to use it in every case. An early decision will need to be taken on the best way to proceed in each case—that decision will take account of all the circumstances of the case, including the particular needs of the witness and the availability and appropriateness of various special measures.

4.11.11 **Compelling victims and witnesses to attend court**

Section 80 of the Police and Criminal Evidence Act 1984 is the statutory provision which governs the competence and compellability of spouses in criminal proceedings.

Spouses are generally competent to give evidence against their partners. The only exception is if the spouses are jointly charged. If they are, neither is competent or compellable to give evidence on behalf of the prosecution against the other, unless the spouse witness has already pleaded guilty, or the proceedings in respect of the spouse witness have been discontinued.

Spouses are competent and compellable to give evidence on behalf of the defendant or the defendant's co-accused. The prosecution can only compel a spouse to give evidence for the prosecution in cases which involve:

- an allegation of violence against the spouse
- an allegation of violence against a person under the age of 16 years
- an alleged sexual offence against a victim under the age of 16 years or
- attempting, conspiring, aiding and abetting, or counselling and procuring to commit the offences in the categories above.

Unmarried partners are competent and compellable witnesses: see s 97 of the Magistrates' Courts Act 1980.

If a spouse witness has become divorced before s/he gives evidence, the spouse becomes a compellable witness in all circumstances.

The decision to compel a witness to attend court against his or her expressed wish is one that should be exercised with sensitivity and discretion. When making the decision to compel a witness to attend court to give evidence against a spouse you should bear in mind that the witness will probably be distressed. It is also important to review the risk assesment and risk-management plan at this stage in light of any additional risks which result from this action.

It is not always possible to know how the witness will react. S/he:

- may become a 'hostile witness'
- may give good evidence or
- may refuse to give evidence and be in contempt of court.

Bear in mind that the refusal of a witness to attend court may be brought about through fear. If you consider that this may be a possibility, you may be asked for further information by the CPS to consider the use of s 116 of the Criminal Justice Act 2003.

The provision of appropriate support from Victim Support, the police, and other agencies may be very important to witnesses in these circumstances.

4.12 **Specialist Domestic Violence Courts (SDVC)**

Once an offender is arrested, the establishment of Specialist Domestic Violence Courts (SDVC) in a local area may improve the outcomes of domestic-violence cases. The SDVC system situates the court system and the CJS as part of a community-wide response to domestic violence, improving local responses to DV cases, and increasing the number of DV offences reported and successfully prosecuted. Specific measures include:

- accredited independent domestic-violence advisers (IDVAs) who offer victims one point of contact during and after a case
- all CJS staff and magistrates trained on DV
- specific court listing practices to enhance the effectiveness of the court and support services.

There are currently 64 operational SDVC schemes in England and Wales. These will be expanded to 100 in England and Wales by April 2008, and be guided by the current evaluation as to next steps in the longer term.

Example

The victim reported to the police a series of incidents of domestic violence that had occurred over the last few years. The latest incident resulted in her losing hearing in one of her ears. The victim made a statement but later **withdrew** it. Medical evidence, however, was obtained. The suspect was arrested for GBH and was later convicted at court despite the defence team trying to throw the case out of court. The case was heard by a **magistrate trained in domestic violence** and the suspect was **convicted** and sentenced to six months custody.

A recent review by the CPS into areas where SDVCs were operating showed:

- There was a 15% increase in the number of cases being prosecuted in 2006/07 compared with 2005/06.
- Successful prosecutions rose from 59.7% in 2005/06 to 65.2% in 2006/07. It is important to note that successful prosecutions increased quarter on quarter during 2006/07—reaching 66% successful outcomes by the fourth quarter (January–March 2007).

- Guilty pleas increased from 52.5% in 2005/06 to 57.6% in 2006/07.
- Cases discontinued by CPS fell from 33% in 2005/06 to 27.9% in 2006/07, as did bind-overs from 14.9% to 9.6%.

4.13 Completion of Crime and Intelligence Reports

All crime and intelligence reports should be completed in as much detail as possible including full details of your investigative strategy. All reports should be cross-referenced against other reports and previous allegations. These reports are vital for building up a history of offending, identifying and managing risks, and documenting your decision-making, which may be challenged at a later time—this could well be several years after the event.

4.13.1 Recording counter-allegations of crime—National Crime Recording Standards (NCRS) compliance

It is not always necessary for you to record counter-allegations of crime. The Home Office Counting Rules provide the following guidance:

> Very often offenders claim that they were acting in self-defence and make counter-allegations of assault. Great care should be taken before routinely recording such allegations as crime. For example, when the offender makes a counter-allegation of assault this should only be recorded as such if on the balance of probability the offence took place. The absence of any evidence such as personal injury or independent witnesses may show that the allegation is false and care should be taken before recording as a crime. Each case should be treated on its own merits. (Home Office Counting Rules for Recorded Crime, April 2007)

Where counter-allegations have been made this should only be recorded as such if on the balance of probability the offence took place. The absence of any evidence, such as personal injury or independent witnesses, could indicate that the allegation is false and care should be taken before recording as a crime. Where multiple offences are alleged, advice should be sought from your crime-management units to ensure that the correct crime-reporting standards are complied with.

105

Further information and reading

ACPO (2004), *Investigative Interviewing Strategy* (London: NPIA).

ACPO (2005e), *Responses to Domestic Violence Modular Training Programme* (London: NPIA).

ACPO (2008), *Guidance on Investigating Domestic Abuse* (London: NPIA).

Criminal Justice System (2005), *The Code of Practice for Victims of Crime* (London: Office for Criminal Justice Reform).

Criminal Justice System (2006), *Working with Intimidated Witnesses: A manual for police and practitioners responsible for identifying and supporting intimidated witnesses* (London: Office for Criminal Justice Reform).

Crown Prosecution Service (2004a), *The Code for Crown Prosecutors* (London: Crown Prosecution Service), available at <http://www.cps.gov.uk/victims_witnesses/code.html>.

Crown Prosecution Service (2004b), *The Use of Expert Witness Testimony in the Prosecution of Domestic Violence* (London: Crown Prosecution Service), available at <http://www.cps.gov.uk/publications/docs/expertwitnessdv.pdf>.

Crown Prosecution Service (2005), *Guidance for Prosecuting Cases of Domestic Violence* (London: Crown Prosecution Service), available at <http://www.cps.gov.uk/publications/prosecution/domestic/>.

Crown Prosecution Service (2006), Domestic Violence Monitoring Snapshot December. Available at <http://www.cps.gov.uk/publications/prosecution/domestic/snapshot_2006_12.html>.

Risk Identification, Assessment, and Management

5.1 **Introduction**

Society is becoming intolerant of mistakes, even honest ones, on the part of public servants. It is now commonplace for citizens to resort to civil law or to complain if harm befalls them. Reflecting social change, and encouraged by the media and legal profession, the victim and/or their family is likely to want to know how the event could have been prevented and who is to blame for not protecting them.

Twenty-first-century policing can no longer simply be understood solely as the activity of the public police institution. It is now the output of a variety of agencies with multiple objectives and lines of accountability. It is no longer acceptable to speak of policing as though it relates to activities of a single organization (Wright, 2002). Policing has tended to be reactive rather than having a proactive and preventative role. This is an important point to make—we are not talking about a predictive role, but a preventative one. Policing, like the insurance business, is now in the risk society and police now have to determine the nature and degree of risk posed by an offender in terms of harm to him or herself and to others.

That having been said, historically the culture of policing has tended to be risk averse. However, more recently a risk culture is being encouraged whereby officers are trained using simulated, immersive exercises so that they can 'practise' using their judgement in different scenarios in a safe environment and learn from this experience. Nevertheless, police work is about making difficult decisions in trying circumstances with incomplete information. It is not about seeking to avoid a risk altogether. There is a growing body of literature on risk and policing, particularly regarding dangerous and serial offenders. Domestic-violence offenders tend to, more often than not, fall into this category. Managing risk is a complex and developing subject and it's one that *all* officers need to be aware of when making investigative decisions that could impact on a victim's life. Assessing and responding to risk is a key element in policing domestic violence. This chapter presents some models to use as good practice frameworks when making decisions about risk.

5.2 **What Positive Obligations are Imposed on Investigators?**

The failure to consider risks and apply an appropriate strategy constitutes negligence. The court interpretation of Art 2 ECHR in *Osman v UK* (1998) 29 EHRR 245 illustrates this point. A positive obligation was held to exist where the 'authorities knew or ought to have known at the time of the existence of a real and immediate risk to life of an identified individual or individuals from the criminal acts of a third party and that they failed to take measures within the scope of their powers which, judged reasonably, might have been expected to avoid that risk'.

Investigators and managers should take reasonable measures to manage foreseeable risks. The advent of the public inquiry, reviews, Art 2 hearings, and Independent Police Complaints Commission (IPCC) investigation are all too familiar these days—particularly regarding domestic homicides where it has been deemed more could have been done to prevent death occurring.

5.2.1 Justifiable and defensible decisions

Risk of harm can only be reduced in terms of likelihood of occurrence and/or the severity of impact. It cannot always be completely removed. Decisions on risk identification, assessment, and management do not always prevent harm and will never be infallible, but they should always be justifiable, defensible, and auditable.

KEY POINTS—JUSTIFIABLE AND DEFENSIBLE DECISION-MAKING

Any justifiable and defensible decision should be based upon:

- all available information having been collected, recorded, and thoroughly evaluated
- policies and procedures having been followed
- reliable risk assessment methods having been used where available
- all reasonable steps having been taken and any information acted upon
- practitioners and their managers having communicated with each other and with other agencies, having been effective and proactive, and having adopted an investigative approach
- decisions having been recorded and subsequently carried out.

All staff should be aware of these elements and include them in any decision-making process related to public protection and the supervision of such processes.

5.3 Benefits of Good Risk Assessment

The processes of assessing and managing risk in the context of domestic violence are intended to achieve the following (ACPO, 2005b):

1. For the victim, children, and other vulnerable persons:

- to inform decisions and actions by the police and other agencies to protect the victim, children, and other vulnerable persons
- to reduce repeat victimization
- to inform and build upon the safety-planning processes of the victim, children, and other vulnerable persons

- to assist in delivering effective multi-agency support for the victim, children, and other vulnerable persons
- to contribute to increased victim satisfaction in police responses to domestic violence.

2. For the police service:

- to assist in the processes of the police protecting the following:
  - adult victim(s)
  - child victims(s)
  - possible future victims of domestic violence, and
  - others who may be at risk. This could include police staff, members of staff from all agencies, members of the public and perpetrators of domestic violence (eg if injured or killed when the victim acts in self-defence)
- to inform child protection processes, including assistance in the fulfilment of legal obligations and commitments to other agencies (eg child protection enquiries, referrals of children to social care, information-sharing protocols, multi-agency public protection panels (MAPPA) and multi-agency risk-assessment conferences (MARAC) and other similar arrangements)
- to prevent and reduce homicides and serious injury (including domestic homicides, child homicides, and honour-based violence-related homicides)
- to mainstream the understanding and use of risk factors in domestic-violence and child-protection cases
- to inform police decision-making and action, including effective investigation and evidence-gathering
- to inform the tasking and coordinating process at strategic and tactical level (see National Intelligence Model)
- to prevent and reduce repeat victimization
- to prevent and reduce repeat and chronic offending
- to increase reporting of domestic violence to the police
- to increase public confidence and the confidence of victims, their families, and other agencies in the police response to domestic violence.

3. For other criminal justice and partner agencies:

- to inform the decision-making processes within the criminal justice system (CJS). Many criminal-justice decisions depend on information about the public interest and risk to victims and others (including historical information, recent events and risks identified). These include decisions relating to rules of evidence, public interest, and case-specific issues (eg charge, bail and remand, prosecution, and sentencing);
- to inform the decision-making processes within and between partner agencies (eg local safeguarding children boards (LSCB), multi-agency public protection arrangements (MAPPA), and multi-agency risk-assessment conferences (MARAC))

- to inform the process of information-sharing according to local information-sharing protocols, including, in some cases, providing 'prompts' or opportunities to share information
- to increase public confidence in the criminal-justice and multi-agency responses to domestic violence
- to increase the understanding of domestic violence and risk in the context of the UK.

Risk identification, assessment, and management cannot eliminate risk or predict with certainty the occurrence of particular behaviour. However, possible risks can and should be identified and the risk of serious harm kept to a minimum. All opportunities for positive action should always be exploited. ·

5.4 **Risk Identification, Assessment, and Management**

The concept is embedded in police practice and procedures in relation to the victim, offender, police officers, the impact of an event, the construction of a case file, as well as the probability of securing a conviction in court. However, the practice of risk assessment and management still requires a more professional, enhanced, and systematic approach, particularly in relation to risks posed to the victim and managing dangerous offenders using a collaboration of highly able personnel from a range of backgrounds, who are both police and non-police specialists.

Police must be prepared to open the door and work with other professionals and practitioners who can bring to the table a range of different disciplines, including behavioural science, forensic psychology, decision-making, leadership, and management studies in order to respond to victims and manage offenders more effectively. An understanding of one another's world is crucial in order to work together effectively.

Appropriate risk identification and accurate risk assessment rely on thorough information-gathering (within the police and across agencies) and the application of approved risk-assessment tools. Unless all relevant information is available to those making assessments, public protection may be compromised. This means that all staff should be familiar with the basics of risk identification so that information can be flagged and assessments kept up to date.

Identification of risk factors should be undertaken by all police staff at all stages of a domestic-violence investigation and should be taken into account when making any decision, with appropriate documentation and notification to relevant police personnel and other police staff.

The risk-management structure is that cases should be managed at the lowest level that is consistent with providing a defensible risk-management plan. Resource allocation is a matter for strategic management, and the rationale and decision-making processes leading to such decisions should be written into force policy and recorded in individual cases. The basis of this is a systematic process of identification, assessment, management, and review of risk.

All mechanisms and processes to assess and manage risk must have a sound knowledge and evidence base and be monitored and evaluated from the outset. This is an obligation on the police service and enhances service to the public. It is in the public interest that finite police resources are directed at preventing or minimizing the most serious harm.

5.4.1 What constitutes risk of serious harm?

Risk refers to risk of serious harm as defined in *Offender Assessment System (OASys) User Manual* (Home Office, 2002, revised in 2006). OASys is a national standardized risk-assessment tool used by the Prison and Probation Services for processing all offenders.

Risk of serious harm is defined as:

Definition of Risk according to OASys

'…a risk which is life-threatening and/or traumatic, and from which recovery, whether physical or psychological, can be expected to be difficult or impossible'.

Home Office (2002) Offender Assessment System (OASys) User Manual

---

5.4.2 Risk factors

There are a number of risk factors for domestic violence which need to be taken into account when assessing risk of serious harm. These factors are indicators of risk that practitioners should identify and record as early as possible. Risk factors for serious harm and homicide in cases of domestic violence will be discussed later on in the chapter.

There are three key stages in considering risk for the purposes of public protection. These are risk identification, risk assessment, and risk management.

5.4.3 Risk identification

This involves identification of the risks using evidence-based risk factors for domestic violence. Risk identification occurs when risk factors and their **context** are identified, so that risk assessment and management are based on full and accurate information. The identification of those persons who pose a risk of serious harm is the first step in establishing the specific risk factors which apply to those individuals, as well as to whom they pose a risk. Thorough gathering of information should be followed by complete analysis to identify harm and risk factors. It is also a dynamic and continuing process, as are the processes of risk assessment and risk management. Risk identification should be undertaken by first-response staff.

5.4.4 **Risk assessment**

Risk assessment is the process of establishing the following:

- the likelihood of a behaviour or event occurring
- the frequency with which it may occur
- whom it will or may affect
- the extent to which that behaviour will cause harm, ie the impact of that event.

Risk assessment sometimes involves each offender being categorized at a particular time as presenting a distinct level of risk (ie standard, medium, or high). It also identifies the specific nature of the risk posed. The process of assessing risk is dynamic and risk levels can increase or decrease depending on the situation. When properly applied, risk assessment can serve as a paradigm for effective case management. Risk assessment should be undertaken by specialist domestic-violence personnel trained in risk assessment.

5.4.5 **Risk management**

This term refers to the management of responses to risk identification and assessment to ensure that risk of further harm by the offender is minimized. Risk management involves the use of various strategies by the police and other agencies to reduce the risk posed by an offender. Increased understanding of the nature of the risk will enable service providers to plan those resources better. Risk management should be targeted at the risk factors identified. Risk management in domestic-violence cases should include, where apt, a multi-agency approach which is based around appropriate information-sharing and the development and implementation of interventions and risk management or action plans.This may be undertaken, for example, through the MARAC.

5.4.6 **Safety planning**

Safety planning describes a structured method whereby victims may consult with other agencies to enable them to make use of their existing and available resources in order to understand the risk posed by the perpetrator and increase their safety and that of their children. Such planning can facilitate a proactive approach to reducing risk of further harm. The plan should focus on the individual victim's and children's needs and circumstances, with their safety and protection being paramount at every stage.This process should be separated from the investigation process and risk assessment, although an effective investigation and risk assessment should inform a victim's safety plan.

> **KEY POINT**
>
> 'Failure to plan is planning to fail'

5.5 The Risk-Assessment Models Available for Police Staff and Officers to Use

Within the context of domestic violence there have previously been two commonly recognized risk tool kits:

- SPECSS+
- South Wales (or CAADA) model

Both have been developed using analysis of risk factors associated with domestic homicide and domestic violence. Both models are also used by partner agencies to inform the MARAC. There is evaluated evidence to show that correct use of both SPECSS+ and the South Wales (or CAADA) model, when used in the originally developed format, can reduce the incidence of domestic violence.

The ACPO Domestic Abuse, Stalking and Harassment, and Honour-Based Violence risk Model (DASH, 2008) has been compiled from research and the best of both SPECSS+ and the South Wales model. It has been developed with CAADA and they will use the non-police version for IDVAs and other non-police agencies for MARAC case identification and prioritization. The intention is for it to be launched by ACPO and CAADA towards the end of 2008/beginning of 2009.

5.5.1 Why use an ACPO-approved model?

An approved risk-assessment model is evidence-based, rooted in research, and more importantly has been tried and tested. It also ensures that a standardized framework is used across police services and in partnership with other agencies in a consistent, open, and transparent way and to allow for a more timely and accurate identification of risk. It also allows for intelligent questions to be asked to find out what is going on and make the links across public protection and offending behaviour.

Currently no scientific 'predictive formula' exists for the occurrence of future harm (including serious injury and homicide) in cases of domestic violence. However, research suggests that certain factors increase the likelihood of future harm, including homicide.

All police personnel who have contact with victims and perpetrators of domestic violence should have appropriate training to ensure knowledge and understanding of the domestic-violence risk factors.

The value of any risk-assessment tool depends on the skill of those using it, and the efficiency of the IT system it runs on. Forces should only use accredited tools operated by trained and accredited practitioners. The outcome of any risk identification assessment, and management tool should be recorded on local and national information systems, and shared with all relevant agencies. All assessments should be reviewed regularly and whenever there is a change in the circumstances of the offender.

There will always be a degree of unreliability in predicting the risk any individual poses. This is because of the nature of human behaviour and the inherent difficulties associated with assessing risk of any kind. Ensuring the most appropriate and accurate risk assessments are made, taking account of all available information and intelligence, and communicating with other agencies, all assist the risk-assessment process. It has been suggested that the use of a structured risk assessment can make police procedures and actions more consistent, more resistant to individual prejudice, and guide decisions to protect victims (Kropp, 2004). All staff should ensure that any decision they make which contributes to risk identification, assessment, and management is recorded and defensible.

5.5.2 **ACPO domestic-violence risk-assessment principles (2007)**

Clearly, it would be desirable if there was a common approach to risk assessment across the service. To introduce a common approach to risk assessment there is a requirement for certain principles to be applied to the tools in use:

I. Forces shall operate one domestic abuse risk identification checklist of risk indicators which is ACPO compliant.
AND
Forces shall operate one domestic abuse risk assessment tool which is ACPO compliant.
II. Forces should not have more than one domestic abuse risk identification checklist and assessment tool operating in the same Force area at the same time (unless for the purpose of conducting a project/pilot approved by the Force).
III. Where one or more MARAC is operating in a Force area, each MARAC should operate to the guidelines and principles contained within the CAADA MARAC implementation guide.
IV. The Force risk identification checklist and assessment tool shall be compatible with the MARAC(s) risk management process in that area.
V. Where one or more MARAC is/are operating in a Force area, all Police referrals should be made using a single Police risk assessment tool.
VI. The ACPO Domestic Abuse Policy Lead will advise on whether models proposed by Forces are ACPO compliant.

In due course, the police service and partners should rely upon one accredited risk-assessment tool which is developed and revised in light of any new academic research and evaluated good practice. This is currently being compiled in the form of DASH (2008).

If a risk-assessment model has been implemented correctly and is being supervised effectively, there are a number of signs of success that should be measured and monitored. Some of those measures include:

- increased arrests
- improved standards of investigation
- charges increased
- compliance with positive action through the criminal justice system
- improved recording of intelligence
- better risk identification and intervention
- sharing of information between agencies
- support and safety planning for victims
- reduction of repeat victimization
- monitoring and targeting of perpetrators
- reduction in homicide, rape, and serious violence.

5.5.3 Risk assessment and the investigation

Risk assessment and management processes must NOT be used to decide whether or not to conduct an effective investigation or in place of an effective investigation (ACPO, 2005). The questions which make up the risk assessment will be part of an effective investigation by the investigating officer, and should not be seen as an ancillary process to the investigation.

Identification of risk factors should be undertaken by all police staff at all stages of a domestic-violence investigation and should be taken into account when making any decision, with appropriate documentation and notification to relevant police personnel and other police staff.

Effective processes of assessing and managing risk in the context of policing domestic violence require information from and consultation with the victim, the children, and other vulnerable persons. The focus should be on increasing the safety and protection of victims, children, and others, rather than short-term organizational goals.

Information from and intelligence relating to the perpetrator acquired during an effective investigation (particularly at the stage of interview with the alleged offender) should be used in assessing and managing risk. Early and appropriate intervention in domestic-violence situations is a key element of the police response to domestic violence. Risk assessment and management should enhance rather than undermine the police response to domestic violence.

Identification of risk factors is an integral part of every stage of an effective investigation of all domestic-violence cases. However, officers should note the importance of following good practice in relation to investigation (including evidence-gathering and interviewing of suspects, victims and witnesses—refer to *Guidance on Investigating Domestic Abuse* (ACPO, 2008)). Formal processes of risk assessment and management should not undermine an effective investigation (for example, by avoiding 'leading' questions and being aware of police and CPS responsibilities relating to disclosure).

The process of identifying, assessing, and managing risk is intended to assist police forces and other agencies in meeting the positive obligations to protect individuals within the Human Rights Act, particularly Arts 2 and 3 of the European Convention on Human Rights.

5.5.4 Disclosure and risk assessment

Information and material gathered during the course of risk assessment will be treated in the same way as any other information and material in accordance with the Criminal Procedure and Investigation Act (CPIA) 1996 and the Attorney General's Guidelines (AGG) 2000.

Any information relevant to a prosecution should be conveyed to the CPS—the police officer will make a decision on the category of the material (ie, sensitive or non-sensitive), record it on the appropriate schedule and attach it to the file for the CPS. The crown prosecutor is then under a duty to review the material and decide on the issue of disclosure. Once a decision has been made about whether disclosure is necessary, consideration can then be given to whether there is a public interest immunity (PII) issue. This is likely to be in the minority of cases. If it is deemed necessary to disclose material and a PII application is unsuccessful, a decision would then have to be made whether to proceed and disclose the material or discontinue the proceedings.

5.5.5 Information-sharing and risk assessment

Assessing and managing risk effectively cannot be undertaken by the police service in isolation and must be a process undertaken in partnership with other relevant agencies and based on a shared understanding of the nature of risk. In cases where risk is identified as particularly high it is useful to have arrangements in place for multi-agency case conferences, as well as local information-sharing protocols (ISPs) or standard operating procedures (SOPS).

Any risk identification and assessment information acquired by team members should be dealt with according to *Guidance on the Management of Police Information* (ACPO, 2006). Any risk action plan that relates to the management of identified domestic-violence issues or is case-specific should be prepared by the police domestic-violence coordinator and should take into account any existing relevant risk management plans that are in place. Effective multi-agency information-sharing is crucial to a comprehensive process of risk assessment and risk management. Information-sharing should be careful, balanced, and should always focus upon ensuring the safety of the victims.

In order that the CPS can make an informed decision about a particular case, the police should provide them with as much information as possible. This also assists in the effective prosecution of the case, and can be used in the protection of the victim and any children when applying for a remand in custody. The CPS will also require information contained on the risk-assessment form.

The responsibility for assessing and managing the risk posed by perpetrators is held by agencies not victims.

5.5.6 **Reviewing the risk assessment**

Any intervention by police officers or others, including the process of assessing and managing risk, has the potential to increase the risk of harm to adult and child victims and others. The possibility of increased risk must be acknowledged within risk-assessment and management processes.

The process of assessing and managing risk in the context of domestic violence is dynamic and complex. Particular domestic-violence situations can undergo rapid and frequent change. As and when events change or new information is obtained from any source about the case, the risk assessment must be reviewed. All systems for assessing and managing risk must reflect this reality.

Police domestic-violence coordinators should monitor domestic-violence cases to evaluate and update risk assessments. Coordinators should generate further risk assessments after locally agreed periods of time to ensure that risk factors are managed and are part of a risk action plan, where appropriate.

5.5.7 **Risk identification and custody**

In conjunction with the officer in the case (OIC), you should ensure that a custody risk assessment is undertaken and recorded on the custody record for ALL domestic-violence offenders regardless of risk level. Risk identification and assessments often rely exclusively on information provided by the victim.

This can result in an incomplete assessment of the circumstances. Any information about comments or behaviour observed during the period of custody, including those made during police interview, should be inserted into the risk-identification and assessment tool. Officers should be particularly alert to any information which indicates further harm, escalation, or imminence of harm. Any intelligence should also be considered as part of this process, as should existing risk assessments carried out on the offender as part of any previous cases.

5.5.8 **Risk identification and police bail**

Officers should use the established risk factors, listed at 5.76, to make their decisions relating to police bail. The primary consideration of an officer determining bail conditions should be the safety and protection of the victim, children, and the suspect.

If a suspect is charged with an offence and released on police bail to appear at court, *The Code of Practice for Victims of Crime* (Criminal Justice System, 2005) requires that the police notify the victim of this, and of the date of the court hearing and any relevant bail conditions, within one working day for vulnerable or intimidated victims, and within five working days for other victims. In practice, in domestic-violence cases involving identified risk factors, case officers should, if possible, inform the victim of the police bail decision and any conditions prior to release. However, once a decision has been made to bail a suspect, release must not be delayed by difficulties in contacting the victim or their representative.

5.5.9 Risk identification, domestic sieges, and hostage taking

Many siege and hostage-taking incidents managed by the police are domestic in nature. Therefore the links with domestic violence should be made at the earliest stage to safeguard lives of victim(s), suspects and police personnel. Police operations should use domestic-violence intelligence and the expertise of domestic-violence officers to assist with the safe conclusion of incidents and the effectiveness of any associated investigation.

Domestic-violence officers should be ready to provide the following information to siege commanders and hostage negotiators:

- any intelligence or a criminal history suggesting previous domestic violence or child abuse in current or previous relationships
- any current or past civil order which has been in place
- any known child-contact restrictions under the Children Act 1989 or disputes relating to child contact
- domestic-violence risk factors associated with the case or the incident such as suicide threats or threats to kill
- details of any safety planning carried out with the victim or previous victims
- details of any relevant risk assessments
- any relevant information that would inform negotiation/communication tactics with the suspect.

5.6 The Domestic Abuse, Stalking and Harassment, and Honour-Based Violence Risk Model (DASH, 2008)

This DASH (2008) model complements and builds on the two existing ACPO compliant domestic abuse risk models (SPECSS+ and South Wales). It is a natural development as our understanding and responses to domestic abuse improve. It also incorporates risk factors relating to Stalking and Harassment and Honour-Based Violence. It has been developed in conjuction with Coordinated Action against Domestic Abuse (CAADA) to create one common risk framework for police and non-police agencies to refer high risk cases to multi-agency Risk Assessment Conferences (MARAC).

The DASH (2008) risk model is about prevention, not prediction. It ensures that a risk-management plan aimed at specific risk factors is put into place. When properly applied, risk assessment can serve as a paradigm for effective case management for domestic violence.

Risk assessment is based on structured professional judgement. It structures and informs decisions that are already being made by you. It is only a guide/

aide-memoire and does not provide an absolute or relative measure of risk using cut-off scores.

Assessment of risk is complex and not related to the number of risks appearing alone. Rather, the imminent risk posed to the victim or others in a particular situation will be dependent upon what they are and how they apply in that context.

There are three parts to the DASH (2008) risk model:

- Part 1: risk identification by first response police staff
- Part 2: the full risk assessment by trained police staff
- Part 3: the risk-management and intervention plan by trained police staff.

Figure 5.1 Part 1: Risk identification by the first response police staff

Guidance and Practice Advice on Risk Identification

There are two approaches to implementation—the 'big force' and the 'smaller force' approach. In the bigger forces the first response can ask about the 15 high risk factors alone (as detailed—Part1). In some smaller forces, first responders are able to ask ALL the questions contained in the Part 2 risk assessment for risk identification. Therefore, Part 2 CAN be used by the first responders in order to identify the risks and then the specialist officer will conduct risk assessment in full. Whichever approach is taken, the first response staff and their supervisor should IDENTIFY risk factors, WHO is at risk and decide WHAT level of intervention is required. This should be completed for EVERY incident. The next stage will be dependent on the identified level of risk.

Please search all relevant public protection databases such as intelligence, the IMPACT Nominal Index (INI), ViSOR, firearms and child protection, for example. Details of children resident at the address must be provided. Consider the nature of the information and what it means in terms of the investigation (lines of inquiry), as well as public protection (preservation of life, reduction and prevention of harm to victim and others). Remember a quality investigation can reduce the risk. All injuries must be photographed as well as the scene, if appropriate.

Officers should ensure that victims understand why questions are being asked—it is about their safety and protection. Particular sensitivity and attention is required when asking about whether the victim has been assaulted, physically and/or sexually by the perpetrator. These questions will also inform what level of intervention is required at the time of first contact and what measures need to be taken to protect the victim and prevent repeat victimization. Positive action should be taken in all cases and decisions must be recorded.

The vulnerability of victims cannot be overstated. This could be further compounded by issues such as traditional gender roles, literacy, language and/or immigration or refugee status. Consider honour based violence (HBV) and that there could be multiple perpetrators, for example. Considerable care should be taken when conducting a risk assessment. **Please take into consideration the victim's perception of risk.**

Please ensure you ask the victim about the abuser's behaviour when stalking and honour based violence are present and consider the context of their behaviour. **There are risk factors that relate to these areas as well.**

The risk assessment process must remain dynamic. Events and circumstances may undergo rapid and frequent change. Where this is the case, the assessment must be kept under review.

Crime Number			
Is there a history of violence, domestic or other?	☐ Yes	☐ No	
Is there intelligence on offender?	☐ Violence/ Sexual	☐ Other (please specify)	☐ None
Does the offender have access to firearms?	☐ Yes	☐ No	☐ Not known
ViSOR check and Nominal Number	☐ Yes Nominal No.:	☐ No	☐ Not known
Impact Nominal Index (INI)	☐ Yes	☐ No	☐ Not known
DNA confirmed on database	☐ Yes	☐ No	☐ Not known
Civil orders check i.e. injunctions, non-molestation orders etc	☐ Yes	☐ No	☐ Not known
Other names used (please specify)	☐ Yes	☐ No	☐ Not known
MG11 from all witnesses including attending officers	☐ Yes	☐ No	☐ Not known
Photographs/video injuries of victim and scene	☐ Yes	☐ No	☐ Not known
CCTV evidence	☐ Yes ☐ Secured and obtained?	☐ No ☐ Yes	☐ Not known ☐ No
SOCO requested	☐ Yes	☐ No	☐ Not known
House to House enquiries (including local enquiries)	☐ Yes	☐ No	☐ Not known

The 'Big Force' Approach—the 15 high risk factor questions or for the 'Smaller Force' Approach refer to Part 2 (Fig. 5.2):

Please ensure victims know why you are asking these questions—it is about their safety and protection. **These are all high risk factors.** Use the comment box to expand. Tick box if factor is present ☑	Yes ☑	No ☑
1. Victim's perception Are you afraid of what (___) might do to you and/or anyone else? (Please give an indication of what you think (name of abuser(s))'..... might do and to whom) Kill: Self ☐ Children ☐ Other (please specify) ☐ Further injury and violence: Self ☐ Children ☐ Other (please specify)	☐	☐
2. Separation (child contact) Have you separated or told (name of abuser(s) ___) you want to separate from them within the past year? (Comment) _____ Is there conflict over child contact? (Comment)	☐ ☐	☐ ☐
3. Pregnancy/New birth Are you currently pregnant or have you recently had a baby? _____	☐	☐
4. Escalation Is the abuse happening more often? (Comment on how often) _____ Is the abuse getting worse?	☐ ☐	☐ ☐
5. Community issues and isolation Are there any personal or cultural issues which make it harder for you to seek support/help? (Consider honour based violence. For example, is the victim being forced to marry, under house arrest, being 'policed' at home, self harming or being forced to go abroad? Consider LGBT, travellers, disability and further vulnerability. Comment) _____ Is there any other person that has threatened you or that you are afraid of? _____ Are you isolated from support or help? _____	☐ ☐ ☐	☐ ☐ ☐

Please use the comment box to expand. Tick box if factor is present.	Yes ☑	No ☑
6. Stalking and Harassment Does (__) text, call, contact, follow, stalk or harass you? (Please explain what has been done and whether this was to deliberately intimidate you. Ask about the context and behaviour and whether this causes significant concern) _____ _____	☐	☐
7. Sexual assault Does (__) say or do things of a sexual nature which make you feel bad or that physically hurts you or someone else? _____ _____	☐	☐
8. Child abuse Has (__) ever hurt the child(ren)? _____	☐	☐
Has (__) ever threatened to hurt the child(ren)? (Comment) _____	☐	☐
9. Use of/access to weapons and Credible threats to kill? Has (__) ever used weapons or objects to hurt you in the past? _____	☐	☐
Has (__) ever threatened to hurt or kill you and you believed them? _____	☐	☐
10. Strangulation (Choking/Suffocation/Drowning/Attempt to block airway) Has (__) ever attempted to strangle/choke/suffocate/ drown you? _____	☐	☐
11. Suicide-homicide Has (__) ever threatened or attempted suicide? _____	☐	☐

Please ensure victims know why you are asking these questions – it is about their safety and protection. **These are all high risk factors.** Use the comment box to expand. Tick box if factor is present	Yes ☑	No ☑
12. Controlling and/or jealous behaviour Does (___) try to control everything you do and/or are they excessively jealous? (I.e. relationships, who you see, being 'policed at home', telling you what to wear for example. Consider honour based violence and stalking and specify behaviour) _____	☐	☐
13. Animal/ Pets Abuse Has (___) ever hurt the family pet/animals? _____	☐	☐
14. Alcohol/drugs Abuse Has (___) had problems in the past year with drugs, alcohol, prescription drugs leading to problems in leading a normal life? (Please specify which) _____ _____	☐	☐
15. Mental health Has (___) had problems in the past year with their mental health leading to problems in leading a normal life? (Please specify) _____	☐	☐
Other relevant information (from victim or officer) which may alter risk levels. Describe: (consider for example victim's vulnerability—disability, mental health, alcohol/substance misuse and/or the abuser's occupation/interests—does this give unique access to weapons i.e. ex-military, police, pest control and whether the abuser has ever broken an injunction, molestation order, breached bail and/or agreement?)		
Is there anything else you would like to add to this?		

In all cases an initial risk assessment is required: STANDARD, MEDIUM, HIGH:

Imminent risk to victim:		
STANDARD ☐	MEDIUM ☐	HIGH ☐

Risk Identification Categorization

This is based on the OASys (Offender Assessment System developed by the Prison and Probation Services) definitions of what constitutes standard, medium, high risk:

Standard	Current evidence does not indicate likelihood of causing serious harm.
Medium	There are identifiable indicators of risk of serious harm. The offender has the potential to cause serious harm but is unlikely to do so unless there is a change in circumstances, for example, failure to take medication, loss of accommodation, relationship breakdown, drug or alcohol misuse.
High	There are identifiable indicators of risk of serious harm. The potential event could happen at any time and the impact would be serious.
	Risk of serious harm (Home Office 2002 and OASys 2006):
	'A risk which is life threatening and/or traumatic, and from which recovery, whether physical or psychological, can be expected to be difficult or impossible'.

Actions taken by the Investigating Officer

You must take all reasonable steps to manage the immediate risk

Review

The risk is:

Imminent risk to victim:		
STANDARD ☐	MEDIUM ☐	HIGH ☐

Actions assigned by the Supervisor

The following actions have been allocated to manage risk (show officer responsible and result)

| |
| |
| |
| |
| |

This model is most effective when undertaken by officers who have been fully trained in its use.

I have reviewed this form, the risks identified and the quality of the investigation to date. I confirm that they have been completed to a satisfactory standard and all reasonable risk management actions have been taken

Supervisor Name _____

Date and Time _____

Guidance on risk management

A crucial part to risk identification is risk management. Please refer to Part 4—the domestic abuse tactical menu of intervention options for victims and offender for use by trained police staff. If honour based violence features, please use the ACPO HBV Tactical Menu of Intervention Options for Victims and Offenders.

Several levels of intervention/prevention should be considered once a risk(s) has been identified. The risk management plan should be targeted at the risk factors identified. A carefully planned and co-ordinated response is needed from the agencies working in close partnership. Victim's views should be incorporated into the assessment process.

The level of risk identified (be it Standard, Medium or High) is not linked to a prescriptive risk management/safety plan as each case that presents will be different. You will need to identify the risks first off in order to create a bespoke risk management/safety plan for each victim aimed at the risk factors identified. Flexibility is required for this reason. Use the tactical menu of intervention options list (at Part 4 Section 5) as a prompt for what might be available to you. Please note some of the options listed may not be available to you in your force area.

Risk management frameworks

Use the **RARA** model when compiling safety plans for victims. What are you seeking to do?

Remove the risk:	By arresting the suspect and obtaining a remand in custody.
Avoid the risk:	By re-housing victim/significant witnesses or placement in refuge/shelter in location unknown to suspect.
Reduce the risk:	By joint intervention/victim safety planning, target hardening, enforcing breaches of bail conditions, use of protective legislation and referring high risk cases to Multi-Agency Risk Assessment Conference (MARAC).
Accept the risk:	By continued reference to the Risk Assessment Model, continual multi-agency intervention planning, support and consent of the victim and offender targeting within Proactive Assessment and Tasking pro forma (PATP), or Risk Management Panel format (such as Multi-Agency Risk Assessment Conference (MARAC) or Multi-agency Public Protection Panel (MAPPP).

Please refer to the ACPO Guidance on Investigating Domestic Abuse (2008) for further information on the options listed. If stalking features, please refer to the ACPO Practice Advice on Investigating Harassment (2005).

Please use the PLANBI for Human Rights
Proportionality:
Police actions must be fair and achieve a balance between the needs of society and the rights of the individual. You should consider different options to achieve the objective and select the least intrusive.

Legality:
Police actions must be supported by legislation or stated cases. You must know your basic police powers.

Accountability:
Police actions will be open to scrutiny. You should fully record your actions and the options considered. Show what factors influenced your decisions, include reasons for ***not*** taking action. ***Your decisions must be defensible and auditable. This is your decision log***.

Necessity:
Police actions must be 'necessary in a democratic society'. You must be able to justify any infringements of rights.

Based on the

Best Information/Intelligence:
Police actions must be based on the best information and intelligence *available at that time.*

Domestic Abuse High Risk Factor Definitions for Serious Harm and Homicide
Q1. Separation (child contact): have you separated or tried to separate from (name of the abuser(s).....) within the past year?
Research and analysis shows that attempts to end a relationship are strongly linked to intimate partner homicide. Websdale (1999) states that attempts to leave violent men are one of the most significant correlates with domestic death. Notions of *'If I can't have her, then no-one can'* are recurring features of such cases and the killer frequently intends to kill themselves (Wilson and Daly, 1993; Richards, 2003).

Threats that begin with *'if you were to ever leave me...'* must be taken seriously. Victims who stay with the abuser because they are afraid to leave may correctly anticipate that leaving would increase the risk of serious harm. The data on time-since-separation further suggest that women are particularly at risk within the first three months (Wilson and Daly, 1993; Richards, 2003). Further, many incidents happen as a result of discussions and issues around child contact or disputes over custody (Richards, 2003 and 2004). Children must be considered in the assessment process.

Q2. Pregnancy/new birth: Are you currently pregnant or have you recently had a baby?
Pregnancy can be a time when abuse begins or intensifies (Mezey, 1997). Gelles (1988) found that pregnant women had a greater risk of both minor and severe violence than non-pregnant women. Domestic violence is associated with increases in rates of miscarriage, low birth weight, premature birth, foetal injury and foetal death (Mezey, 1997). Domestic violence was disclosed as a feature of the lives of women in at least 12% of maternal deaths in the UK during 1997–1999 (Confidential inquiries into Maternal Deaths, UK 1999).

Young children are extremely vulnerable in situations of domestic abuse and consideration must be given both to the risks that they face and the risks to the mother. Research suggests that children under 18 months are the most vulnerable in these situations.

More recent research, Jasinski (2004), has confirmed that serious consequences remain for those who suffer domestic abuse during pregnancy. If the victim responds positively to this question, you should note whether she is pregnant or has just given birth.

Q3. Escalation: Is the abuse happening more often? Is the abuse getting worse?
Previous domestic violence is the most effective indicator that further domestic violence will occur. 35% of households have a second incident within five weeks of the first (Walby and Myhill, 2000). There is a very real need to identify repeat victimization and escalation. Victims of domestic violence are more likely to become repeat victims than any other type of crime. Research indicates that general violence tends to escalate as it is repeated. Analysis indicates that the time between incidents seems to decrease as the number of contacts escalate (Understanding and Responding to

Hate Crime Team, 2001). Men who have demonstrated violent behaviour in either past or current intimate relationships are at risk for future violence (Sonkin, 1987).

Q4. Community issues and isolation: Are there any personal or cultural issues which make it harder for you to seek support/help? Are you isolated from support or help? (Consider honour based violence. For example, is the victim being forced to marry, under house arrest, being 'policed' at home, self harming or being forced to go abroad? Consider LGBT, disability and further vulnerability. Comment)

Needs may differ amongst community groups. This might be in terms of issues of perceived racism, language, culture, insecure immigration status and accessing relevant support services. Domestic violence may take on different forms within specific communities. Reduced access to services and social isolation can combine to increase lethal risks. For example, this could apply to newly arrived communities, asylum seekers, older people, people with disabilities, as well as travelling, ethnic minority and/or gay, lesbian, bisexual or transgender people. There may be difficulties speaking/reading English, not working outside the home, service access issues – not knowing who, how or where to go for help.

Consider issues relating to Honour Based Violence (HBV)[1]:

'HBV is a crime or incident, which has or may have been committed to protect or defend the honour of the family and/or community' (ACPO, 2008). It can be distinguished from other forms of violence, as it is often committed with some degree of approval and/or collusion from family and/or community members. Examples may include murder, un-explained death (suicide), fear of or actual forced marriage, controlling sexual activity, domestic violence, child abuse, rape, kidnapping, false imprisonment, threats to kill, assault, harassment, forced abortion. This list is not exhaustive.

Officers should assess the situational context and consider asking further questions of victims who are particularly vulnerable or socially isolated in terms of:

- ✓ Truanting—this is risk a factor amongst teenage girls;
- ✓ Self-harm—more prevalent amongst young Asian women and a predictor for suicide;
- ✓ House arrest and being 'policed at home';
- ✓ Threats to kill, harm or that they will never see the children again;
- ✓ Fear of being forced into an engagement/marriage;
- ✓ Isolation—this is one of the biggest problems facing victims of forced marriage. There may be difficulties speaking/reading English, not working outside the home and/or living in an isolated community;
- ✓ Pressure to go abroad;
- ✓ Insecure immigration status;
- ✓ Disability (physical or mental).

---

[1] Refer to ACPO HBV advice leaflet, tactical menu of intervention options for HBV offenders and victims and the HBV resource documents. They are available on the NPIA Genesis website: www.genesis.pnn.police.uk

Evidence from research and analysis shows that where such murders occur, most often wives are killed by their husbands and daughters by their fathers (Richards and Dhothar, 2007). HBV is often a child protection issue. Males can also be victims, sometimes as a consequence of their involvement in what is deemed to be an inappropriate relationship, if they are gay, or if they are believed to be supporting the victim. Relatives, including females, may conspire, aid, abet or participate in the killing. Younger relatives may be selected to undertake the killing, to avoid senior family members being arrested and prosecuted. Sometimes contract killers (bounty hunters) are employed. HBV cuts across all cultures, nationalities, faith groups and communities.

Do not underestimate that perpetrators of HBV really do kill their closest relatives and/or others for what might seem a trivial transgression. Just the perception or rumour of immoral behaviour may be sufficient to kill. Such trigger incidents may include (this list is not exhaustive):

- ✓ Smoking in public;
- ✓ Inappropriate make up or dress;
- ✓ Truanting;
- ✓ A relationship not being approved of by family and/or community;
- ✓ Interfaith relationships;
- ✓ Rejection of religion or religious instruction;
- ✓ Rejection of an arranged marriage;
- ✓ Pre-marital conflict;
- ✓ Pre-marital or extra marital affair;
- ✓ Objection to being removed from education;
- ✓ Reporting domestic abuse;
- ✓ Escalation—threats, violence, restrictions;
- ✓ Running away;
- ✓ Sexual conduct—talking, kissing, intimacy in a public place;
- ✓ Pregnancy outside of marriage;
- ✓ Rape;
- ✓ Being a reluctant immigration sponsor;
- ✓ Attempts to separate/divorce;
- ✓ Sexual orientation (including being gay, lesbian, bisexual or transgender).

Q5. Stalking: Does (…..) text, call, contact, follow, stalk or harass you? (Please explain what has been done and whether this was to deliberately intimidate you. Ask about the context and behaviour and whether this causes significant concern)

Most female victims know their stalker. Stalking commonly occurs after the relationship but can also occur before the relationship ends (McFarlane, Campbell, Wilt, Sachs, Ulrich & Xu, 1999). Stalkers are more likely to be violent if they have had an intimate relationship with the victim. A prior intimate relationship is the most powerful predictor of violence in stalking cases (Mohandie, Meloy, McGowan and Williams, 2006). Intimate stalkers are more likely to exhibit higher levels of behaviour indicative of dangerousness (Palarea et al.1999). Furthermore, stalking is revealed to be related to lethal and near lethal violence against women and, coupled with physical assault, is significantly associated with murder and attempted murder.

Sheridan and Davies (2001) found that ex-intimate stalkers were the most aggressive of all stalkers. Ex-partners were overall the most intrusive in their behaviour and were also the most likely to threaten and assault third parties as well as their principal victim. Sheridan and Davies (2001) research suggests that being stalked carries a high violence risk.

Please ensure you ask the victim about the abuser's behaviour when stalking is a factor and consider the context of their behaviour. Risk factors for future violence for domestic stalkers include:

- ✓ If the victim is very frightened;
- ✓ Previous domestic abuse and harassment history;
- ✓ Vandalizing or destroying property;
- ✓ Turning up unannounced more than three times a week;
- ✓ Following the victim or loitering near the victim;
- ✓ Threats of a physical or sexual violence;
- ✓ Harassing any third party since the harassment began (i.e. family, children, friends, neighbours, colleagues);
- ✓ Acting violently to anyone else during the stalking incident;
- ✓ Engaging others to help (wittingly or unwittingly);
- ✓ Abuser abusing alcohol/drugs;
- ✓ Previous violence in past (intelligence or reported).

Q6. Sexual assault: Does (…..) say or do things of a sexual nature which make you feel bad or that physically hurts you or someone else?
The analysis of domestic sexual assaults reported to the police demonstrates that those who are sexually assaulted are subjected to more serious injury (Richards, 2004). Further, those who report a domestic sexual assault tend to have a history of domestic abuse whether or not it has been reported previously.

One in twelve of all reported domestic sexual offenders were considered to be very high risk and potentially dangerous offenders (Richards, 2004). There is a link between domestic and stranger sexual offending. Further, Browne (1987) reported that over 75% of the abused women who killed their abuser were raped by him. Men who have sexually assaulted their partners and/or have demonstrated significant sexual jealousy are more at risk for violent recidivism (Stuart and Campbell, 1989).

Q7. Child abuse: Has (…….) ever hurt the child(ren)? Has (…….) ever threatened to hurt or kill the child(ren)?
It is also important to note whether the child(ren) have witnessed or heard the abuse. There is compelling evidence that both domestic violence and child abuse can occur in the same family. Child abuse can therefore act as an indicator of domestic violence in the family and vice versa. Websdale (1999) outlines three antecedents to child homicide: prior history of child abuse; prior agency contact; and a history of adult domestic violence in the family. In a recent analysis of serious review cases

of child deaths, one of the commonly reoccurring features was the existence of domestic violence (Department of Health, 2002).

There is a significant association between risk and the number of children in a household, the greater the number the higher the risk (Barmish 2004 and sidebottom and Heron 2006.) The presence of step children in particular increases the risk to both the child and the woman (Cavanagh et al. 2007).

Q8. Use of weapons and/or credible threats to kill: Has (……..) ever used weapons or objects to hurt you in the past. Has (……..) ever threatened to hurt or kill you and you believed them?

The use of weapons and/or threats which the victim believe to be credible are important to note for the purposes of risk assessment. Abusers who have used a weapon on intimate partners or others, or have threatened to use a weapon, are at increased risk of violent recidivism (Sonkin, Martin and Walker, 1985).

Both sub-lethal assaults and threats to kill can be interpreted as coercive tactics to terrorize victims and thus keep them under the abusers control (Wilson and Daly, 1993). A credible threat of violent death can very effectively control people and some may carry out this threat. Evidence suggests that such threats to estranged partners by the abuser are more often than not sincere.

Q9. Strangulation (Choking/Suffocation/Drowning or blocking the airway): Has (……..) ever attempted to strangle/choke/suffocate/drown you?

It is important that escalating violence, including attempts at strangulation, are recorded for the purposes of assessing risk (Richards, 2003). Strangulation or 'choking' is a common method of killing by male perpetrators of female victims (Dobash et al., 2004). Bruising may not be immediately obvious around the neck and skin pigmentation may compound marks being seen. Petichae (burst blood capillaries) may be evident in the eyes or on the skin. Any attempt at closing down the victim's airway should be considered high risk.

Q10. Suicidal or homicidal ideation/intent: Has (…….) ever threatened or attempted suicide?

If step children (not the biological children of the abuser) are present it is worth exploring the quality of the relationship between the abuser and step child and whether to refer to children services.

Suicidal behaviour is evidenced by history of suicide attempts, self-harm or thoughts about it. Homicidal behaviour is evidenced by the same. There is a link between dangerousness to self and dangerousness to others; that is the two factors co-exist more often than expected on the basis of chance (Menzies, Webster and Sepejak, 1985).

The homicide victims in such cases are almost always female. The person who usually kills, cannot let the victim go. Homicide-suicide rarely involves strangers. The most common factor in homicide-suicide is that the male needs to control the relationship. If a wife or girlfriend tries to leave, the man will often threaten to kill himself. This is a manipulative move and one that needs to be taken seriously. The perpetrator should be assessed not just for suicide but possibly homicide-suicide.

Q11. Controlling and/or Jealous Behaviour: Does (.......) try to control everything you do and/or are they excessively jealous? (i.e. relationships, who you see, being 'policed at home', telling you what to wear for example. Consider honour based violence and stalking and specify behaviour)

Men who believe that they 'should be in charge' are more likely to use violence against their partner. Consider honour based violence—a victim may not have the freedom of choice, may be heavily 'policed' at home or unable to leave the home address except under escort or children may be used to control the victim's behaviour.

Complete control of the woman's activities and extreme jealousy have both been associated with severe battering (Richards, 2004; Campbell, 1986). Furthermore, jealous/controlling behaviour also has been shown to increase the likelihood of other risk factors for violence and abuse (Robinson, 2004, 2006a). A perpetrator's obsessive possessiveness and morbid jealousy, has been listed as one antecedent to domestic homicide (Websdale, 1999). Possessiveness, jealousy and 'stalking' behaviour include following the victim, persistent telephone calls, visits, texting, and sending letters. A large proportion of harassment and 'stalking' cases involve former partners and there are clear links between this behaviour and domestic violence and domestic homicide by men against women (Morris, Anderson and Murray, 2002).

Q12. Animals/Pet Abuse: Has (........) ever hurt the family pet/animals?

Experts increasingly recognise a disturbing correlation between cruelty to animals and domestic violence (Cohen and Kweller, 2000). For families suffering domestic violence or abuse, the use or threat of abuse against companion animals is often used for leverage by the controlling/violent member of the family to keep others in line or silent. The violence may be in the form of spousal abuse, child abuse (both physical and sexual), or elder abuse. It is estimated that 88% of pets living in households with domestic abuse are either abused or killed. Of all the women who enter shelters to escape abuse, 57% have had a pet killed by their abuser (http://www.healthypet.com/Library/animal_bond-14.html). Common types of cruelty include torture, shooting, stabbing, drowning, burning, and bone-breaking. The main reason for animal abuse within a domestic relationship is control. Threatening, harming, and killing companion animals can powerfully demonstrate someone's power over a partner or child (http://www.vachss.com/guest_dispatches/ascione_1.html). Abuse of animals by the perpetrator may also indicate a risk of future harm (NSPCC, 2003).

Q13. Alcohol/Drugs Abuse: Has (........) had problems in the past year with drugs, alcohol, prescription drugs leading to problems in leading a normal life?

This includes serious problems in the past year with illicit drugs, alcohol or prescription drugs that lead to impairment in social functioning (health, relationships etc.). Research shows that when perpetrators have aggravating problems (alcohol, drug, and/or mental health issues), they are also more likely to injure the victim, to use weapons, and to escalate the frequency or severity of the domestic violence (Robinson, 2003, 2006b). Coker et al (2000) found the male partner's drug or alcohol use to be the strongest correlate of intimate partner violence and Robinson (2003) found that those who used drugs were more likely to inflict injuries and emotionally abuse their partners. Substance abuse is related to criminality and recidivism in general. Recent substance abuse is associated with risk for violent recidivism among partner assaults (Stuart and Campbell, 1989).

Q14. Mental Health: Has (.......) had problems in the past year with their mental health leading to problems in leading a normal life?

Physical and mental ill health does appear to increase the risk of domestic violence, but again conclusions relating to causation are complex as the health issues may be the results of the violence (Walby and Myhill, 2001). Disability and issues of physical and mental ill health (for example depression and/or suicidal feelings) can be important in assessing the victim's vulnerability to future harm. Alcohol and drugs misuse can also relate to mental and physical ill health and can also be a response to continued abuse.

Q15. Victim's perception that they are at risk of future harm: Are you afraid of what (.....) might do to you and/or anyone else? (Please give an indication of what you think (name of abuser(s).....) might do and to whom).

The victim's perception of the level of risk is an important element that should be included in risk assessment as the victim has the most detailed knowledge of the suspect (Weisz et al., 2000). Officers should also be aware that victims frequently underestimate their risk of harm from domestic abusers. However, it is important that fears for their own safety are integral in assessing the risk to them.

Other relevant information (from victim or officer) which may alter risk levels. Describe: (consider for example victim's vulnerability i.e. disability, mental health, alcohol/substance misuse and/or the abuser in terms of previous history or occupation/interests—does this give unique access to weapons i.e. ex-military, police, pest control).

This question is intended to pick up other issues that might change the risk level. This could relate to the victim in terms of their vulnerability (i.e. disability, mental health or alcohol /substance misuse), or something that might come to your notice or that might relate directly to the abuser (i.e. if ex-military/police and engaged in stalking behaviour the abuser may well have been trained in surveillance techniques or have unique access to weapons). Any of these things would increase the risk.

KEY POINTS—RISK IDENTIFICATION

Any risk identification process should be:

- compliant with *Guidance on Identifying, Assessing and Managing the Risk in the Context of Policing Domestic Violence* (ACPO, 2005)
- carried out in all domestic-violence cases, including both incidents and crimes
- based upon the ACPO-established risk factors for domestic violence, which are based on empirical research
- inclusive of information relating to frequency and repeat victimization, severity, and escalation of abuse
- part of the entire investigation, there should be opportunities for all relevant staff to incorporate information into the risk-identification process (eg, call-takers, custody officers, suspect interviewing officers)

- established with an awareness training programme for all first responders (police officers and staff)
- separate from risk-assessment processes, which should be carried out by a trained member of staff
- communicated to victims at the earliest appropriate stage of the investigation
- reviewed and supervised by a domestic-violence officer
- supported by a mentoring system for less experienced officers or those requiring refresher training
- victim- and offender-focused, identifying factors relating to both parties
- defensible, justifiable, and auditable—therefore decision-making should be recorded.

Figure 5.2 Part 2: – risk assessment by trained officer (refer to guidance notes and factors definitions)

If your force has used Part 1 for first responders then this form should be completed for MEDIUM and HIGH risk domestic crime and incidents. If your force has used the 'Smaller Force' approach (first response officers are able to ask all questions in Part 2 in terms of risk identification), as the risk assessor you should complete this for MEDIUM and HIGH risk cases as well. If not, this should be completed for ALL incidents of domestic abuse.

Please search all relevant public protection databases such as intelligence, Impact Nominal Index (INI), ViSOR, firearms and child protection, for example. Details of children resident at the address must be provided. Consider the nature of the information and what it means in terms of the investigation (lines of inquiry), as well as public protection (preservation of life, reduction and prevention of harm to victim and others). Remember a quality investigation can reduce the risk. All injuries must be photographed as well as the scene, if appropriate.

The Part 2 Risk Assessment should be undertaken by a trained officer and the information obtained should be used to inform the risk management safety plan. Please refer to Part 3: the DA or HBV Tactical Menu of Intervention Options in full.

Please ensure that when you conduct the risk assessment, the victim is comfortable and understands why you are asking certain questions. Particular sensitivity and attention is required when asking about whether the victim has been assaulted, physically and/or sexually by the perpetrator.

The vulnerability of victims cannot be overstated. This could be further compounded by issues such as traditional gender roles, literacy, language and/or immigration or refugee status. Consider honour based violence (HBV), for example. Considerable care should be taken when conducting a risk assessment. **Please take into consideration the victim's perception of risk.**

Please ensure you ask the victim about the abuser's behaviour when stalking and honour based violence are present and consider the context of their behaviour. **There are risk factors that relate to these areas as well.**

The risk assessment process must remain dynamic. Events and circumstances may undergo rapid and frequent change. Where this is the case, the assessment must be kept under review.

Guidance and Practice Advice on Risk Assessment

Crime Reference Number:				
Sources of Information:	☐ Victim	☐ Other sources, please state		
Does the offender have a criminal record?	☐ Domestic	☐ Other (specify)		☐ None
Is there a history of violence, domestic or other?	☐ Violence	☐ Sexual	☐ Other (specify)	☐ None
Is there a history of violence with other partners or anyone else?	☐ Yes	☐ No	☐ Not known	
Is there intelligence on offender?	☐ Violence	☐ Sexual	☐ Other (specify)	☐ None
Does the offender have access to firearms?	☐ Yes	☐ No		☐ Not known
ViSOR check and Nominal Number	☐ Yes Nominal No:	☐ No	☐ Not known	
Child To Notice (CTN)	☐ Yes	☐ No	☐ Not known	
DNA confirmed on database	☐ Yes	☐ No	☐ Not known	
PHA Notices	☐ Yes	☐ No	☐ Not known	
Existing Bail Conditions	☐ Yes	☐ No	☐ Not known	
Civil orders check i.e. injunctions, non-molestation etc	☐ Yes	☐ No	☐ Not known	
Other names used (please specify) Other dates of birth (please specify)	☐ Yes	☐ No	☐ Not known	

Current situation The context and detail of what is happening is very important. The questions highlighted in bold are high risk factors. Tick the relevant box and add comment where necessary to expand.	Yes ☑	No ☑
1. Has the current incident resulted in injury?	☐	☐
2. Are you very frightened?* (Please note extreme levels of fear)	☐	☐
3. Are you afraid of further injury or violence? (Please give an indication of what you think (name of abuser(s)) __ might do and to whom)	☐	☐
Kill: Self ☐ Children ☐ Other (please specify) ☐		
Further injury and violence: Self ☐ Children ☐ Other (please specify) ☐		
Other (please clarify): Self ☐ Children ☐ Other (please specify) ☐		
4. Do you feel isolated from family/ friends i.e. does (name of abuser(s) __) try to stop you from seeing friends/family/Dr or others?*	☐	☐
5. Have you separated or told (name of abuser(s) __) you want to separate from them within the past year?	☐	☐
6. Is there conflict over child contact?	☐	☐
7. Does (__) constantly text, call, contact, follow, stalk or harass you?* (Please expand to identify what and whether you believe that this is done deliberately to intimidate you? Consider the context and behaviour of what is being done)	☐	☐
8. Are you feeling depressed or suicidal?	☐	☐
Children/Dependants (If no children/dependants, please go to the next section)	Yes	No
9. Are you currently pregnant or have you recently had a baby?*	☐	☐
10. Are there any children, step-children that aren't (__) in the household? Or are there other dependants in the household (i.e. older relative)?	☐	☐
11. Has (__) ever hurt the children/dependants?	☐	☐
12. Has (__) ever threatened to hurt or kill the children/dependants?	☐	☐

Domestic Violence History	Yes	No
13. Is the abuse happening more often?*	☐	☐
14. Is the abuse getting worse?*	☐	☐
15. Has (__) ever used weapons or objects to hurt you?*	☐	☐
16. Has (__) ever threatened to kill you or anyone else and you believed them?*	☐	☐
17. Has (__) ever attempted to strangle/choke/suffocate/drown you?*	☐	☐
18. Do they do or say things of a sexual nature that makes you feel bad or that physically hurt you or someone else?* (Please specify who)	☐	☐
19. Does (__) try to control everything you do and/or are they excessively jealous? (I.e. relationships, who you see, being 'policed at home', telling you what to wear. Consider honour based violence and stalking and specify behaviour)*	☐	☐
20. Is there any other person that has threatened you or that you are afraid of?* (Consider extended family if honour based violence. Please specify who)	☐	☐
21. Do you know if (__) has hurt anyone else in the family, anyone else they have had a relationship with or anyone else? (children/siblings/elderly relative/stranger, for example. Consider HBV. Please specify who and what)	☐	☐
22. Has (__) ever hurt the family pet/animals?*	☐	☐
Abuser(s)	Yes	No
23. Are there any financial issues? For example, are you dependent on (__) for money/have they recently lost their job/ other financial issues?	☐	☐
24. Has (__) had problems in the past year with drugs (prescription or other), alcohol or mental health leading to problems in leading a normal life?* (Please specify what) **Drugs ☐ Alcohol ☐ Mental Health ☐**	☐	☐
25. Has (__) ever threatened or attempted suicide?*	☐	☐
26. Has (__) ever broken an injunction, molestation order, breached bail and/or agreement for when they can see you and/or the children? (If yes, please specify i.e. breach of civil/ criminal order or bail conditions)	☐	☐

27. Do you know if (___) is involved in any other criminal activity? (If yes, please specify) DV☐ Sexual violence ☐ Other violence ☐ Other ☐	☐	☐
Other relevant information (from victim or officer) which may alter risk levels. Describe: (consider for example victim's vulnerability—disability, mental health, alcohol/substance misuse and/or the abuser's occupation/interests—does this give unique access to weapons i.e. ex-military, police, pest control?)		
Is there anything else you would like to add to this?		

Imminent risk to victim:

STANDARD ☐   MEDIUM ☐   HIGH ☐

Investigating officer's signature: _____

Date: _____

Part 2 of the Risk Assessment: Risk Factor Definitions

Q1. Has the current incident resulted in injury?

Research from Browne et al. (1999) concluded that 'the greatest risk factor for partner homicide by men appears to be estrangement and prior assaultive and controlling behaviour'.

Q2. and Q3 How frightened are you? And Q3. What are you afraid of? Is it further injury or violence?

The victim's perception of the level of risk is an important element that should be included in risk assessment as the victim has the most detailed knowledge of the suspect (Weisz et al., 2000). When victims are very frightened, when they report being afraid of further injury or violence, when they are afraid of being killed, and when they are afraid of their children being harmed, they are significantly more likely to experience additional violence, threats and emotional abuse (Robinson, 2006a). Thus, victim perception cannot be ignored. Officers also should be aware that victims frequently underestimate their risk of harm from domestic abusers. Whilst not every assessment on the victim's part will be accurate, their fears for their own safety are integral in assessing the risks to them.

Practitioners need to keep in mind the wider risks to other family members, especially children. Websdale (1999) outlines three antecedents to child homicide: prior history of child abuse; prior agency contact and a history of adult domestic violence in the family. In a recent analysis of serious case reviews of child deaths, one of the commonly reoccurring features was the existence of domestic violence (Department of Health, 2002).

Q4. Do you feel isolated from family/friends i.e. does (name of abuser(s) ___) try to stop you from seeing friends/family/Dr or others?

Isolation is a common feature of domestic abuse but may also have a culturally specific context. Factors which may influence isolation can include: a lack of financial resources to leave; greater social isolation; less access to informal and formal support networks; a disability or issues relating to an individual's sexual orientation or gender identity (LGBT) and/or practical issues including living in a very rural area will also affect this.

In 'honour cultures' isolation can be particularly acute and can be reinforced by the risk of forced marriage. Normal support network of siblings and parents may not be available and sexual assault, 'inappropriate relationships' and failed marriages are seen to dishonour not just the woman or girl but the family as well (Hayward, 2000). Threats that a victim will be killed or that they will never see the children again can be very real and persistent. The chances that they will be carried out are high, either in this country or outside it (Richards, Findings from the Multi-agency Domestic Violence Homicide Review Analysis, 2003; Huisman, 1996). HBV cuts across all cultures, nationalities, faith groups and communities.

Further questions should be asked of victims who are particularly vulnerable or socially isolated in terms of:

✓ Truanting: this is a risk factor amongst teenage girls;
✓ Self-harm: more prevalent amongst young Asian women and a predictor for suicide;
✓ House arrest and being 'policed at home';
✓ 'Threats to kill' or that they will never see the children again;
✓ Fear of being forced into an engagement/marriage;
✓ Pressure to go abroad to the country of the family's origin.

Equally, complete control of the woman's activities and extreme jealousy have both been associated with severe violence and homicide (Richards, 2004; Campbell, 1986). Violence against the female functions to deter the victims from pursuing alternative relationships or opportunities that are not in the interests of the abuser (Wilson and Daly, 1993).

Q5. Have you separated or tried to separate from (name of the abuser(s) ___) **within the past year?**

Women's attempts to end a relationship are strongly linked to intimate partner homicide and it has been stated that: 'attempts to leave violent men are one of the most significant correlates with domestic death' (Websdale, 1999). Threats that begin with *'if you were to ever leave me...'* must be taken seriously. Victims who stay with the abuser because they are afraid to leave may correctly anticipate that leaving would increase the risk of serious harm. The data on time-since-separation further suggest that women are particularly at risk within the first two months (Wilson and Daly, 1993; Richards, Findings from the Multi-agency Domestic Violence Homicide Review Analysis, 2003).

Q6. Is there conflict over child contact?

Many incidents happen as a result of discussions and issues around child contact or disputes over custody (Richards, 2003, 2004). One study found that more than three-fourths of a sample of separated women suffered further abuse and harassment from their former partners and that child contact was a point of particular vulnerability for both the women and their children (Humphreys and Thiara, 2003). Conflict over child contact also has been shown to increase the likelihood of other risk factors for violence and abuse (Robinson, 2004, 2006a). Consequently, children **must** be considered in the assessment process and appropriate referrals made where they are at risk.

Q7. Does (___) constantly text, call, contact, follow, stalk or harass you? (Please expand to identify what and whether you believe that this is done deliberately to intimidate you? Consider the context and behaviour of what is being done)

Most female victims know their stalker. Stalking commonly occurs after the relationship but can also occur before the relationship ends (McFarlane, Campbell, Wilt, Sachs, Ulrich & Xu, 1999). Stalkers are more likely to be violent if they have had an intimate relationship with the victim. A prior intimate relationship is the most powerful predictor of violence in stalking cases (Mohandie, Meloy, McGowan and Williams, 2006). Intimate stalkers are more likely to exhibit higher levels of behaviour indicative of dangerousness (Palarea et al.,1999). Furthermore, stalking is revealed to be related to lethal and near lethal violence against women and, coupled with physical assault, is significantly associated with murder and attempted murder.

Sheridan and Davies (2001) found that ex-intimate stalkers were the most aggressive of all stalkers. Ex-partners were overall the most intrusive in their behaviour and were also the most likely to threaten and assault third parties as well as their principal victim. Sheridan and Davies (2001c) research suggests that being stalked carries a high violence risk.

Please ensure you ask the victim about the abuser's behaviour when stalking is a factor and consider the context of their behaviour. Risk factors for future violence in domestic stalking cases include:

- ✓ If the victim is very frightened;
- ✓ Previous domestic abuse and harassment history;
- ✓ Vandalizing or destroying property;
- ✓ Turning up unannounced more than three times a week;
- ✓ Following the victim or loitering near the victim;
- ✓ Threats of a physical or sexual violence;
- ✓ Harassing any third party since the harassment began (i.e. family, children, friends, neighbours, colleagues);
- ✓ Acting violently to anyone else during the stalking incident;

- ✓ Engaging others to help (wittingly or unwittingly);
- ✓ Abuser abusing alcohol/drugs;
- ✓ Previous violence in past (intelligence or reported).

Q8. Are you feeling depressed or suicidal?

Suicidal behaviour is evidenced by a history of suicide attempts, self-harm or thoughts about it. Homicidal behaviour is evidenced by the same. There is a link between dangerousness to self and dangerousness to others; that is the two factors co-exist more often than expected on the basis of chance (Menzies, Webster and Sepejak, 1985).

Q9. Are you pregnant or have you recently had a baby?

Pregnancy can be a time when abuse begins or intensifies (Mezey, 1997). Gelles (1988) found that pregnant women had a greater risk of both minor and severe violence than non-pregnant women. The consequences for pregnant women experiencing domestic violence remain serious. Domestic violence is associated with increases in rates of miscarriage, low birth weight, premature birth, foetal injury and foetal death (Mezey 1997). Domestic violence was disclosed as a feature of the lives of women in at least 12% of maternal deaths in the UK during 1997–1999 (Confidential inquiries into Maternal Deaths, UK 1999).

Young children are extremely vulnerable in situations of domestic abuse and consideration must be given both to the risks they face and the risks to the mother. Research suggests that children under 18 months are the most vulnerable in these situations.

More recent research, Jasinski (2004), has confirmed that serious consequences remain for those who suffer domestic abuse during pregnancy. If the victim responds positively to this question, you should note whether she is pregnant or has just given birth.

Q10. Are there any children, step-children that aren't (___) in the household? Or are there other dependants in the household (i.e. older relative)?

It is important to know who else might be living in the household and whether they have been a victim of abuse. There is a significant association between risk and the number of children in a household, the greater the number the higher the risk (Barmish 2004 and Sidebottom and Heron 2006). The presence of step children in particular increases the risk to both the child and the woman (Cavanagh et al. 2007). If step children (not the biological children of the abuser) are present it is worth exploring the quality of the relationship between the abuser and step child and whether to refer to children's services. Elder abuse, like other types of DV, is complex. Generally a combination of psychological, social and economic factors along with the mental and physical conditions of the victim and the offender, contribute to the occurrence of elder abuse. Types of abuser tend to be paid carers (31%)—usually associated with physical abuse and neglect and family members or relatives (47%) usually associated with psychological and financial abuse (House of Commons, 2004). The risk factors associated with elder abuse are (WHO, 2002):

- ✓ Cognitive or physical impairment;
- ✓ Shared living arrangements;

✓ Social isolation;

✓ Abuser dependency;

✓ Refusal of outside services, and;

✓ History of family violence.

Q11. and 12. Has (___) ever hurt the child(ren)? Has (___) ever threatened to hurt or kill the child(ren)?

It is also important to note whether the child(ren) have witnessed or heard the abuse. There is compelling evidence that both domestic violence and child abuse can occur in the same family. Child abuse can therefore act as an indicator of domestic violence in the family and vice versa. Websdale (1999) outlines three antecedents to child homicide: prior history of child abuse; prior agency contact; and a history of adult domestic violence in the family. In a recent analysis of serious review cases of child deaths, one of the commonly reoccurring features was the existence of domestic violence (Department of Health, 2002).

Clearly, young children are extremely vulnerable in situations of domestic abuse and consideration must be given both to the risks that they face and the risks to the mother.

Q13 and Q14. Is the abuse happening more often? Q14. Is the abuse getting worse?

Previous domestic violence is the most effective indicator that further domestic violence will occur. 35% of households have a second incident within five weeks of the first (Walby and Myhill, 2000). Research indicates that general violence tends to escalate as it is repeated. Analysis indicates that the time between incidents seems to decrease as the number of contacts escalates. (Understanding and Responding to Hate Crime Team, 2001).

Q15. Has (___) ever used weapons or objects to hurt you?*

The use of weapons and/or threats which the victim believes to be credible are important to note for the purposes of risk assessment. Domestic violence perpetrators who have used a weapon on intimate partners or others, or have threatened to use a weapon, are more likely to be violent again (Sonkin, Martin and Walker, 1985). Research evidence shows that often a variety of household objects are used as weapons.

Supplementary questions may cover:

✓ Has this incident or the previous incident involved the use of any weapons?

✓ Does the abuser have access to weapons through friends/acquaintances/ employment?

✓ Does the abuser have military or martial arts training?

✓ Does this significantly concern the victim?

Q16. Has (___) ever threatened to kill you or someone else and you believed them?

Both sub-lethal assaults and threats to kill can be interpreted as coercive tactics to terrorize wives and thus keep them under their husband's control (Wilson and Daly, 1993). Violence against women functions to deter them from pursuing alternative relationships or opportunities that are not in the interests of the abuser (Wilson and

Daly, 1993). A credible threat of violent death can very effectively control people. Evidence suggests that such threats to estranged partners by abusers should be taken seriously. Threats do precede physical attacks and have been included in risk assessment tools as good predictors of future violence (Hemphill et al., 1998).

Q17. Has (___) ever attempted to strangle/choke/suffocate/drown you?*
Strangulation, choking and/or stabbing are common methods of killing in domestic homicides. It is important that escalating violence, including the use of weapons and attempts at strangulation/choking/suffocation/drowning are recorded for the purposes of assessing risk (Richards, 2003). Strangulation or 'choking' is a common method of killing by male perpetrators of female victims (Dobash et al., 2004). Any attempt at closing down the victim's airway should be considered high risk.

Q18. Does (___) do or say things of a sexual nature that make you feel bad or that physically hurt you or someone else? (If someone else, please specify who)
The analysis of domestic sexual assaults reported to the Police demonstrates that those who are sexually assaulted are subjected to more serious injury (Richards, 2004). Further, those who report a domestic sexual assault tend to have a history of domestic abuse whether or not it has been reported previously. 1 in 12 of all reported domestic sexual offenders were considered to be very high risk and potentially dangerous offenders (Richards, 2004). Further, Browne (1987) reported that over 75% of the abused women who killed their abuser were raped by him, while only 59% of the non-homicidal abused women were similarly sexually assaulted.

Men who have sexually assaulted their partners and/or have demonstrated significant sexual jealousy are more at risk for violent recidivism (Stuart and Campbell 1989). Research in Cardiff showed that perpetrators with previous domestic violence complaints were much more likely to inflict sexual abuse on an intimate partner (Robinson, 2003). Risk of future violence and risk of sexual abuse perpetrated by the same person would therefore appear to be strongly correlated.

Q19. Controlling and/or Jealous Behaviour: Does (___) try to control everything you do and/or are they excessively jealous? (i.e. relationships, who you see, threats you will not see the children. Consider Honour Based Violence and stalking. Please specify behaviour)
Men who believe that they 'should be in charge' are more likely to use violence against their partner.

Complete control of the woman's activities and extreme jealousy have both been associated with severe battering (Richards, 2004; Campbell, 1986). Furthermore, jealous/controlling behaviour also has been shown to increase the likelihood of other risk factors for violence and abuse (Robinson, 2004, 2006a). A perpetrator's obsessive possessiveness and morbid jealousy, has been listed as one antecedent to domestic homicide (Websdale, 1999). Possessiveness, jealousy and 'stalking' behaviour include following the victim, persistent telephone calls, visits, texting, and sending letters. A large proportion of harassment and 'stalking' cases involve former partners and there are clear links between this behaviour and domestic violence and domestic homicide by men against women (Morris, Anderson and Murray, 2002).

Consider honour based violence – a victim may not have the freedom of choice, may be heavily 'policed' at home or unable to leave the home address except under escort or children may be used to control the victim's behaviour.

Q20. Is there any other person who has threatened you or who you are afraid of? (If yes, please specify who and why. If honour based violence, consider extended family)

The victim may also have been threatened by someone else and/or living in fear. This is a substantive feature of extended family violence, such as in the traveller community or 'honour' based violence. Relatives, including females, may conspire, aid, abet or participate in the abuse or killing. Younger relatives may be selected to undertake the killing, to avoid senior family members being arrested and prosecuted. Sometimes contract killers (bounty hunters) are employed.

You may think you have the perpetrator in custody but consider who else may be involved in the abuse in terms of who the victim may be at risk from. Evidence shows that these types of murders are often planned and are sometimes made to look like a suicide, or an accident. A decision to kill may be preceded by a family council. There often tends to be a degree of premeditation, family conspiracy and a belief that the victim deserves to die. Consider whether the victim's partner, children, associates or their siblings are also at risk.

Professionals should assess the context and consider the following factors in relation to the nature of the risk, actions they may take as part of a safety plan, as well as all others who might be at risk:

- ✓ The ongoing relationship or connection between the perpetrator(s) and victim may enhance vulnerability to future abuse and act as a barrier to help-seeking options;
- ✓ Other siblings being subject of similar issues;
- ✓ Strong extended family network;
- ✓ Family may seek to locate and pressurize victim;
- ✓ Family may seek to remove/abduct victim;
- ✓ Overseas threat;
- ✓ Threat to boyfriend/girlfriend;
- ✓ The perpetrator(s) may have a history of abusing others in a domestic context, and;
- ✓ They may also be offending outside the home.

Q21. Do you know if (___) has hurt anyone else in the family, anyone else they have had a relationship with or anyone else? (children/siblings/elderly relative/stranger, for example. Consider honour based violence. Please specify who and what)

Offenders with a history of violence are at increased risk of spousal violence, even if the past violence was not directed towards intimate partners or family members (Stuart and Campbell, 1989). Research has shown that generally violent men engage in more frequent and more severe spousal violence than other wife assaulters. Those who have demonstrated violent behaviour in either past or current intimate relationships are more likely to commit future violence (Sonkin, 1987).

Abusers do not tend to discriminate in terms of who they are abusive towards. Research shows that it tends to be part of a perpetrator's pattern of repeated aggression toward other persons persisting over the life course, with a series of victims from siblings to schoolmates to dating partners to strangers to spouse (Richards, 2004; Fagan, Stewart and Hansen, 1983).

Q22. Has (___) ever hurt the family pet/animals?

Experts increasingly recognise a correlation between cruelty to animals and domestic violence (Cohen and Kweller, 2000). For families suffering domestic violence or abuse, the use or threat of abuse against companion animals is often used for leverage by the controlling/violent member of the family to keep others in line or silent. The violence may be in the form of intimate partner violence, child abuse (both physical and sexual), or elder abuse. It is estimated that 88% of pets living in households with domestic abuse are either abused or killed. Of all the women who enter shelters to escape abuse, 57% have had a pet killed by their abuser (http://www. healthypet.com/Library/animal_bond-14.html).

Q23. Are there any financial issues? For example, are you dependent on (___) for money/have they recently lost their job/other financial issues?

Factors such as unemployment are associated with an increased risk for general recidivism. Low income and financial stresses are also a risk factor for involvement in domestic violence (Campbell, 1986). A sudden change in employment status, such as being fired/made redundant, may be associated with increased risk for violence (McNeil, 1987).

Q24. Has (___) had problems in the past year with drugs (prescription or other), alcohol or mental health leading to problems in leading a normal life? (If yes, please specify which and give relevant details if known)

This includes serious problems in the past year with illicit drugs, alcohol or prescription drugs that lead to impairment in social functioning (health, relationships etc.). Research shows that when perpetrators have aggravating problems (alcohol, drug, and/or mental health issues), they are also more likely to injure the victim, to use weapons, and to escalate the frequency or severity of the domestic violence (Robinson, 2003, 2006b). Coker et al. (2000) found the male partner's drug or alcohol use to be the strongest correlate of intimate partner violence and Robinson (2003) found that those who used drugs were more likely to inflict injuries and emotionally abuse their partners.

Substance abuse is related to criminality and recidivism in general. Recent substance abuse is associated with risk for violent recidivism among wife assaults (Stuart and Campbell, 1989).

In relation to any mental health conditions, consider:

✓ Have they been diagnosed with a mental health condition?
✓ Are they receiving support or intervention for this (this could be in the form of counselling, prescription drugs etc)?
✓ Has there been a recent change in the perpetrator's mental health?
✓ Are there any other triggers to violent behaviour?

Q25. Has (__) ever threatened or attempted suicide?

Suicidal behaviour is evidenced by a history of suicide attempts, self-harm or thoughts about it. Homicidal behaviour is evidenced by the same. There is a link between dangerousness to self and dangerousness to others; that is the two factors co-exist more often than expected on the basis of chance (Menzies, Webster and Sepejak, 1985).

Homicide-suicide rarely involves strangers. The most common factor in homicide-suicide is that the male needs to control the relationship. If a wife or girlfriend tries to leave, the man will often threaten to kill himself. Declarations such as *'If I can't have her, then no-one can'* are recurring features of domestic homicides and the killer frequently intends to kill themselves too (Wilson and Daly, 1993; Richards, 2003). This is a manipulative move and one that needs to be taken seriously. The perpetrator should be assessed not just for suicide but possibly homicide-suicide.

Q26. Has (__) ever broken an injunction molestation order, breached bail and/or agreement for when they can see you and/or the children? (If yes, please specify i.e. breach of civil or criminal order or bail conditions, for example)

Previous violations of criminal or civil orders may be associated with an increased risk of future violence. Equally a breach of bail or order shows commitment to carry out the offence regardless of restrictions based on the abuser's behaviour.

Q27. Do you know if (__) has a criminal record for violence or anything else? (If yes, please specify)

Offenders with a history of violence are at increased risk of harming their partner, even if the past violence was not directed towards intimate partners or family members (Stuart and Campbell, 1989). Research into offending behaviour and studies of groups of offenders, their previous convictions and offending history demonstrates that often offenders do not restrict their criminal activity to a single offence type (i.e. sexual offences or violent offences) or to a single category of victim (i.e. partner, child, adult, male, female, individuals in a particular age group or with a particular appearance).

Rather research shows that abuse tends to be part of a perpetrator's pattern of repeated aggression toward other persons persisting over the life course, with a series of victims from siblings to schoolmates to dating partners to strangers to spouse (Richards, 2004; Fagan, Stewart and Hansen, 1983). When histories of violent people are examined, a consistency begins to emerge in their approaches to interpersonal relationships (Richards, 2004). Note that the victim may not know about their partner's criminal record.

The exception to this relates to honour based violence where generally the perpetrator(s) will not have a recorded criminal history.

Other relevant information (from victim or officer) which may alter risk levels. Describe: (consider for example victim's vulnerability i.e. disability, mental health, alcohol/substance misuse and/or the abuser in terms of previous history or occupation/interests—does this give unique access to weapons i.e. ex-military, police, pest control?)

This question is intended to pick up other issues that might change the risk level. This could relate to the victim in terms of their vulnerability (i.e. disability, mental health or alcohol/substance misuse), or something that might come to your notice or that might relate directly to the abuser (i.e. if ex-military/police and engaged in stalking behaviour the abuser may well have been trained in surveillance techniques or have unique access to weapons). Any of these things would increase the risk.

Further guidance on risk assessing lesbian, gay, bisexual, and transgender (LGBT) related incidents

Domestic abuse is a significant issue within the LGBT communities (Donovan et al. 2006), though accurately assessing risk is challenging given a small research base, limited awareness (either by practitioners or within the LGBT communities) and low levels of reporting. Practitioners should be aware of the impact of unique risks that may be associated with someone's sexual orientation or gender identity. This can include victim's confidence in reporting. Whilst abuse may occur in LGBT relationships, it may arise from other perpetrators, including extended family members (this includes links to HBV) or from former or current heterosexual partners. Practitioners should consider that an LGBT person accessing services will have to disclose both domestic abuse and their sexual orientation or gender identity. Creating a safe and accessible environment where victims feel they can do this is essential.

While the risk factors contained within the checklist are largely relevant, professionals should assess the context of the relationship and consider the additional factors in relation to the nature of the risk (specifically related to sexual orientation or gender identity) and during safety planning:

- ✓ Identity abuse: is the perpetrator(s) using someone's sexual orientation or gender identify (e.g. saying they deserve the abuse because they are LGBT or that no-one will help them);
- ✓ Normalizing abuse: telling someone that domestic abuse is a 'normal' part of LGBT relationships or suggesting that abuse is 'mutual';
- ✓ Threats: the perpetrator(s) threatening to disclose someone's sexual orientation or gender identity if they are not out (e.g. to extended family or to work colleagues); this may also be relevant in relation to health (e.g. disclosing or making allegations about HIV status);
- ✓ Sexual abuse: as with heterosexual women, sexual abuse may be present in an abusive relationship. This may include being forced into sexual activity, having requests for safer sex refused or having 'safe words' and boundaries disrespected.

Practitioners should recognise that LGBT victims have historically had difficulty accessing services because abuse has been inappropriately labelled as 'mutual'. Practitioners should consider how to screen referrals in order to identify counter-allegation and abuse. This could include using the ACPO Guidance 2008.

Further guidance of risk assessing HBV related incidents

Do not underestimate that perpetrators of HBV really do kill their closest relatives and/or others for what might seem a trivial transgression. Just the perception or rumour of immoral behaviour may be sufficient to kill. Trigger invents may include (this list is not exhaustive):

- ✓ Smoking in public;
- ✓ Inappropriate make up or dress;

- ✓ Truanting;
- ✓ A relationship not being approved of by family and/or community;
- ✓ Interfaith relationships;
- ✓ Rejection of religion or religious instruction;
- ✓ Rejection of an arranged marriage;
- ✓ Pre-marital conflict;
- ✓ Pre-marital or extra marital affair;
- ✓ Objection to being removed from education;
- ✓ Reporting domestic abuse;
- ✓ Escalation—threats, violence, restrictions;
- ✓ Running away;
- ✓ Sexual conduct—talking, kissing, intimacy in a public place;
- ✓ Pregnancy outside of marriage;
- ✓ Rape;
- ✓ Being a reluctant immigration sponsor;
- ✓ Attempts to separate/divorce;
- ✓ Sexual orientation (including being gay, lesbian, bisexual or transgender).

Risk Factors for HBV

The risks, and therefore, risk management plan are different for those who *fear* a forced marriage to those who are actually in a forced marriage. The following can combine to raise unique risk factors for honour based violence:

Truanting

This is a risk factor amongst teenage girls, in particular. The reasons for this appear to be twofold. First, if a girl is in a controlling environment, for example being dropped off and collected from school and escorted everywhere, she may not have any other opportunities to socialize. Therefore truanting may be the only time for any form of independence. Equally, many girls know that they will not finish their education and once they leave school they may be sent abroad to be married, where a British education may be of little use. Care must be taken to ensure that if girls are truanting that schools or other officials do not inadvertently up the ante by alerting parents to this fact if there are HBV issues to be considered.

Self-harm

Studies show that more women than men self-harm[2]. In the UK it has been found that the prevalence of self-harm is disproportionately high among young Asian women (Bhardwaj, 2001). It is likely that the reasons behind this stem from a lack of support and the clash that can occur when an individual has to conform to differing cultural ideals, some of which are directly associated with HBV i.e. Forced Marriage. Self-harm is a strong predictor for future suicide or suicide attempts[3].

House arrest and being 'policed at home'

This may include not being allowed out, being supervised by family members and/or escorted to places outside of the home address, restricting access to telephone, internet, finances, passport and friends, for example.

---

[2] http://news.bbc.co.uk/1/hi/health/medical_notes/4067129.stm
[3] http://www.selfharm.org/what/overview.html

Fear of being forced into an engagement/marriage

This might be reported to officials or to friends. The risk tends to elevate if the victim is non-compliant with the family's wishes. This is heightened further if they have a partner that the family do not approve of. Care needs to be taken if the victim believes s/he will be taken overseas against her will. Forced marriage places individuals at risk of rape and possible physical harm. Some cases have resulted in the reluctant spouse being murdered.

Pressure to go abroad

This normally happens just before the summer holidays. Reports to police increase at this time and victims fear they will be taken overseas and forced to marry. If a person holds the nationality of two countries, they are a dual national and will have two passports. Be mindful of this if you believe they will be taken out the country. For many young people it may be their first time travelling overseas. If they are being held against their will and forced to marry there are various difficulties they may face if they want to return to the UK. They may find it impossible to communicate by telephone, letter and e-mail. They may not have access to their passport and money. Women may not be allowed to leave the house unescorted. They may not be able to speak the local language. Often individuals find themselves in remote areas where even getting to the nearest road can be hazardous. They may not receive the assistance they might expect from the local police, neighbours, family, friends or taxi drivers.

Isolation

Individuals forced into marriage often become estranged from their families. Sometimes they find themselves trapped in a cycle of abuse. Many suffer for many years from domestic violence. They may feel unable to leave because of their children, a lack of family support, economic pressures and other social circumstances. Isolation is one of the biggest problems facing victims of forced marriage. They may feel they have no one to speak to about their situation. These feelings are very similar to those experienced by victims for domestic violence and child abuse. Isolation is very real for those who have escaped a forced marriage or the threat of one. For many, running away is their first experience of living away from home and they suffer without their family and friends and usual environment. They often live in fear for being tracked down by their family who may solicit the help of others. In addition to leaving, they may be seen as bringing shame on the honour of the individual and the family in the eyes of the community.

Attempts to separate or divorce (child contact issues)

Research and analysis shows that attempts to end a relationship are strongly linked to intimate partner homicide. Websdale (1999) states that attempts to leave violent men are one of the most significant correlates with domestic death. Notions of *'If I can't have her, then no-one can'* are recurring features of such cases and the killer frequently intends to kill themselves (Wilson and Daly, 1993; Richards, 2003). Threats that begin with *'if you were to ever leave me…'* must be taken seriously. Victims who stay with the abuser because they are afraid to leave may correctly anticipate that leaving would elevate or spread the risk of lethal assault. The data on time-since-separation further suggest that women are particularly at risk within the first two months (Wilson and Daly, 1993; Richards, 2003).

Further, many incidents happen as a result of discussions around child contact or disputes over custody (Richards, 2004). Children should also be considered in the assessment process. Unique risks are raised in terms of shame and honour. Those who leave are seen to bring shame on the honour of the family in the eyes of the community. This may lead to social ostracism and harassment by the family.

Threats that they will never see the children again

This can have a huge impact on a woman, particularly if she believes she has insecure immigration status where she is concerned about being deported while her children remain in the UK. This is often used as a lever to coerce and gain compliance from the victim.

A pre-marital relationship or extra marital affairs

This could be real or perceived by the perpetrator(s).

Threats to kill

Tend to be credible and should be treated as such. Assess the antecedents to the incident and the victimology. Care should be taken around networks/organisations being used to track down victims that flee, for example accessing IT networks, minicabs, employing associates within statutory organisations (i.e. Police, Benefits Agency, Family Law Solicitors).

Further guidance on risk assessing domestic and non domestic stalking and harassment related incidents

Remember that domestic stalkers are the most dangerous group of stalkers. A prior intimate relationship is the most powerful predictor of violence in stalking cases (Mohandie, Meloy, McGowan and Williams, 2006). There could be a shorter duration of stalking and rapid escalation—which could signal High risk of serious harm. If you have a domestic stalking and harassment case refer to the full explanation of the risk factors.

Risk Factors in Domestic Stalking Cases:

- ✓ If the victim is very frightened;
- ✓ Previous domestic abuse and harassment history;
- ✓ Vandalizing or destroying property;
- ✓ Turning up unannounced more than three times a week;
- ✓ Following the victim or loitering near the victim;
- ✓ Threats of a physical or sexual violence;
- ✓ Harassing any third party since the harassment began (i.e. family, children, friends, neighbours, colleagues);
- ✓ Acting violently to anyone else during the stalking incident;
- ✓ Engaging others to help (wittingly or unwittingly);
- ✓ Abuser abusing alcohol/drugs;
- ✓ Previous violence in past (intelligence or reported).

In both domestic and non domestic cases assess the context of how frightened the victim is. This is a good indicator. Consider other relevant information such as:

- ✓ Details of the threats and the violence;
- ✓ The attitude and demeanour of the offender;
- ✓ The duration of the harassment;
- ✓ The harassing behaviours engaged in by the offender;
- ✓ The victim's belief concerning motive of the offender;
- ✓ The nature of unwanted 'gifts' left by the offender;
- ✓ Whether the victim has responded in any way to the offender.

High Risk Factors for Stalking and Harassment Related Incidents
Victim feeling very frightened

Research demonstrates that the victim is frequently the best assessor of risk posed to them (Heckert and Gondolf, 2004). Stalking often consists of behaviours that, when taken at face value, may appear to be quite ordinary (e.g. walking past the victim's house, asking the victim to go out on dates). With repetition however, these behaviours can becoming menacing, and the victim can feel unsafe and threatened. In all cases (even those where no direct threat has been made or where the victim does not yet have a great deal of evidence) it is important that the extent of the victim's fear is recorded. Research indicates that victims are often reluctant to be labelled as 'stalking victims', despite being very frightened, feeling that no one will take their fears seriously (Sheridan et al., 2002).

The offender engaging in harassment on previous occasions(s) (this victim and/or other victims)

One of the best predictors of future behaviour is past behaviour, and stalkers are no exception to this general rule. Those who stalk strangers and public figures are particularly prone to serial stalking (Dietz et al., 1991a,b; Sheridan, 2001). Even though the victim may not know the stalker very well, he or she may be aware of a local reputation the stalker has for this type of behaviour. Stalkers may also seem to stop stalking their victim (usually for reasons unclear to anyone but the stalker), only to suddenly resume the harassment at a later date.

The offender ever destroyed or vandalised the victim's property

Various studies have identified that a sizeable proportion of stalkers (up to two thirds) will damage their victim's property (Blaauw et al., 2002) and this includes stalking engaged in by adolescents (McCann, 2000). Property damage may be associated with rage or frustration (perhaps because the offender is unable to attack the victim directly), revenge, a desire to harm something the victim cares about (i.e. destroying her wedding photographs), a wish to undermine her belief in a safe environment (i.e. by cutting brake cables), as a form of threat, or it may be connected with breaking and entering the victim's property or spying on the victim. Property damage has been identified by researchers as preceding or co-occurring with physical attacks on the victim (Harmon et al., 1995, 1998).

The offender visiting the victim at work, home, etc., more than three times per week

Stalking rarely takes place entirely at a distance. Research tells us that nearly all stalking cases will ultimately involve face-to-face contact between victim and stalker (Mullen et al., 2000). Some stalkers may appear or approach their victims regularly (i.e. on the victim's daily route to work). Others, particularly stalkers with an obvious mental illness, will appear in diverse places at unpredictable times (Sheridan and Boon, 2002). The research informs us that those stalkers who visit the victim's home, workplace, or other places frequented by the victim more than three times in a week are those who are most likely to attack. It should be borne in mind, however, that some stalkers will have no regular pattern of harassment and in such cases an average of stalker visits could be estimated.

The offender loitered around the victim's home, workplace etc

As noted in relation to Q4, most stalkers will be seen by their victims. The positive aspect of this is that evidence can be collected, particularly if the victim keeps a log of stalker sightings and behaviour. Stalkers who loiter around places frequented by the victim tend to be those who are most likely to attack their victim. Such stalkers may be compiling victim-related information or tracking the victim's habits. Alternatively, an attack may be prompted by the stalker's frustration at not achieving his or her aims (such as a relationship with the victim), despite devoting a great many hours to the harassment. Stalkers are a varied group and some will attempt to loiter secretly (even camping out on or in the victim's property), whilst others will make no attempt at concealment. Whether secretive or overt, whether mentally disordered or not, most stalkers will share a belief that their behaviour is an appropriate response to circumstances.

The offender making any threats of physical or sexual violence in the current harassment incident

Stalkers frequently threaten their victims, either directly or indirectly. Examples of indirect threats include sending wreaths or violent images to the victim (often anonymously). Stalkers will often make specific written or verbal threats, however, and research demonstrates that these should be taken particularly seriously. Stalkers have been known to threaten violence months or even years into the future, and have indeed followed through on their threats. A review of eight studies by Rosenfeld (2004) revealed that the strongest predictors of stalker violence were threats to the victim. Threats have been found to be even stronger predictors in cases of very serious violence (James and Farnham, 2003).

The offender harassed any third party since the harassment began (i.e. friends, family, children, colleagues, partners or neighbours of the victim)

In the majority of stalking cases, secondary victims will be identified. Although stalkers may stalk more than one person at a time, this question relates to associates of a primary victim. Stalkers will involve third parties for several reasons, principally to upset the victim (i.e. by harassing the victim's children), to obtain information on the victim (i.e. by hounding the victim's friends), to remove perceived obstacles between the stalker and victim (i.e. by harassing the victim's partner), and to punish those perceived as helping or shielding the victim (i.e. work colleagues who state that the victim is not available). Individual stalkers have been known to harass hundreds of third parties who they perceive as connected with the primary victim (Mohandie et al., 2006; Mullen et al., 1999).

The offender acting out violently towards people within the current stalking incident

As noted immediately above, secondary victims will be identified in a majority of stalking cases, and these can be a valuable source of evidential information. Research suggests that third parties will be physically attacked by the stalker in between 6% and 17% of cases (Mohandie et al., 2006; Mullen, Pathé, Purcell, and Stuart, 1999; Sheridan and Davies, 2001). Stalkers who attack those associated with the victim are more likely to also attack the primary victim. Persons perceived as preventing access to the victim or protecting the victim are at particular risk.

The offender persuading other people to help him/her (wittingly or unwittingly)

The abilities of a stalker to pose as other persons and/or to draw information out of third parties should never be under-estimated. Many stalkers will devote hours each day to their stalking campaign, and are capable of stalking their victims for many years (Meloy, 1996). New technologies can facilitate harassment, enabling stalkers to impersonate another on-line; to send or post hostile material, misinformation and false messages (i.e. to usenet groups); and to trick other internet users into harassing or threatening a victim (i.e. by posting the victim's personal details on a bulletin board along with a controversial invitation or message) (Sheridan and Grant, 2007).

The offender abusing drugs and/or alcohol

Substance abuse by the stalker has been found to be associated with physical assault on the victim in a significant number of cases (Rosenfeld's 2004 review of 13 relevant studies). The abuse of various substances by stalkers can contribute both to the basis from which the stalking occurs and to individual violent episodes. Binge drinking or drug taking may directly precede an attack, fuelling obsessional, yearning or angry thought patterns, or by lending the stalker the confidence to approach or attack the victim. It is well known that substance abuse compounds the violence risk among those who are already mentally ill (Steadman et al., 1998), although non-mentally ill stalkers may also abuse alcohol and drugs.

Previous violence in the past (intelligence or reported)

One of the best predictors of future behaviour is past behaviour. Generally speaking, stalkers who have been violent before—whether as part of a stalking campaign or in relation to separate offences—are more likely to be violent again. It should be noted, however, that some of the most seriously violent stalkers identified in the past had no criminal history (James and Farnham, 2003).

KEY POINTS—RISK ASSESSMENT

Any risk-assessment process should:

- comply with *Guidance on Identifying, Assessing and Managing the Risk in the Context of Policing Domestic Violence* (ACPO, 2005)
- be undertaken by a trained member of staff
- provide a common understanding of the terms used to describe risk assessment and categorization
- include categories of risk and the consequence or meaning of different categories
- define the risk categorizations used and communicate these to police officers and staff and partner agencies
- allow the practitioner to exercise their professional judgement while conducting the assessment or categorization
- include a process for sharing the risk categorization with the victim and making appropriate links to safety measures and the identification of protective factors.
- provide a source of supplementary information and regular training which is readily available to officers and staff and relates to information about the nature of risk
- allow for inputting free text to describe circumstances not covered by the established risk factors but relevant to the investigation and risk assessment
- identify cases which are categorized as high risk
- include review processes for closing or removing cases which are no longer categorized as high risk from the risk-assessment process
- ensure that decision-making is recorded and that it is auditable.

Figure 5.3 Part 3: Risk management by trained officer management

Each incident should be risk-assessed using the DASH (2008) and recorded on the force crime reporting system and/or other appropriate databases. Once the assessment has been conducted, the intervention plan **must** be implemented to manage the risks. The Senior Investigating Officer/Investigating Officer (SIO/IO) should work with crisis intervention teams, Independent Domestic Violence Advisers (IDVA) and community partners to develop support packages/safety plans for victims.

Consider liaison with the local/central Intelligence Unit. An analyst can be tasked to aid and support the investigation by building a profile of the offender. Those **victims** who are HIGH risk should be referred to either a:

- Child Protection Case Conference;
- Domestic Violence Forum;
- Risk Management Panel (RMP) (such as the Risk Assessment Management Panels (RAMP) being piloted in the MPS or Priority Offender Panels currently being used in West Midlands Police);
- Multi-agency Risk Assessment Conference (MARAC) for a multi-agency response;

Those **offenders** who are at HIGH risk should be referred to either a:

- Risk Management Panel (RMP), such as the Risk Assessment Management Panels (RAMP) being piloted in the MPS or Priority Offender Panels currently being used in West Midlands Police;
- Multi-Agency Public Protection Panel Arrangement (MAPPA) for a multi-agency response.

Intelligence logs should be completed detailing all the prominent and high risk victims/perpetrators for each borough. It should detail and specify a brief history of the relationship, the address, the personal details of those involved including date of birth, description, CRO/PNCs and a summary of the calls to that address. Cases should be reviewed and a detailed proposed action plan should be compiled using a tactical menu of options. Agencies should be working together to safeguard victims (Section 115 of the Crime and Disorder Act 1998). The action taken must be:

- **P**roportionate;
- **L**egal;
- **A**ppropriate and;
- **N**ecessary based on the
- **B**est Information/**I**ntelligence **(PLANBI)** available at the time the offence is disclosed. It must also comply with Human Rights legislation.

A crucial part to risk assessment is risk management. Several levels of intervention/prevention should be considered once a risk(s) has been identified. A carefully planned and co-ordinated response is needed from the agencies working in close partnership. The safety plan should be aimed at the risk factors identified in order to **R**emove, **A**void, **R**educe or **A**ccept the Risks.

Remove the risk:	By arresting the suspect and obtaining a remand in custody.
Avoid the risk:	By re-housing victim / significant witnesses or placement in refuge / shelter in location unknown to suspect.
Reduce the risk:	By joint intervention/victim safety planning, target hardening, enforcing breaches of bail conditions, use of protective legislation and referring high risk cases to Multi-Agency Risk Assessment Conference (MARAC).
Accept the risk:	By continued reference to the Risk Assessment Model, continual multi-agency intervention planning, support and consent of the victim and offender targeting within Pro-active Assessment and Tasking pro forma (PATP), or Risk Management Panel format (such as Multi-Agency Risk Assessment Conference (MARAC) or Multi-agency Public Protection Panel (MAPPP))

The victim should be an active participant in determining the degree of danger and what s/he should do next. Victim's views should be incorporated into the assessment process. It is advisable to refer to the 'ACPO Domestic Abuse or Honour Based Violence Tactical Interventions Menu of intervention Options for Victims and Offenders'. If stalking features, please refer to the ACPO Practice Advice on Investigating Harassment (2005).

Tactical Menu of Intervention Options for Domestic Violence Victims and Offenders

Profiling and targeting of perpetrator	
Perpetrator	**Details to be recorded on Intelligence System**
Criminality	Consider that the offender may be involved in other areas of crime. Search for previous intelligence entries, use cross force intelligence and crime reporting system for offender, accused, victim, vehicle fields, for example.
	Check PNC, ViSOR, Impact Nominal Index (INI) and firearms licences.
	Use information from victim, witnesses, family etc. as well as considering Community Intelligence about offender. Outstanding warrants, breach of bail/contact orders or failure to conform to CROs or CPROs (Community Rehabilitation Order or Community and Punishment Rehabilitation Order), non-payment of fines etc. Utilise Open Source for checks on offender.
	Consider referral to TT&CG and/or a risk management panel such as MARAC.
Addresses	Details of all known addresses (relatives, friends etc), alternative place of arrest, location and risk to victim(s).
Children	Child Abuse Investigation Units (CAIU), Child abuse Coming to notice record, Youth Offending/Action Teams (YO/ATs), Child Protection Register, Schools Liaison Officer. If under 18 consider making Ward of Court if necessary. Liaise with Social Services.
Previous partners	Existing risk to previous partner(s), history of abuse, intelligence / statement available from previous partner(s). Are you dealing with a serial offender?
Associates	Criminality known about associates, alternative place of arrest, etc.
Vehicle	All vehicles that the offender has access to (private, relatives', work). To be used for information reports, details of bail restrictions, curfews, information to Investigating Officer etc.

Profiling and targeting of perpetrator	
Perpetrator	**Details to be recorded on Intelligence System**
Phone numbers	Details of landlines, mobile phones and pagers. Lists of numbers stored within phones, details of associates etc.
Work	Details of offender's workplace, access to information, relevant skills, alternative place of arrest.
Places frequented	Pubs, clubs, sport centres etc.

Investigation of Offences	Investigative considerations and actions
Crime reporting and intelligence databases	Detail a clear investigative strategy. Complete crime report and intelligence reports in as much detail regarding the victim, offender (description, relationship, CRO/PNC, etc), venue, offence behaviour including significant language, children being present at time of assault or in household, for example. Crime reports should be created as per National Crime Recording Standards (NCRS) rules. Cross-reference all crime reports and intelligence reports. Restrict report if necessary. Recognize and record the victim's wishes.
Statements and supporting documents	See the victim on their own in a secure and private place. Reassure the victim about confidentiality. ABE/video interview the victim on first report. Obtain a statement from the victim as soon as practicable to support the alleged offence, as well as statements from witnesses, neighbours, family members, ambulance staff, doctors, Forensic Medical Examiners (FMEs), midwives, previous partner(s) etc. Obtain a full account of the family tree, both immediate and extended. Police officer's notes and statements should fully detail all aspects of the abuse/violence including previous incidents, levels of violence and injury, damage to property, crime scene, emotional abuse, behaviour of both the offender and victim and other relevant factors including the impact on victim/family.

	Use a specialist sexual offences officer where allegations of sexual assault are made. Consider documenting victim's negative statement when they do not want to take a specific course of action and a community impact assessment. Consider deploying an accredited Family Liaison Officer (FLO).
Using 999 tapes	Examine demeanour of caller, background noise including comments from witnesses, suspects and victims; Any first description (*res gestae* or things done) of the incident as provided by the witness or victim.
Risk Assessment	Clear and effective risk assessment must be documented. Complete a risk assessment of the threat including risks to the victim and anyone else involved, such as their partner, friends or relatives. The assessment must take account of suicide and self-harm behaviour. Refer it on for action. Use an ACPO compliant risk model, such as the DASH (2008) risk identification/assessment model. Put an appropriate intervention plan into place. Identify dates/times of risk to victim, location for bail objections, etc. If there is an immediate, real and credible threat to life and the perpetrator is assessed as having the intention and ability to carry out that threat check your 'Threats to life' policy. This procedure is for threats to life only but it may also apply to certain threats to cause serious injury that may prove fatal (i.e., a threat to shoot someone in the legs). It may be appropriate and reasonable to follow this procedure when dealing with threats of that nature. Consider the use of Osman warnings/options.
Risk Management Panels	Consider referral of high risk cases to relevant risk management panels such as MARAC or MAPPA.
Forensic	Treat victim, suspect, other persons at premises and venue as a crime scene: secure, preserve and control the scenes to limit any access until sufficient information is available to make an informed assessment of the situation. Request a Crime Scene Investigator (CSI) to attend or record the reasons why one could not attend or was not called.

INVESTIGATION OF OFFENCES

Investigation of Offences	Investigative considerations and actions
	Ensure preservation of all other forensic opportunities such as victim's swabs from injuries (if bite or skin not broken), seize clothing, bedding, objects or weapons used, taking fingerprints, firearms and scene preservation. Consider blood or liquid distribution, footwear impressions, DNA, signs of a disturbance, injuries and evidence from the forensic medical examination. Use FME or forensic identification officer. Use Sexual Offences Kit, obtain DNA from offender (buccal swab).
Photographic/Video	Use of digital camera instant evidence capture, photograph victim, scene, damage to property etc. Consideration of use of video evidence at scene and/or body worn video can be used on oficers first deployed. Consider hospital images recorded for internal damage prognosis (X-ray) may also be required to support the investigation.
CCTV	Evidence of offence(s), offender placed at scene, area, verification or elimination of alibi. Existing overt CCTV facilities can be used to monitor and target subjects. In some areas it may be possible to reposition CCTV to cover a subject's address or an area known to be of interest to a subject. The local/central intelligence unit will have access to covert video surveillance, which can be deployed to monitor a subject and establish intelligence as to their lifestyle, with appropriate covert surveillance authorities.
Surveillance	Use of level 1, 2 or 3 surveillance teams. Covert surveillance is a potential investigative tool to gather evidence in certain domestic abuse cases, particularly where harassment is an issue. Covert policing techniques should only be contemplated when due consideration has been given to all of the circumstances of the case and conventional policing methods have failed or are likely to fail. Police forces should comply with the Regulation of Investigatory Powers Act (RIPA) 2000 and Home Office (2002) Covert Surveillance Code of Practice.

Proactive targeting	Consider the use of level 1 or 2 resources to target offender for all areas of criminality. Use first-response officers, targeted patrols, specialist teams. Capture of evidence though itemized phone billing, answer phone messages, text messages, e-mail, forensic examination of letters, tracking devices, mobile phone triangulation, for example.
Covert Human Intelligence Sources (CHIS)	There may be circumstances where victims or witnesses of domestic abuse seek to provide intelligence regarding other criminal activities of the suspect. Any victim or witness of domestic abuse providing intelligence to police officers should be subject to further risk assessment and safety planning measures. Officers should ensure that established risk factors for domestic abuse are identified and monitored. The first priority for the police is to ensure the safety and protection of victims and witnesses. In situations where the domestic abuse victim or witness provides information about offences, other than domestic abuse, the information should be forwarded to the intelligence unit for evaluation.
Seeking evidence from other agencies	Other agencies may hold relevant evidence that could assist in supporting a prosecution. This might be photographic evidence, body maps, witness evidence, items or samples that they are safeguarding on behalf of a victim. Partner agencies might, on occasions, be better placed to obtain evidence from victims. For example, victims may consent to have photographs taken of their injuries, or body maps completed, by medical staff at a time when they are not ready to disclose the abuse formally to the police.
Use of Interpreters	General guidance is that interpreters live in close proximity to the interview premises, but in domestic abuse and HBV cases it might be prudent to use interpreters that meet the criteria of the suspect, victim or witness but who do not live within the immediate community.
Communication	Agree a means of discreet future contact with victim. Ask the victim to keep their passport in a safe place and also inform passport office to flag their details. Consider letters to victim explaining what is happening and other agencies they can contact for help.

INVESTIGATION OF OFFENCES

Investigation of Offences	Investigative considerations and actions
Special Measures	Victims may want to speak to their employers to maximize their safety at work. It may be necessary for the victim to inform child minders, nurseries and schools of who exactly is permitted to pick the children up and what action to take if attempts are made to take the children. Consider whether the victim's name needs to be removed from computerized agency systems such as the electoral roll, DVLA, DHSS, National Insurance, for example. Consider what other measures need to be in place for protection pusposes for the victim, partners, siblings as well as witness. Speak to the Criminal Justice Protection Unit (CJPU), if appropriate.

Prevention of repeat victimization, support to victim and formation of a safety plan	
Safety Planning	**Action**
Target hardening	Crime prevention advice from Crime Reduction Officers and Crime Prevention Design Officers, consideration around victim's home address, workplace, schools, other places frequented and other vulnerable areas.
Panic Alarms	Panic alarms are available to victims who wish to remain in their own homes and for whom the perpetrator presents a significant risk. They will generally only be suitable where the perpetrator has no legal right of access to the premises concerned.
Mobile phones	Issue of '999' mobile phones to victims—some of which have a facility to record live to the police control room.
Alarms/Sanctuary Schemes	Use of Mascot or other similar systems to be installed within victim's premises. Update caller aided despatch around installation of alarms and previous history. Consider issue of personal attack alarms to victims and witnesses. Consider a Sanctuary Project or other target hardening service referral. The Sanctuary Scheme is a victim centred and innovative approach to homelessness

	prevention. DV victims are encouraged to remain in their own homes by installation of additional security measures.
Police Watch/ Community Officers	Neighbourhood policing team are tasked to provide regular visible presence in close proximity to the victim's address and in some circumstances pay welfare visits to the victim provided that consent is given. Officers may also be tasked in relation to the offending behaviour of the perpetrator.
Cocoon Watch	Similar to Neighbourhood Watch, this scheme engages nominated family, friends and neighbours to provide a support network for the victim and their children. This has to have the knowledge and consent of the victim as the nominated persons would need to be made aware of their situation.
Escape plan	Nominated safe contact, access to funds and credit card/bank account numbers, passport, identification, insurance documents, birth certificate, social security cards, driver's licence, lease or mortgage papers, school and medical records, welfare and immigration papers, court documents, transport (spare car keys), a change of clothes, child(ren's) favourite toy/blanket etc. Children need to be included in safety plan and alternative escape plan for them may be necessary. Rehearse escape plans with children and ensure children know how to contact police.
Special Schemes/ warning flags on systems for call outs to address	Implementation of Special Schemes or warning flags on systems relating to victim's and offender address. Detail further action to be taken as the result of further calls to the premises.
Specialist Refuge Service Provider	Refuge/Women's Aid, for example, provide places of safety for women fleeing domestic violence across the UK. They also provide specialist Refuge places for women with specific ethnic or cultural backgrounds.
Integrated Domestic Abuse Programme (IDAP)/ Offender Tracking	IDAP is a perpetrator programme aimed at challenging violent and abusive behaviour by men against their female partner/ex-partner. Run by Probation it can be part of the sentence delivered to domestic violence perpetrators under a Community Order or part of the requirement of a Post Custody licence.

Prevention of repeat victimization, support to victim and formation of a safety plan	
Safety Planning	**Action**
	Liaise with Probation Officer. Establish whether offender is subject to a Community Sentence (Community Rehabilitation Order or Community and Punishment Rehabilitation Order). Track offender to ensure compliance with Order. Keep Probation informed of re-offending behaviour. Ensure Order is enforced by executing warrants as soon as possible. Consider using ViSOR.
Independent Domestic Violence Advisers (IDVA)	IDVAs give personal advice and support direct to high risk victims to help them make decisions about their future and also help them access the range of services they need. Referrals are normally made from the point of crisis. The role of the advocate IDVA is to advise and support victims to help ensure their safety independently of any other organization. Generally, IDVAs provide intervention assistance to victims of domestic abuse, identified as high risk, whose cases are referred to a MARAC and/or are progressing through the criminal justice system. All cases that are being discussed at MARAC should be referred to the IDVA service so that they can contact the victim beforehand wherever it is safe to do so. IDVAs should maintain current information about victims and witnesses in domestic abuse cases. They should also update police officers responsible for the case and attend and contribute to MARACs, as required.
Support Groups	Local, national, VSS, Women's Aid, Refuge, Southall Black Sisters (SBS), Iranian and Kurdish Women's Rights Organisation (IKWRO), Karma Nirvana, Newham Asian Women's Project (NAWP), cultural, religious, LGBT, advisory groups, etc.
Injunctions/Orders	Liaise with partner agencies re: Ward of court, Injunctions etc. Consider: **Restraining Order** under s. 5 Protection from Harassment Act 1997 and Section 3(a) Protection from Harassment 1997 allows a civil injunction to be sought by the victim for actual or apprehended breach of section 1 harassment, by application to the High Court.

Non-Molestation Injunction forbids the perpetrator from using or threatening violence, harassing, pestering or intimidating the victim. The court can attach a power of arrest to the order, which if breached will ensure that the perpetrator is arrested and placed before a court. Domestic Violence Crime and Victims Act 2007 makes breaches of non-molestation a criminal offence. Note that sections 2, 3 and 4 of the Domestic Violence, Crime and Victims Act 2004 extend the provision of the Family Law Act 1996 to same sex couples and to those who have had an intimate personal relationship with each other which is, or was, of significant duration, thus allowing those individuals to apply for a non-molestation order. If non-contact or molestation orders exist, speak to neighbours to warn them of this. Advise them to contact victim and/or police if offender or his car is seen in the area. Set up local agreements with housing, local government.

Occupation Order provides a remedy to have the perpetrator removed from the home and to forbid him or her from returning within a specified distance, entering or attempting to enter. A power of arrest can be attached to the order to ensure that the perpetrator is placed before a court should they breach any part of it. Residence Order is an order setting the arrangements made as to the person or people with whom a child is to live. The court will undertake a welfare check and make the order.

Prohibited Steps Order is an order that no step, of a kind set out on the order, can be taken by a person in meeting their parental responsibility for a child without the comment of the court, for example, to prevent a child being removed from the country.

Contact Order is an order requiring the person with whom the child lives or is to live to allow the child to visit or stay with the person named in the order, or to otherwise have contact with each other.

Deportation orders for foreign and EU nationals.

Anti-social Behaviour Orders (ASBOs) are civil orders made by a court which prohibit the perpetrator from specific anti-social acts and from entering defined areas on a map (exclusion zones).

Prevention of repeat victimization, support to victim and formation of a safety plan	
Safety Planning	**Action**
	Sexual Offences Prevention Orders (SOPOS) Minimum of 5 yrs. Similar to ASBOs. Need to liaise with CPS and obtain SOPOs on conviction for Sexual or Violent offences. **Notification Orders**—Result in offenders who committed sexual offences abroad having to comply with registration requirements in the UK. **Risk of Sexual Harm Orders** RoSHOs (Min 2 yrs). No need for any conviction! Only for persons over 18 who are deemed to pose a risk of sexual harm to under 16s. Breaching a RoSHO will result in registration. **Disqualification Orders** (Always Life) (CJCSA 2000). Can be obtained on conviction at Crown Court for sexual or violent offences against children.
Court Liaison	Dedicated officer to update victim and witnesses of case progression for both criminal and civil cases.
Breaches of conditions	Enforce breaches of bail conditions, injunctions or family court orders.
Bail Objections	Previous convictions of offender, previous history known to police, relevant call outs/crime/intelligence reports relating to offender, past relations. Highlight bail address if in close proximity to victim's address and previous breaches of conditions/arrangements. All relevant information to be passed to Crown Prosecution Service (CPS) with a view to informing the court. The Investigating Officer must ensure that objections to bail are comprehensively documented and the CPS effectively briefed (if necessary attend court and support the CPS).
Child access	Formalized agreements, risk assessment, supervised visits, etc.
Victim Log	Advise victim to record details of all interactions that take place between the victim and the offender.
The Code of Practice for Victims of Crime	Victims of sexual offences or domestic abuse are eligible for enhanced service under the Code, unless the victim informs the service provider of their wish not to have this.

KEY POINT—THREATS TO LIFE

If there is an immediate, real and credible threat to life, and the perpetrator(s) has been assessed as having the intention and ability to carry out that threat check your force's 'threats to life' policy. This procedure is for threats to life only but it may also apply to certain threats to cause serious injury that may prove fatal (ie, a threat to shoot someone in the legs). It may be appropriate and reasonable to follow this procedure when dealing with threats of that nature.

KEY POINTS—RISK MANAGEMENT

Any risk management process should:

- Comply with *Guidance on Identifying, Assessing and Managing the Risk in the Context of Policing Domestic Violence* (ACPO, 2005)
- be extended post the initial investigation, right through to court and beyond including a risk management framework such as PLANBI—Proportionality, Legality, Accountability, Necessity, and based on best intelligence/information at the time—and RARA—Remove, Avoid, Reduce, or Accept the Risk
- remain dynamic so that significant changes to the case may be reflected easily within assessments and management plans
- use a tactical menu of intervention options for victims and offenders which describe the whole array of tactics available to minimize risk of harm
- be subject to review at set intervals which are appropriate to the risk categorization
- inform decision-making processes within the criminal justice system, eg some criminal-justice decisions may depend on information about the public interest and risk to victims and others
- be linked to multi-agency risk-management processes which focus on high-risk cases, eg MARACs
- provide clarity on which internal unit and/or external agency takes the lead, or is responsible for certain actions as part of the risk-management plan
- include the review of actions from the risk-management plan as part of ongoing safety planning
- be communicated to the victim(s) to ensure that they are kept up to date throughout the process, where appropriate and achievable.

5.7 **MARACs and the Non Police Risk Identification Checklist**

5.7.1 **MARAC aims?**

The MARAC's aims are:

- to share information to increase the safety, health and well-being of victims—adults and their children
- to determine whether the perpetrator poses a significant risk to any particular individual or to the general community
- to construct and jointly implement a risk-management plan that provides professional support to all those at risk and that reduces the risk of harm
- to reduce repeat victimization
- to improve agency accountability and
- improve support for staff involved in high-risk domestic-violence cases.

The responsibility to take appropriate actions rests with the individual agencies. The role of the MARAC is to facilitate, monitor, and evaluate information to enable appropriate actions to be taken to increase public safety.

The MARAC is underpinned by trust between agencies to share information, a common understanding of risk so that all agencies can refer cases into the MARAC, not just CJS ones, and that there is some clarity about what a high-risk case looks like so that we are above the threshold for confidentiality.

5.7.2 **The IDVA (independent domestic-violence adviser)**

The IDVA allows police officers to carry out essential policing functions at the fast-track and investigative development stages, while providing a support mechanism for the victim. Arrangements should be made to ensure the safety of IDVAs during the course of their work. Police domestic-violence coordinators should ensure that accurate and timely information is given to IDVAs, to make certain that they will be as safe as possible when carrying out their role. Police domestic-violence coordinators working with IDVAs should also ensure that communication links between IDVAs and police officers are maintained. IDVAs should be consulted over changes in police working practices, and routinely included in briefings and update meetings.

5.7.2.1 Main duties of an independent domestic-violence adviser

The main duties of an independent domestic-violence adviser (ACPO, 2008a) are as follows:

- provide proactive service and advice to victims to keep them and their children safe
- risk-assess and deliver service in keeping with the result
- explain housing and civil and criminal legal options to clients

- conduct safety planning with clients to secure practical safety measures
- develop an individual service plan to meet individual risks the client faces
- refer high-risk clients on to a MARAC
- ensure that clients receive the services to which they are entitled
- understand the legal framework relating to the protection of children, including the policy and procedures of the Local Safeguarding Children Board (LSCB)
- support clients through the criminal justice system, explaining the procedures and their role and rights within that system
- help clients to develop their own support networks
- refer on and arrange meetings with other agencies and services as necessary, eg solicitors, benefit agency
- manage a caseload
- maintain and update records of all cases
- follow procedures and protocols with other services so that the safety of the clients remains central to any process
- keep other relevant agencies informed about important changes in the client's situation
- participate in the MARAC framework by referring clients, attending and participating in meetings, and following-up on actions agreed at a MARAC
- refer regular difficulties clients are having in order to manage and contribute to efforts to improve procedures and services
- note and feed back to other agencies any consistent difficulties clients are having accessing their service.

5.7.3 **The referral process**

The risk-assessment process is carried out by the agency. In most cases this is the police, although many other agencies such as health, social care, and health visitors, for example, may also identify clients. It is more than likely that most victims will disclose more information about their case to a non-statutory agency such as the IDVA.

The MARAC meeting is only for high-risk victims.

5.7.4 **The MARAC meeting**

The following should attend the MARAC meeting:

- police
- social care
- independent domestic-violence advisers (IDVA)
- specialist domestic-violence services including local Women's Aid or other refuge provider and specialist projects supporting minority communities and group

- health representatives (midwifery, health visitors, child-protection nurse, and hospital staff as appropriate)
- housing
- probation
- education
- mental health
- homelessness team
- local drug and alcohol services
- Children and Family Court Advisory and Support Service (CAFCASS).

This list is not exhaustive as there may be additional attendees as individual cases dictate, such as community-based and voluntary perpetrator programmes or children's support organizations for example.

5.7.5 **Developing an action plan**

Only accurate information that is directly relevant to the safety of the victim should be shared by the attending agencies. This information falls into four main categories:

1. basic demographic information including pseudonyms used and whether there are any children and their ages
2. information on key risk indicators including, where appropriate, professional judgement on the risks faced
3. any relevant history of domestic violence or other associated behaviour (child abuse, sexual assault) by the perpetrator or victim
4. the 'voice' of the victim—typically the IDVA or another support agency should represent the perspective of the victim on the risks faced.

Information-sharing at MARAC conferences is strictly limited to the aims of the meeting and attendees should sign a declaration to the effect at the start of each conference. Information gained at the meeting cannot be used for other purposes without reference to the person/agency that originally supplied it.

There is further guidance on legal grounds for information-sharing. Key laws and guidance governing disclosure made during or following a MARAC meeting are:

- Data Protection Act (DPA) 1998
- common-law duty of confidence
- Human Rights Act (HRA) 1998
- Caldicott guidance
- Crime and Disorder Act 1998.

5.7.6 **Risk-identification checklist for use by IDVAs and other non-police agencies for MARAC case identification**

There needs to be a common understanding of risk among the practitioners. This checklist can be used by IDVAs and other non-police agencies for MARAC case identification. It is the mechanism for referring in to a MARAC.

CAADA has been working with ACPO to develop a single risk-indicator checklist for use by IDVAs, multi-agency partners and police in relation to MARAC referrals. This aims to incorporate risks linked to extended family violence including honour-based violence and stalking. The latest draft is currently being piloted by Advance (Brent), Blackburn with Darwen Women's Aid and East Berkshire Women's Aid for the months of June and July. The feedback from practitioners and their partner agencies will be incorporated and the amended checklist will be published in September 2008.

Figure 5.4   Risk Identification Checklist for Use by IDVAs and other Non-Police Agencies for Multi-Agency Risk Assessment Conference (MARAC) Case Identification

This form is designed for agencies who are part of the MARAC[4] process and who do not have their own assessment tool or who would like a supplementary form for identifying domestic violence risk. The purpose of the form is to identify risk to the victim and/or others and to be able to offer appropriate resources/support in the form of the MARAC for the most serious cases. Furthermore, the information from the checklist will support agencies to make defensible decisions based on the evidence from extensive research of cases, including domestic homicides and 'near misses' which forms the basis of the most recognised models of risk assessment.

Important notice: responsibility for the use of this checklist and the associated guidance rests entirely with the user. CAADA can take no responsibility for any actions or decisions taken as a result of this information. CAADA May 2008

> Practitioners must be aware that this is a risk identification checklist and not a full risk assessment. It is a practical tool that can help you to identify which of your clients should be referred to MARAC and where you should be prioritizing the use of your resources. Risk is dynamic and practitioners need to be alert to the fact that risk can change very suddenly.

---

[4] For further information about MARAC please refer to the CAADA MARAC Implementation Guide www.caada.org.uk

Introduction

Why have we updated the risk identification checklist?

There are two main reasons why we have decided to publish a revised checklist of risk indicators for use at MARAC. The first is that we are aware of a growing need to identify and support victims of family violence, including forced marriage and honour based violence (HBV). One of the options available to do this is the MARAC. Hence it has become crucial that a multi-agency risk tool includes these issues. The second reason relates to the practical issues that arise locally where the police and multi-agency partners are using different risk tools to identify cases to refer to MARAC. This checklist forms part of a wider task to create a common risk identification, assessment and management model for all police forces. The questions on this checklist form a subset of a somewhat longer list that is being reviewed currently by ACPO for use by police forces nationally. We believe that this consistency in approach to identifying risk factors will help all multi agency partners by simplifying the process.

What are the key changes from the original CAADA recommended checklist?

✓ The number of questions has been increased from 20 to 24. The additional questions include separating the original question 'is the abuse getting worse and/or happening more often' into two questions, adding a specific question about breaches of court orders including formal child contact arrangements, adding a question on abuse by other family or community members, specific reference to strangulation/choking/suffocation and finally, one on abuse of pets.

✓ The wording of some questions has been slightly amended to improve ease of use. All questions now reflect the possibility that this is being used in a case where there might be multiple potential or actual perpetrators, such as in HBV.

✓ The ordering of questions has also been amended to reflect the latest research and feedback from survivors and practitioners.

✓ The research base remains predominantly related to intimate partner violence and honour based violence. We are aware of other cases of family violence being referred to MARAC. Many of the risk factors are generic to homicide and serious harm, but professionals should use their judgement when referring these cases to the meeting.

✓ The criteria for referral have been amended somewhat. The need for professional judgement in all cases is stressed more strongly although it should **never** be used to downgrade the apparent severity of a case. We have suggested increasing the number of 'ticks' from 10 to 12 for the initial threshold but will review this during the next few months as the checklist is used in practice. The concept of weighting certain factors based on the victim's 'serious concerns' is replaced with stronger guidance on the need to take the victim's perception of risk very seriously and by asking for more specific information in relation to those factors where the victim's perception is particularly relevant.

Which cases should be reviewed at MARAC?

It is recommended that a MARAC should aim to review the top 10% of cases in terms of risk profile in its area. We know from the British Crime Survey that less than 45% of people who sustain a serious injury report this to the police, but less than one third where the injury is less serious. One of the strengths of MARAC is that it can accept referrals from any of the agencies who are signed up to the Information Sharing Protocol and so potentially has the ability to address the risks faced by a broad range of victims. Individual agencies such as the police, probation and children's services may have their own criteria for identifying high risk cases. You may wish to use the checklist below as a way of identifying cases from your own practice that should be referred to this meeting.

Risk Indicator Checklist for use by IDVAs and other non-police agencies[5] for MARAC case identification when domestic abuse, honour based violence and/or stalking are disclosed

Sources of Information:	☐ Client ☐ Other sources, please indicate		
Please ensure victims know why you are asking these questions – it is about their safety and protection. Tick box if factor is present ☑. Please use the comment box to expand.	Yes	No	Don't Know
1. Has the current incident resulted in injury? (Please state what)	☐	☐	☐
2. Are you frightened? If yes, indicate: Somewhat ☐ Very ☐ Extremely ☐	☐	☐	☐
3. What are you afraid of? Is it further injury or violence? (Please give an indication of what you think (name of abuser(s)....) might do) Kill : Victim ☐ Children ☐ Other (please specify) ☐ Further injury and violence: Victim ☐ Children ☐ Other (please specify) ☐ Other (please clarify): Victim ☐ Children ☐ Other (please specify) ☐	☐	☐	☐
4. Do you feel isolated from family/friends i.e. do (name of abuser(s)...........) try to stop you from seeing friends/ family/Dr or others?	☐	☐	☐

[5] Note: Work is underway to create more consistency between multi agency and police risk identification.

Tick box if factor is present ☑. Please use the comment box to expand.	Yes	No	Don't Know
5. Have you separated or tried to separate from (name of abuser(s)....) within the past year?	☐	☐	☐
6. Is there conflict over child contact?	☐	☐	☐
7. Does (......) constantly text, call, contact, follow, stalk or harass you? (Please expand to identify what and whether you believe that this is done deliberately to intimidate you? Consider the context and behaviour of what is being done)	☐	☐	☐
8. Are you feeling depressed or suicidal?	☐	☐	☐
9. Are you pregnant or have you recently had a baby?	☐	☐	☐
10. Is the abuse happening more often?	☐	☐	☐
11. Is the abuse getting worse?	☐	☐	☐
12. Has (........) ever used weapons or objects to hurt you?	☐	☐	☐
13. Has (......) ever threatened to kill you or someone else and you believed them? (if yes, tick whom)	☐	☐	☐
Self ☐ Children ☐ Other (please specify) ☐	☐	☐	☐
14. Has (.........) ever attempted to strangle/ choke/suffocate/drown you?	☐	☐	☐
15. Does (......) do or say things of a sexual nature that make you feel bad or that physically hurt you or someone else? (If someone else, specify who)	☐	☐	☐
16. Is (.......) controlling and/or are they excessively jealous? (In terms of relationships, who you see, being 'policed at home', telling you what to wear for example. Consider honour based violence and specify behaviour.)	☐	☐	☐
17. Is there any other person who has threatened you or who you are afraid of? (If yes, please specify who and why. Consider extended family if HBV)	☐	☐	☐
18. Do you know if (...........) has hurt anyone else in the family, anyone else they have had a relationship with, or anyone else? (Please specify who including the children, siblings or elderly relatives. Consider HBV) Children ☐ Someone from a previous relationship ☐ Other (please specify) ☐	☐	☐	☐
19. Has (..........) ever hurt the family pet/animals?	☐	☐	☐

20. Are there any financial issues? For example, are you dependent on (.....) for money/have they recently lost their job/other financial issues?	☐	☐	☐
21. Has (........) had problems in the past year with drugs (prescription or other), alcohol or mental health leading to problems in leading a normal life? (If yes, please specify which and give relevant details if known) Drugs ☐ Alcohol ☐ Mental Health ☐	☐	☐	☐
22. Has (......) ever threatened or attempted suicide?	☐	☐	☐
23. Do you know if (........) has a criminal record for violence or anything else? (If yes, please specify) DV ☐ Sexual violence ☐ Other violence ☐ Other ☐	☐	☐	☐
24. Has (.........) ever broken an injunction and/or formal agreement for when they can see you and/or the children? (If yes, please specify i.e. breach of civil or criminal court order or bail conditions by the suspect)	☐	☐	☐
Total			

Is there any other relevant information (from victim or professional) which may alter risk levels? Consider victim's situation in relation to disability, substance misuse, mental health issues, cultural/language barriers and minimisation. Describe:

Also abuser's occupation/interests-does this give unique access to weapons? Describe:

What are the victim's greatest priorities to address their safety?

Do you believe that there are reasonable grounds for referring this case to MARAC? Does it meet the local threshold for referral?   **Yes / No**

Signed: **Date:**

Guidance on Making a MARAC Referral

There are commonly three criteria for referring a case to a MARAC. The first is if a professional believes the victim to be at high and imminent risk of harm even if they are not prepared or able to indicate this by giving a significant number of 'yes' responses to the questions on the checklist. The second would apply where a case might be described as visibly high risk, namely that the victim has answered yes to a significant number of the questions on the checklist. The third is if escalation in violence appears likely to be occurring. This is captured in point 3 below.

We recommend that you consider the following when setting your local MARAC referral criteria:

1. Professional judgement: if a professional has serious concerns about a victim's situation, they should refer the case to MARAC. There will be occasions where the particular context of a case gives rise to serious concerns even if the victim has been unable to disclose the information that might highlight their risk more clearly. **This could reflect extreme levels of fear, cultural barriers to disclosure, immigration issues or language barriers such as in cases of honour based violence.** This judgement would be based on the professional's experience and/or the victim's perception of their risk even if they do not meet criteria 2 and/or 3 below.

2. 'Visible High Risk': the number of 'ticks' on this checklist. If you have ticked 12 or more boxes the case would normally meet the MARAC referral criteria OR

3. Potential Escalation: the number of police callouts to the victim as a result of domestic violence in the past 12 months. This criterion can be used to identify cases where there is not a positive identification of a majority of the risk factors on the list, but where abuse appears to be escalating and where it is appropriate to assess the situation more fully by sharing information at MARAC. It is common practice to start with 3 or more police callouts in a 12 month period but this may need to be reviewed depending on your local volume.

Please note that the evidence base for the number of 'ticks' in the 'yes' box relates to research on the original risk indicator checklist developed by South Wales Police and which had 20 questions. The guidance above on referral thresholds is based on recent research from a multi site evaluation of IDVA services. It includes a more detailed analysis of the pattern of abuse suffered by almost 1000 victims.[6] We are suggesting that 12 ticks would be a rational starting point but we will be working closely with a number of areas to analyse how this works in practice. You may need to adjust these levels to ensure that the volume of cases referred to your MARAC is in line with the recommended level of the top 10% in risk terms. You will need to analyse whether it would be more appropriate to adjust the number of call outs (say from 3 per annum to 5 per annum) or the number of 'ticks' on the checklist. The importance of professional judgement remains unchanged whatever the level of actuarial threshold.

During this 'pilot period' please pay particular attention to a practitioner's professional judgement in all cases. The results from a checklist are not a definitive assessment of risk. They should provide you with a structure to inform your judgement and act as prompts to further questioning, analysis and risk management whether via a MARAC or in another way.

---

[6] http://www.caada.org.uk/library_resources.html#14

The responsibility for identifying your local referral threshold rests with your local MARAC.

How to use this checklist

The purpose of this checklist is to give a practical tool to all the agencies that are part of the MARAC process to help them identify suitable cases to be reviewed by a multi-agency group and to become familiar with the risk factors that are associated with homicide and serious harm. **It is very important to ask all of the questions on the checklist.** Please note that the 'don't know' option is included where the victim does not know the answer to a specific question and where ticking 'no' would give a misleadingly low risk level.

These indicators can be organised into factors relating to the behaviour and circumstances of the alleged perpetrator and to the circumstances of the victim. Most of the available research evidence, upon which the following factors are based, is focused on male abusers and female victims in a current or previous intimate relationship. Generally these risk factors refer to the risk of further assault, although some are also linked to the risk of homicide and where this is the case, it is highlighted in the explanations below. Other risk factors relating to different groups or partnerships and children are less developed.

We **have also highlighted factors linked to honour based violence which must always be taken extremely seriously**. Do not underestimate that perpetrators of HBV really do kill their closest relatives and/or others for what might seem a trivial transgression. Just the perception or rumour of immoral behaviour may be sufficient to kill.

The notes below (same as the risk factor explanations for the police tool – so please refer to 5.6) give brief references to research base for each question on the checklist and some suggestions about how they should be interpreted in practice. It should be noted that the bulk of the research relates to cases where the perpetrator has been male and the victim has been female. Please note that there is some additional information regarding specific issues relating to lesbian, gay, bi-sexual and transgender (LGBT) victims.

5.8 **Common-Risk Framework**

In time there will be a consistent approach to risk assessment and the police and non-police agencies will be asking a common set of questions about the risks posed. This has been work-in-progress for some time and is a huge step forward in terms of ensuring a joined-up approach to keeping victims safe.

Checklist—Risk identification, assessment, and management

- There are three parts to the process: risk identification, assessment, and management.

- Risk identification must form part of an effective evidence-gathering. It should be undertaken by first-response staff.

- Risk assessment is a dynamic and fluid process. When events change, the risk assessment should be re-worked.

- The risk assessment should inform lines of inquiry. It should be undertaken by specially trained staff.

- Risk assessment is not a predictive process and there is no existing procedure to calculate or foresee which cases will result in a homicide, further assault, or harm.

- Risk assessment is based on professional judgement. It informs decisions that are already being made by you.

- Assessment of risk is complex and not related to the number of risks appearing alone. Rather, the imminent risk posed to the victims and others in a particular situation will be dependent on what they are and how they apply in that particular context.

- Police actions will be open to scrutiny. You should fully record your actions and the options considered. Show what factors influenced your decisions, and include reasons for NOT taking action.

- Your decisions must be defensible and auditable. Use the risk assessment as your decision log and RECORD all decision-making.

- The risk assessment allows for a standardized framework to ensure that questions are asked in a consistent, open, and transparent way, to enable more timely and accurate identification of risk.

- A risk-assessment model ensures that a risk-management plan is aimed at specific factors.

- When properly applied, risk assessment can serve as a paradigm of effective case management

- High-risk, vulnerable, repeat victims and high-risk offenders should be flagged to this MARAC.

Further information and reading

ACPO (2005), *Guidance on Identifying, Assessing and Managing Risk in the context of Policing Domestic Violence* (London: NPIA).

ACPO (2005), Practice Advice on Investigating Harassment (London: NPIA).

ACPO (2007), *Protecting the Public: Managing sexual and violent offenders* (London: NPIA).

ACPO (2008a), *Guidance on Investigating Domestic Abuse* (London: NPIA).

ACPO (2008), *Guidance on the Lawful and Effective Use of Covert Techniques: The legal framework and covert operational management* (London: NPIA).

ACPO/HMRC/SOCA (2008), *Guidance on the Use and Management of Specialist Surveillance Techniques [Restricted]* (London: NPIA).

CAADA (2007), *Multi-Agency Risk Assessment Conferences: Implementation guide.* Bruton: CAADA. Available at <http://www.caada.org.uk/library_resources.html>.

Criminal Justice System (2005), *The Code of Practice for Victims of Crime* (London: Office for Criminal Justice Reform).

6

Children and Domestic Violence

6.1 **Introduction**

Children are often referred to as the 'hidden victims' of domestic violence, which implies that the welfare of children involved in incidents is not being considered alongside those of adult victims. Therefore, it is imperative that when responding to cases of domestic violence, police and their partner agencies ensure that children are not ignored in the process and that every regard is given to their safety and protection.

Rather than describe how to conduct an effective investigation in child-abuse cases, which is clearly defined within the *Guidance on Investigating Child Abuse* (ACPO, 2005a), this chapter seeks to make the links between the abuse of children and the abuse of adults in a domestic context and provides practical guidance on the appropriate police response.

6.1.1 **The extent to which children are involved in domestic-violence incidents**

Police data in relation to the presence of children at domestic incidents is patchy. Younger children are rarely shown as witnesses on recorded allegations and, historically, the compliance with the requirement to complete the appropriate form or database regarding the incident and the child/children, for the notification of child abuse investigation units (CAIU) and children's social care, has been poor. Police **must** be robust in ensuring effective recording and dissemination of information regarding children.

Where there are children of the relationship who are not present at the incident or where there is an unborn child, then there is even less compliance with this requirement. Therefore, police statistics available cannot be relied upon to provide the true picture.

KEY FACTS—DOMESTIC VIOLENCE AND CHILD VICTIMS

- Domestic violence is a child-protection issue; in over half of known domestic-violence cases children were also directly abused (Farmer and Owen, 1995).
- About 750,000 children witness domestic violence every year (Department of Health, 2002).
- In **90%** of domestic-violence incidents occurring within the home, the children are in the same or the next room (Hughes, 1992).
- In **30%** of cases domestic violence started during pregnancy (McWilliams and McKiernan, 1993).
- **75%** of children on the 'at risk' register live in households where domestic violence occurs (Department of Health, 2003).
- **70%** of children living in UK refuges have been abused by their father (Bowker, Arbitell and McFerron, 1998).
- **30%** of domestic-violence murders are witnessed by children (Bowker, Arbitell and McFerron, 1998).

6.1.2 **Effects of domestic violence on children**

The effects of experiencing domestic violence as a child are reported in several pieces of research with varying findings. Children living within abusive relationships and witnessing or experiencing domestic abuse may suffer devastating effects during the developing years and potentially later on in life when they are entering into their own relationships or becoming parents themselves.

Children might be used as a 'tool' to effect power and control over the adult victim; children may sustain injuries when they intervene to protect the non-abusing parent; quite often they are forced by the perpetrator to take part in the abuse; when the victim has fled or the perpetrator been excluded or kept away from the victim, it is not uncommon for the perpetrator to use child-contact arrangements as a way of accessing the victim to continue the abuse. There have been several cases of homicide of children, or mothers and their children, at arranged contact visits. In some of these cases it is apparent that the motive for killing the children was ultimate revenge for the partner leaving the abuser. In addition, some children who suffer abuse at the hand of a parent may then go on to murder them.

The extent of the effects will be different in each child and will depend on various factors. This will include, for example, the levels of violence, whether they are directly abused or witnessing the abuse, or how long and how often they have been subject to the abuses. In addition, the child's age and development stage, levels of resilience, race, gender, disability, and social isolation may have a direct bearing on the levels of abuse experienced and how the child reacts. It may manifest in many forms, both physical and psychological, short and long term.

The following are some of the symptoms and signs that children may display if they are suffering the effects of domestic violence. However, not all children will react in the same way. Some may be quite resilient; others may have developed excellent coping strategies. Therefore, it would be wrong to assume that a child displaying any of the following physical, psychological, or behavioral effects are necessarily experiencing domestic violence; but it is important that agencies recognize that it may be the cause, especially where it is known that the child's parent is a victim of domestic abuse.

Table 6.1 Possible effects of domestic abuse on children

Physical effects	Physiological/behavioural effects
Stab wounds	Low self-esteem
Bruising	Fear, panic, guilt, anxiety
Broken bones	Depression/mental health
Welts	problems
Burns	Withdrawal
Death	Suicidal thoughts

Table 6.1 Possible effects of domestic abuse on children

Physical effects	Physiological/behavioural effects
Mental illness	Angry, aggressive behaviour
General poor health	Drug or alcohol misuse
Stress-related illnesses	Lack of self-confidence
Homelessness	Thoughts of running away
Eating difficulties	Hyperactivity
Teenage pregnancy	Tension
Tiredness/disturbed sleep	Sexual problems/promiscuity
Failure to thrive	Suicide
Damaged foetus	Eating disorders
Gynaecological problems	Truancy /schooling problems
Sexual abuse	Criminality
Gun shot wounds	Assumes a parental role
Strangulation	Self-harm
	Harming pets

In addition, experiencing domestic violence may have serious consequences on a child's ability to relate to other people and may cause problems forming healthy relationships in the future.

It is also apparent that domestic violence at home or in young people's own relationships increases their vulnerability to a range of poor outcomes, often as a result of poor social, emotional, and economic grounding. This includes joining gangs where youths have described how they see gangs as an 'alternative' family where a safe home is not an option to them. Young girls may be at risk of sexual exploitation or teenage pregnancy, with many teenage mothers experiencing violent relationships themselves.

Mothers who are living in abusive relationships may find it difficult to protect their children from direct or indirect effects of abuse. This is important for police officers to bear in mind when responding to incidents and ensure that the safety of the child is considered in all cases.

6.2 Effective Police Responses to Domestic-Violence Cases Affecting Children

In addition to legal obligations under the United Nations Convention on the Rights of the Child and the Human Rights Act 1998, there is specific legislation within the Children Act 1989 and the Children Act 2004 which places an onus on the police service and other public authorities to protect the lives of children.

Every Child Matters: Change for children (HM Government, 2006) is a government initiative to ensure that agencies work together to provide that children and young people from birth to age 19:

- are healthy
- stay safe
- enjoy and achieve
- make a positive contribution
- achieve economic well-being.

When children come to notice, police action will be aligned to the above aims for safeguarding children.

Other priorities for the police service, as outlined in the Guidance on Investigating Domestic Abuse (ACPO, 2008) and the Guidance on Investigating Child Abuse (ACPO, 2005), include:

- ensuring that in the policing of domestic violence and child abuse the safety and welfare of all victims and children are paramount
- investigating all reports of domestic violence and child abuse and to protect the rights of the victims
- facilitating effective action against offenders so that they are held accountable through the criminal justice system
- adopting a proactive multi-agency approach to prevent and reduce further offending.

It is therefore important that relative service policies and standard operating procedures (SOP) for domestic-violence and child-abuse investigations reflect the cross-overs between the two.

6.2.1 Learning from the past

Serious-case reviews relating to children and domestic-violence homicide reviews enquire into the background of the circumstances leading up to the incident of serious harm or death, to ascertain whether lessons might be learnt and make recommendations for improvement in services across relevant agencies including health, social services, and police. Lessons and recommendations must be taken into account when developing policies and regularly updated to reflect lessons learnt from recent reviews.

Recommendations from these reviews and other high-profile enquiries, including Lord Laming's enquiry into the death of Victoria Climbié and the Bichard enquiry into the murders of Holly Wells and Jessica Chapman, must be implemented at all levels in an effort to prevent homicide or serious harm. A failure to comply with the SOP may constitute a neglect of duty; indeed a recent enquiry in Derbyshire into the domestic murder of Tania Moore resulted in the demotion and dismissal of police officers. There are currently several similar enquiries being conducted by the Independent Police Complaints Commission (IPCC) across the United Kingdom.

6.2.2 **Support and training**

Chief officers should ensure that policy and strategy is adopted at a strategic and local level and must take responsibility for implementing systems and processes to support officers in providing a professional service and to prevent omissions and mistakes.

Adequate training in domestic violence for officers employed in the areas of public protection is imperative, especially for officers specializing in the field of domestic-violence or child-abuse. In other areas training is necessary for officers engaged where links to other criminality have been identified, for example human trafficking, prostitution, and youth offending.

6.2.3 **Examples of lessons learnt in serious-case reviews**

Whilst not exhaustive, the following summary puts into practical context those failings which have given rise to the recommendations resulting from some of the reviews where children have been involved in domestic incidents, and which may assist in ensuring that policies and operating procedures for domestic violence are fit for purpose (Saunders, 2004; Richards, 2004; Laming, 2003, and Bichard, 2004):

- levels of notification to children's social care not reflecting number of domestic calls to incidents where children are present within the relationship
- calls to incidents not being recorded on crime report or incident databases
- lack of referrals into the police service when children's social care workers discover criminal offences
- child homicide and family murders where the perpetrator believes or is aware that the mother wants to separate or recent separation combined with disputes over child contact
- lack of positive action in relation to the arrest and charge of the perpetrator
- investigations not carried out in a timely fashion (initial response)
- separate charges in relation to children not being preferred
- investigation of offences, particularly sexual offences, halted when it becomes apparent that the victim does not wish to pursue a prosecution
- failure to ensure that the criminal justice system effectively addresses victim safety whilst ensuring that perpetrators are brought to justice
- inadequate recording of intelligence
- inadequate sharing or accessing of intelligence cross-border, nationally, and internationally either electronically or manually
- lack of common language, risk-assessment tools, or risk-management strategies amongst partner agencies
- male perpetrators controlling and manipulating professionals
- failure to address mental-health matters in relation to the perpetrator.

In response, the government strategy outlined in *Every Child Matters: Change for children* (HM Government, 2004) and the provisions of *Every Child Matters: Working together to safeguard children* (HM Government, 2006) seeks to address all areas for improvement in a multi-agency context.

Section 5 of the Domestic Violence Crimes and Victims Act 2004 provides a criminal offence of causing or allowing the death of a child or vulnerable adult as an alternative charge to murder where the evidence of direct abuse by the perpetrator is lacking and places an obligation on family members to protect a vulnerable family member from other family members.

6.3 Considerations when Investigating Cases of Domestic Violence where Children are Affected

The role of investigators, supervisors, and managers responding to domestic violence are fully covered in Chapter 4 above. It is acknowledged that investigating officers have to consider and make many decisions when dealing with domestic incidents and good practice has shown that an aide memoire with checklists, guidance, and facility for recording information and actions at the scene, not only assists the officers with investigations, but improves the response in relation to the safety of victims and enables effective service delivery through the criminal justice system.

Officers should be alert to the fact, when dealing with an allegation of abuse against the child, that there may be domestic violence against the parent and vice versa. The following considerations need to be addressed when children are involved in the incidents.

6.3.1 **The initial response**

6.3.1.1 Call-takers

Emergency calls will often be made by children and it is important that this is recorded as it could be vital evidence in any subsequent investigation. Advice and reassurance should be given to the child in relation to their safety. It is **not** the child's role to protect the victim of the abuse.

The use of 999 tapes in investigations and prosecutions is invaluable and it is important that this is recognized by call-takers and included within their initial training to ensure that they understand the importance of effective evidence-gathering from the point of initial contact. Where it is known that a child is present at an ongoing incident this must be imparted to the attending officer, as this will affect the response, investigation, and risk assessment.

There is an onus on staff within command and control centres to ensure that attending officers are provided with any information or intelligence in relation to the parties or the address. Where children are involved this might include:

- history of domestic incidents where the child has been present
- history of child-abuse allegations
- presence of high-risk factors (see Chapter 5 above)
- information in relation to placement on the child-protection register
- details of non-molestation orders
- details of restraining orders
- details of care orders
- details of contact orders
- details of residence orders
- details of emergency protection orders
- details of prohibited steps orders
- details of exclusion orders
- details of specific issue orders
- details of recovery orders
- details of undertakings.

Further details regarding the above orders in relation to children are covered in Chapter 10 below.

Command and control supervisors have a role to play in ensuring that information in relation to children is gathered, recorded, and disseminated effectively. Managers of staff in this area should ensure that systems are in place for this to be addressed and that policies are clear in relation to the role of the staff.

6.3.2 **Initial investigating officers**

6.3.2.1 **Station reception officers**

Domestic-violence incidents are frequently reported at the front counter and it is important that the training schedules for station reception officers include training on domestic-violence and child-abuse issues.

The welfare of the child is paramount and any first aid or medical needs must first be addressed. Where an incident is reported the officer **must ask questions in relation to children within the relationship** whether or not they were present at the incident and ensure that details are recorded both on the crime report and other forms or databases which are designed to share information with the appropriate agencies for children's welfare (this will include unborn children). Children that were present during the incident should be shown as witnesses as this will have an effect on the subsequent investigation and risk assessment process. When questions are being asked about children, it is important to stress to the victim that this information is required to ensure a multi-agency response to the welfare of the child and to ensure support for both the child and the abused parent. It is not to facilitate the removal of the child into care.

The officer **must ask questions to ascertain the risk posed to the child** and take any steps necessary to reduce the risk pending the allocation of a secondary investigator or DV specialist.

If a child is present at the station office, where it is believed that they have been directly abused or thought to be at risk of future harm the presence of a domestic-violence or child-abuse investigator must be requested to prevent loss of vital evidence and ensure an effective response and support to the child.

It is important that supervisors with responsibility for station reception officers proactively check their reports at the earliest opportunity to ensure that they have dealt with the case effectively and in accordance with operating procedures. Information will then be shared with local authority children's social care in accordance with local protocol.

6.3.2.2 Response officers

Prior to attending the scene, the officer will have enquired as to what information and intelligence is known about the parties and the address. This will assist the officer to make a professional judgement in relation to the risks posed, both to the adult and to the child and any dangers that the attending officers may be presented with.

At this stage it may not be obvious to the officer that a child is present at the scene or is part of the relationship but away from the address. There may be signs such as toys, clothing, and high chairs but in any event the officer must be intrusive and enquire as to the fact. The officer **must ask questions in relation to children within the relationship** and ensure that details are recorded both on the crime report and other forms or databases which are designed to share information with the appropriate agencies for children's welfare (this will include unborn children). Where children are present, officers must physically check on their welfare. The safety and welfare of the victim and any children will be paramount on arrival and first aid or medical needs must be addressed.

Where criminal offences have been committed and the perpetrator is present, then an arrest will be effected in accordance with s 110 SOCPA 2005. It is not uncommon for cross-allegations to be made at domestic-violence incidents and both parties may present with visible injuries. Officers should be able, at this stage, to identify, through a thorough investigation, who is the 'primary' aggressor and who has acted in self-defence. This is especially pertinent in cases where children are present as the arrest of a 'victim' or of both parents may leave the children with a lasting mistrust of police.

The importance of early evidence-gathering cannot be over-emphasized and at this stage officers must act on the presumption that a prosecution will follow. This will include any evidence in relation to offences against the child. Corroborative evidence—in the form of photographs, forensic evidence retrieval for scene interpretation, evidence of officer's observations, a comprehensive record of significant statements, admissions, unsolicited comments, and demeanour of all parties—may be invaluable in refuting any defence given by the perpetrator, providing a fuller picture to the court and supporting the prosecution where the victim's statement cannot be relied upon.

Where children are involved as witnesses or victims, it is likely that their evidence will need to be gathered in accordance with guidance on *Achieving Best Evidence in Criminal Proceedings* (Criminal Justice System, 2007) and their statement may later be obtained using video/audio equipment. However, this does not preclude the need for the officer to question the child to check on their welfare and ascertain the facts in relation to the incident, provided that a record is made of the questions and answers. This activity must take place away from the alleged perpetrator where the child feels comfortable to speak.

Officers must ask questions to enable effective identification of the risk posed to the child and ensure that immediate steps are taken to reduce the risk and prevent harm coming to the child. Risk management will be retained by response officers pending handover to the specialist investigator, where this is an option, ie ensuring safety of the victim(s) where the perpetrator has left the scene. It is important that this activity is recorded in full, as this will guide the subsequent investigation and level of multi-agency response. Again, it should be stressed to the adult victim that this information is required to ensure a multi-agency response to the welfare of the child to ensure support for both the child and the abused parent. It is not to facilitate the removal of the child into care.

Where a child has witnessed abuse, been directly abused themselves, or otherwise appears to be suffering from the effects of domestic violence, officers are reminded of their powers under s 46 of the Children Act 1989, which enables officers to take children into police protection where they consider that the child may be at risk of significant harm. It should be noted at this point that s 120 of the Adoption and Children Act 2002 adds 'impairment suffered from seeing or hearing the ill-treatment of another' to the list of those incidents which might amount to 'significant harm' when investigating child abuse cases. These powers should only be necessary where there is a risk to the life of the child or a likelihood of immediate serious harm and it is considered that it would be unsafe to leave the child with a parent or relative. Where these risks are not present but the child has no one with legal responsibility to care for them, for example because the parent or carer has been taken to hospital or there are other reasons why the child is in need of care, then the child may be consulted and children's social care services contacted to make decisions on where they might be placed. Any powers attached to orders that are in existence in relation to the child must be executed.

Unless absolutely unavoidable, children must not be used as interpreters where English is not the first language, but assistance gained via Language Line or by using an officer with appropriate linguistic skills.

It is important to mention at this stage, and will need to be borne in mind when responding to reports of domestic violence incidents, that for some communities violence is often perpetrated where the child or young person is perceived to have brought 'shame and dishonour' to the family or are refusing to enter into an arranged marriage. Parents, siblings, and other relatives may take part in the abuse or collude with the perpetrator. Officers should not allow issues of race or culture to blur the investigation or influence their activities. This topic is covered in depth in Chapter 7 below.

High-risk cases must be brought to the attention of the duty officer. Officer's reports must be supervised at the earliest opportunity to ensure that an effective investigation has been conducted in relation to the children.

Checklist—Key issues for first response officers

- Ascertain history and intelligence on family.
- Check on welfare of children.
- Address first aid or medical needs.
- Gather evidence in relation to offences against children in the relationship.
- Take positive action against the perpetrator of offences committed against the children.
- Identify and record risk factors in relation to children within the relationship.
- Remember that risk assessment remains dynamic and must be revisited when circumstances change.
- Ensure the safety of the children is secured pending handover to the secondary investigator.
- Record details of all children within the relationship, whether present or not.
- Do not use children as interpreters.
- Ensure that full details of the incident and associated risks are passed to children's social care.
- Conduct early supervision to ensure effective investigation and protection in relation to the children.

6.3.3 Secondary investigation

Where forces have separate teams for investigating domestic violence and child abuse, decisions will need to be made at an early stage to determine who will take primacy in the investigation. Where the child is directly abused, then the child abuse investigation unit (CAIU) should take primacy, in consultation with the domestic violence investigator or specialist. In cases where the victim is an adult but children are featured, then the domestic-violence team should lead, in consultation with the child-abuse investigator and/or children's social care worker.

Where a child has witnessed domestic violence against a parent, then consideration should be given in relation to the child suffering 'significant harm' and an investigation under s 1 of the Children and Young Persons Act 1933 pursued for evidence against the perpetrator of wilful neglect.

The investigator should identify any gaps or omissions in the investigation so far and take any necessary action to remedy. Further lines of enquiry for investigation might include:

- the child's school records
- strategy discussions with social care
- joint visits with social care
- the child's GP or medical records
- civil proceedings in relation to child contact
- child-protection registers
- other means of accessing history and evidence in relation to the offence against the child.

The investigator may need to consider further assessment in relation to the risk to the child based on the initial identification of risk and information gathered during the course of the investigation. It will then be the responsibility of that officer to ensure that appropriate action is taken to manage the risk and prevent further harm to the child.

Where forensic medical examination of the child by a medical practitioner or paediatrician is required, then the consent of the child, if they have the capacity to do so, or consent of the parent, carer, or person with parental responsibility, should be sought. Where this is refused then the local authority can apply for an emergency protection order and child assessment order.

Investigators responsible for interviewing children must be trained in accordance with guidance outlined in *Achieving Best Evidence in Criminal Proceedings* (Criminal Justice System, 2007). In most cases, the child will be video interviewed. The child to be interviewed must be consulted throughout according to their age and understanding. In most cases, the consent of the parent or carer will also be required. However, there may be exceptional circumstances where the interview takes place without their knowledge. The child themselves may also request that they are interviewed without knowledge of their parent and, where the child has the capacity to make this decision, this may be honoured; but there may be circumstances where complete confidentiality cannot be guaranteed and this must be explained to the child.

Victim personal statements (or impact statements) may be required from the child as well as the adult victim in domestic-violence cases as the effect of the abuse on the child may have a bearing on both sentencing decisions and decisions in relation to bail. This statement must be taken in the same format as the original statement.

It is incumbent on investigating officers to notify the CPS of special-measure requirements at the earliest opportunity to enable the child to be fully supported when giving evidence at court. Officers may also make arrangements with the court for the child to visit the court before the trial. In addition, there may be facilities at the court for the child to be accompanied by a child-witness supporter or domestic-violence advocate throughout the trial.

6.3.3.1 Information-sharing

All forces must ensure that there are local processes in place to enable effective information-sharing in relation to children experiencing domestic violence. This will include all children coming to notice in such circumstances, whether they were present at the incident or not, and will include unborn children.

Whatever decisions are made in relation to the child as a victim or witness to domestic abuse, notification to the local authority children's social care team is essential as they have the responsibility to carry out an initial assessment of the child's needs using the common assessment framework (CAF) and to ensure that child-protection matters under ss 17 or 47 of the Children Act 1989 are considered.

It is important that information regarding the risk posed by the perpetrator is shared, not only in relation to the risk posed to the child, but also to staff, as it may be necessary for home visits to be conducted. When carrying out assessments, the care team may contact the police for further information to assist the process and the sharing of information may, and should, take place in accordance with current protocol outlined in Chapter 9 below.

Requests for information in relation to police reports for domestic violence or other matters may also be requested where proceedings are taking place in the Family Law Court and it is important that officers comply with requests in a timely fashion. (For details of the current protocol see the Ministry of Justice website at <http://www.justice.gov.uk>.)

Officers should ensure that there is input on appropriate police databases, including the Police National Computer (PNC), Impact Nominal Index (INI), and Violent and Sexual Offenders Register (ViSOR) where the relevant case criteria are met.

Checklist—Issues for secondary investigators

- Gather further evidence.

- Interview in accordance with *Achieving Best Evidence* guidelines.

- Consider obtaining victim's personal statement (or impact statement).

- Request 'special measures' at the earliest opportunity.

- Consider arrangements for the child to visit the court.

- Ensure early consultation with children's social care.

- Consider further risk assessment and risk management.

6.4 **Risk Identification/Management and the Needs of the Children**

Risk identification, assessment, and management processes are fully document-ed in Chapter 5 above. As a general rule, risk management in relation to the adult victim should address the risks to the child. However, each individual family history and situation will be unique and risk must be considered on all the avail-able information without prejudice. There may be occasions where the parenting abilities of the non-abusing parent are severely undermined by the effects of the abuse on them: this must be borne in mind when making decisions in the inter-est of the child. What must be remembered in risk-management processes is the perpetrator's ability to access the child at school or leisure and social facilities in addition to the home address and these locations will need to be considered in the safety action plan.

The following checklist outlines risk factors pertinent to children living within abusive relationships. Each factor must be taken in context with the current situa-tion, history of abuse, and what is known about the perpetrator. Risk-identification and assessment tools for children are still being developed, so it is impossible at this stage to add weight to any specific risk or detail higher-risk factors:

Checklist—Factors heightening the risk to children in domestic-violence cases

- **Direct abuse of the child**
  Concurrent child abuse and adult domestic violence is common. Antecedents to do-mestic homicide often include a history of child abuse and a history of adult domestic violence in the family. It is important that automatic screening for domestic violence in all child-abuse cases and vice versa is carried out.

- **Separation and/or child contact concerns**
  Attempts to end a relationship are strongly linked to intimate-partner homicide. Despite the common assumption that leaving a violent partner will end violence, it is apparent that women victims who separate from their partner are at a higher risk of physical violence and sexual assault as well as homicide. Violence that continues after separation tends to be more serious and is more likely to involve stalking-type behaviour and lead to homicide. The early stages of separation (especially the first three months) are particularly dangerous. It is important to note that a child contact dispute can indicate risk of homicide to both the partner and children.

- **Threats to kill or harm child**
  A credible threat of violent death to the victim or the child can very effectively control people and some may carry out this threat. Evidence from serious-case reviews suggests that such threats to estranged partners and their children by the abuser are often acted upon.

- **Threats to abduct child**
  This is another powerful method for controlling the child's parent whereby, if the threat does not obtain the required effect, the threat is carried out and may result in harm to the child.

- **Misuse of drugs or alcohol**
  Alcohol or drugs misuse may affect the ability to care for a child and impact directly on the health of an unborn child. There is also a risk of harm to young children from accessible alcohol, drugs, or drugs paraphernalia. Some children may require particular care such as medication or tube feeding which, if wrongly provided or forgotten by someone influenced by alcohol or drugs, could be fatal.

- **Mental-health issues**
  Having a mental illness does not in itself indicate any heightened risk but when considered with other factors may do so. The impact on the risk to the child will depend on the type and severity of the mental illness. Failure to take prescribed medication may heighten the risk.

- **Animal/pets abuse**
  Research has established links between child abuse and abuse of household pets. Any suspicion of animal abuse should prompt further enquiries into the welfare of children who frequent premises in the control or occupation of the perpetrator. Children in abusive families may show effects of domestic violence by abusing their pets.

- **Pregnancy of adult victim**
  There is a connection between pregnancy and domestic violence. Pregnancy may increase the isolation and dependency of the victim and poses risks in terms of miscarriage and foetal abnormality as well as additional risks to the lives of women themselves. Violence during pregnancy and following the recent birth of a child are both indicators of high risk of future harm.

- **Social isolation**
  Increased entrapment of the victim is an antecedent to domestic homicide. Women who are unemployed or housewives have been found to have the highest risk of domestic violence, but there are a number of ways this could link to vulnerability. These include a lack of financial resources to leave, greater social isolation, less access to informal and formal support networks, and potentially more opportunity for the perpetrator to be unchallenged. Victims may also be particularly vulnerable to future harm if they live in a physically isolated community (ie, in a rural area) or socially isolated communities, for example, people who may be isolated due to their sexuality or lifestyle. Such social isolation may be exacerbated by perceived or actual discrimination from other communities or agencies providing services, such as the police. Some victims from minority ethnic groups may experience particular social isolation due to racism, language, cultural, religious, or immigration issues that can all be barriers

to reporting violence and seeking help. Police officers should be aware of the impact that all of these issues can have on the vulnerability to risk of harm of a particular victim. Research has shown that children who are in families who are socially isolated and do not have access to community resources are at a higher risk of abuse. Other issues that may indicate particular vulnerability include lack of basic amenities such as heating, lighting, indoor sanitation, water, cooking facilities, and overcrowded accommodation. Children who have been forced away from home because of domestic violence within the family may be more vulnerable to abuse.

- **Sexual offences**
  The injuries sustained by domestic sexual-assault victims are often more serious than those experienced in sexual assaults by strangers. Men who have sexually assaulted their partners and/or have demonstrated significant sexual jealousy are more at risk for violent recidivism.

- **Suicidal threats or attempts by the perpetrator/victim**
  Self-harm or the threatened or attempted suicide of a parent or carer should prompt further investigation into the welfare of any children in their care. Close attention should be paid to child-contact arrangements where parents are separated, particularly where there is a history of self-harm, or threats or attempts to commit suicide by a perpetrator of domestic violence. A suicidal suspect with a history of perpetrating domestic violence or child abuse should also be considered as potentially homicidal and a risk to their former or current partner and children.

- **Threats or ideation about committing homicide by the perpetrator**
  Threats or ideation about committing homicide are a risk factor for subsequent violence including homicide of a family member.

- **Perpetrator minimizing or denying the abuse**
  A failure to accept responsibility for abuse or acknowledge that they have problems with their behaviour, particularly in the face of strong evidence, may heighten the impact of other risk factors.

- **Jealousy or excessively controlling behaviour**
  Possessiveness, jealousy, and stalking behaviour include following the victim, unwanted attention, persistent telephone calls, visits, and sending text messages and letters. A large proportion of harassment and stalking cases involve former partners and there are clear links between this behaviour and subsequent domestic-violence assaults and domestic homicide by men against women and children.

- **Young age of the child**
  Pre-verbal children and pre-mobile children are especially vulnerable to abuse, as are children who are not yet old enough to attend school or pre-school groups. Babies under 12 months are particularly vulnerable to violence.

- **Disability**
  Children with disabilities are more vulnerable to abuse for a number of reasons, eg they may receive intimate personal care, have a higher dependency on carers, have fewer outside contacts, and may be less able to complain about abuse due to communication difficulties. Where the child's disability is such that they have experienced little external social interaction, there is potential that any abuse has become normalized and the child may not realize that what they have experienced is wrong. Where necessary, officers should seek advice from social services, which should have information on every disabled child in their area.

- **Cultural considerations**
  For some communities refusal to enter into an arranged marriage, associating with persons not approved by the family or other perceived transgressions might be seen to bring dishonour to the family which can result in violence or even death of the person, often affecting children under 18.

6.5 How Agencies can Work Together to Ensure Children's Safety

Children can only be safeguarded properly if the key agencies work effectively together. Local Safeguarding Children Boards (LSCBs) are designed to help ensure that this happens. They placed the former Area Child Protection Committees (ACPCs) on a statutory footing. The core membership of LSCBs is set out in the Children Act 2004, and includes local authorities, health bodies, the police, probation, and others. The objective of LSCBs is to coordinate and to ensure the effectiveness of their member agencies in safeguarding and promoting the welfare of children. Local safeguarding procedures will be produced and implemented by the LSCBs.

Risk assessment activity in domestic-violence cases where children are involved may be being conducted within individual agencies, eg police, children's social care, domestic-violence support agency, or health. Initial information-sharing across the relevant agencies is likely to take place on the telephone or by secure email or at a strategy meeting. These strategy discussions will be necessary to:

- establish the facts
- identify other agencies already involved
- identify whether a conflict of interest exists by continuing with the lead agency role
- re-assess the needs of the child for protection, support, and redress in the light of additional information
- plan and agree an investigation process or what further action may be necessary.

However, no individual agency's statutory responsibility can be delegated to another. Each agency must act in accordance with its duty when it is satisfied that the action is appropriate. There may be joint investigation but the shared information flowing from that must be constantly evaluated and reviewed by each agency.

6.5.1 **Child-protection conferences**

Any agency working in the interest of the child may identify the need for multi-agency risk management and conferencing to take place and make a referral through the appropriate channels for a conference to be held. The conference will normally be in the form of a child-protection conference but information may arise through a multi-agency risk-assessment conference (MARAC) for high-risk domestic victims, a multi-agency public protection panel (MAPPP) for high-risk sex or violent offenders, or other operational-safety planning panel.

Whatever form the conference takes, **it is important that professionals working both within the field of domestic violence and child protection are present**, as they will both bring vital information and experience on which to base effective interventions. Risk management may be severely undermined where this does not exist. It is imperative that each agency, particularly the police, bring all information on the child, the parents, and siblings (including step-family) to the conference to ensure a holistic overview of the family circumstances.

The purpose of police representatives attending conferences is to:

- ensure that the police service is represented and for an independent police record to be kept of information provided/received and decisions made
- identify and record new and critical information
- fulfil a statutory duty to safeguard children under the Children Act 2004 and comply with 'Working Together to Safeguard Children' 2006
- present the police-service view in accordance with service guidelines
- make decisions on behalf of the child as to whether they should be part of a child protection plan (CPP) after having considered information shared at the conference by police and other agencies
- challenge, where appropriate, the views of other representatives at the conference (These representatives may hold higher positions of authority within their respective organizations and will include doctors, head teachers, social-work managers and local authority solicitors. Any decisions made may be liable to subsequent legal challenge.)
- be in a position to provide reports justifying decisions made or actions proposed, outlining a clear rationale based on the interests of the child and taking into account organizational, personnel, and resource factors
- prepare for the conference summaries of information held by the police service on children and families, and the progress and status of criminal investigations

- identify and record all actions arising from the conference, ensuring those relating to the police service are brought to the attention of the investigating officer or other relevant member of police staff.

Chapter 10 below outlines what protective measures, in addition to the criminal justice process, are available in relation to safeguarding children.

6.6 Serious-Case Reviews and Domestic-Violence Homicide Review

Multi-agency reviews of serious cases concerning children and reviews of deaths of adults in domestic-violence cases conducted under Chapter 8 of *Every Child Matters*: *Working together to safeguard children* (HM Government, 2006) and s 9 of the Domestic Violence Crimes and Victims Act 2004 respectively are intended to examine the circumstances which led up to the incident to determine lessons to be learnt to enable services to improve their response to the protection of children and adults.

Where there are cases involving children as victims of domestic violence, it is important that each agency review includes input on domestic-violence policy, procedures, and practices and similarly where the review concerns the death of an adult with children featured in the relationship, then the review includes input in relation to child-protection policy, procedures, and practices. Where the case involves the adult and child(ren), the decision may be to conduct the two reviews alongside each other.

In any event it is important to ensure that the cross-overs between the services are linked to ensure that gaps in services are identified and that recommendations from reviews are recognized and implemented by both adult- and child-protective services.

6.7 Missing Persons Cases and Children

When dealing with reports of missing children, there are specifics to be aware of in relation to children living within abusive relationships:

- The child may have run away to escape domestic violence or find it hard to cope with the situation at home.
- The child may be escaping a forced marriage or honour-based violence.
- The non-abusing parent may have fled with the children to seek refuge.
- The perpetrator may be using the police to gain access to a victim in refuge.
- The perpetrator may be making the report to cover up a homicide.
- The child may have been abducted in disputes over child contact.

Where domestic violence is suspected, then all relevant databases must be searched. Enquiries with relatives, friends, or associates may reveal further information regarding the domestic violence. Children's teachers, children's social care workers, or local statutory or voluntary support agencies specializing in domestic violence may also hold information. The subsequent debrief of missing persons returned should also include screening for domestic violence.

Further information and reading

ACPO (2005a), *Guidance on Investigating Child Abuse and Safeguarding Children* (London: National Police Improvement Agency).

ACPO (2008), *Guidance on Investigating Domestic Abuse* (London: National Police Improvement Agency).

Crown Prosecution Service (2006), *Policy on Prosecuting Criminal Cases involving Children and Young Persons as Victims and Witnesses* (London: Crown Prosecution Service).

Criminal Justice System (2007), *Achieving Best Evidence in Criminal Proceedings* (London: Office for Criminal Justice Reform).

Department of Health (2003), *What to Do if you are Worried a Child is Being Abused* (Nottingham: Department of Education and Skills).

HM Government (2006), *Every Child Matters: Working together to safeguard children: A guide to inter-agency working to safeguard and promote the welfare of children* (Norwich: The Stationery Office). Available at <http://www.everychildmatters.gov.uk>.

Honour-Based Violence (HBV)

7.1 **Introduction**

This chapter aims to help police and other partner-agency professionals protect individuals from abuse. It sets out an understanding of what HBV is along with its prevalence, explores the unique risks associated with HBV cases, and details a range of practical advice including a tactical menu of intervention options for victims and offenders.

Firstly, it is important to state that although the police need to be sensitive to cultural, religious, and racial differences, they also have a clear overriding duty to identify individuals who are likely to suffer significant harm and to invoke the necessary child-protection procedures if the individual is under 18 years old and that irrespective of whether criminal offences are apparent or prosecuted the police have a duty under Art 2, Right to Life, Human Rights Act 1998, to protect the lives of those that are at risk.

KEY POINT

'Multicultural sensitivity is not an excuse for moral blindness.'
(Mike O'Brien, House of Commons Adjournment Debate on Human Rights (Women) 10 February 1999)

7.2 **What is Honour-Based Violence (HBV)?**

ACPO definition of honour-based violence

'"Honour-based violence" is a crime or incident, which has or may have been committed to protect or defend the honour of the family and/or community.'

(ACPO, 2008b, Working Definition)

HBV is a fundamental abuse of human rights. There is no honour in the commission of murder, rape, kidnap, and the many other acts, behaviours, and conduct which make up 'violence in the name of honour'. The simplicity of the above definition is not intended in any way to minimize the levels of violence, harm, and hurt caused by the perpetration of such acts.

HBV is a collection of practices which are used to control behaviour within families to protect perceived cultural and religious beliefs and/or honour. Such violence can occur when perpetrators perceive that a relative has shamed the family and/or community by breaking their honour code. Women are predominantly (but not exclusively) the victims of HBV, which is used to assert male power in order to control female autonomy and sexuality. HBV can be distinguished from other forms of violence, as it is often committed with some degree of approval and/or collusion from family and/or community members. Examples may include murder, unexplained death (suicide), fear of or actual forced marriage, controlling sexual activity, domestic violence[1] (including psychological, physical, sexual, financial, or emotional abuse), child abuse, rape, kidnapping, false imprisonment, threats to kill, assault, harassment, and forced abortion. This list is not exhaustive. HBV cuts across all cultures, nationalities, faith groups, and communities. Such violence transcends national and international boundaries.

7.2.1 What is 'murder in the name of so-called honour'?

HBV incidents cannot be separated from HBV murder.

ACPO definition of 'murders in the name of so-called honour'

These are murders in which victims, predominantly women, are killed for their perceived immoral behaviour, which is deemed to have breached the honour code of a family or community, causing shame. They are sometimes called 'honour killings'.
There is, however, no honour in murder.

(Richards and Dhothar, 2007a, ACPO Working Definition)

7.3 Forms of HBV

The following crimes make up those which can typically happen when domestic abuse occurs:

- murder/attempted murder
- manslaughter
- rape
- sexual assault
- grievous bodily harm/wounding
- actual bodily harm
- common assault
- threats to kill
- missing persons
- affray
- threatening behaviour
- firearms offences (such as shotguns being discharged through doors)
- harassment
- blackmail
- false imprisonment
- kidnapping
- criminal damage (such as cars being set on fire, house windows being broken)
- malicious communications

---

[1] Refer to ACPO Domestic Violence definition.

- witness intimidation
- obstructing the course of justice
- conspiracy to pervert the course of justice.

There are also other manifestations of HBV. Some of these behaviours are well understood. However, others are not.

7.3.1 What is a forced marriage?

In an arranged marriage, the families take a leading role in choosing the marriage partner. The marriage is entered into freely by both people. However, in some cases, one or both people are 'forced' into a marriage that their families want. A forced marriage is a marriage conducted without the valid consent of both people, where pressure or abuse is used.

Victims might be put under both physical pressure (when someone threatens to or actually does hurt them) or emotional pressure (for example, when someone makes them feel like they're bringing shame on their family) to get married. In some cases people may be taken abroad without knowing that they are to be married. When they arrive in the country their passports may be taken by their family to try and stop them from returning home. They often do not know where to go for help. People at risk need to be aware of this practice, and we need to ensure that they know what to do and where to turn if it happens to them.

7.3.2 Why parents force their child to marry

Parents who force their children to marry often justify their behaviour as protecting their children, building stronger families, preserving cultural or religious traditions, and/or keeping wealth within the family—which is why in so many of these cases they are forced to marry a relative. They may not see anything wrong in their actions.

There is also a difference between 'child marriages', ie cases where parents promise their children to the child of another family at a very young age, and 'child brides' where the bride is very much younger than the groom.

Forced marriage cannot be justified on religious grounds; every major faith condemns it and freely given consent is a prerequisite of Christian, Jewish, Hindu, Muslim, and Sikh marriages. Often parents believe that they are upholding the cultural traditions of their home country.

Some parents come under significant pressure from their extended families to get their children married. In some instances, an agreement may have been made about marriage when a child is in its infancy. Some of the key motives that have been identified are:

- controlling unwanted behaviour and sexuality (including perceived promiscuity, pre-marital relationships or being gay, lesbian, bisexual or transgender)—particularly the behaviour and sexuality of women

- protecting 'family honour'
- responding to peer-group or family pressure
- attempting to strengthen family links
- ensuring land, property, and wealth remain within the family
- protecting perceived cultural ideals (which can often be misguided or out of date)
- protecting perceived religious ideals which are misguided
- preventing 'unsuitable' relationships, eg outside the ethnic, cultural, religious, or caste group
- to provide a carer for a disabled member of the family (there is a stigma within some communities of having a disabled child. One way of hiding such a disabled child is to marry him or her off, outside of the family, to someone who does not have a disability, providing a carer in the process)
- assisting claims for residence and citizenship
- fulfilling long-standing family commitments.

While it is important to have an understanding of the motives that drive parents to force their children to marry, these motives should not be accepted as justification for denying them the right to choose a marriage partner. Equally, where there is forced marriage, there is also likely to be rape and repeated rape.

KEY POINT

Forced marriage is an abuse of human rights, and a form of domestic violence and child abuse.

Case study—Narina (aged 21)

Narina's story: 'I felt that I had no option. Once they had taken me out of the country there was nothing I could do. I had no contact with anyone but the family. My mother was caught between my feelings and the community's expectations. They made me feel that I would dishonour my family if I didn't marry him.'

Narina was 18 when her parents took her back home for a family holiday. She was kept in the family home and was not allowed out on her own. Finally, she and her sister managed to run away and contacted the British Consulate, who found her a place to stay and helped her contact her friends in the UK. She eventually came home and with the help of a women's refuge and her friends, has built a new life for herself and her sister.

7.3.3 **Child marriages**

Child marriage is a practice in which the parents of a small child (even infants) arrange a future marriage with another child's parents. The children are betrothed or promised to each other. Often the two children never even meet each other until the wedding ceremony, when they are both of an acceptable marriageable age—age differs based upon custom. In some cultures, the age is at or even before the onset of puberty. Child marriage has been practised for centuries. It continues to this day, and is most common in sub-Saharan Africa, South Asia and among the Roma gypsies of Eastern Europe. The rationale behind this practice is that a child's parents can arrange a sensible match with the parents of a child from a suitable family, thus securing the child's future at a young age. Parents may feel that marrying off a child at a young age can help them economically—a daughter may be regarded as an economic burden—while also keeping them safe from unwanted sexual advances.

The betrothal is considered a binding contract upon the families. The breaking of a commitment can have serious consequences for both the families and the children themselves. Often girls are married to men many years older. A child bride faces a number of problems, for instance: greater health risks linked with early sexual activity and childbirth; limited economic and social opportunities; an incomplete education; and she can be more vulnerable to domestic violence.

> **KEY POINT**
>
> The majority of child marriages could be classed as FORCED marriages.

7.3.4 **The legal position**

The Marriage Act 1949 and the Matrimonial Causes Act 1973 govern the law on marriage in England and Wales. The minimum age at which a person is able to consent to marriage is 16; a person between the ages of 16 and 18 may not marry without parental consent (unless the young person is a widow/widower).

Section 12(c) of the Matrimonial Causes Act 1973 states that a marriage shall be voidable if 'either party to the marriage did not validly consent to it, whether in consequence of duress, mistake, unsoundness of mind or otherwise'. Voidable means the marriage is valid until it is challenged by one of the parties, at which time the court can award a decree of nullity invalidating the marriage. Although there is no specific criminal offence of 'forcing someone to marry' within England and Wales, criminal offences may nevertheless be committed.

Perpetrators—usually parents or family members—could be prosecuted for offences including threatening behaviour, assault, kidnap, abduction, imprisonment and, in the worst cases, murder. Sexual intercourse without consent is rape, regardless of whether this occurs within the confines of a marriage. A girl who is forced to marry is likely to be raped and may be raped until she becomes pregnant.

7.3.5 Forced repatriation

HBV cases can involve the abduction of victims and children from the UK. This can be undertaken for an array of reasons—most notably forced marriage.

Typically, in such cases, the victim, often a teenager, is induced or forced by their immediate family members to travel abroad for a holiday or to visit relatives. S/he may later reappear, often with a new husband or wife; however, in other incidents s/he may just disappear.

7.3.6 Bride price

Definition of 'Bride price'

'Bride price (in some societies) is an amount of money or goods given to a bride's family by the bridegroom's family.'

(*The Cassell Dictionary*, 1997)

The tradition of giving bride price is still practised in many countries. Bride price is revered as a symbol of sincerity and good faith that brings together the bride and groom's families. In some cases it is derided as a means to enrich a bride's family. However, it can become a licence for a man to treat a woman as a *purchased* good.

7.3.7 Dowry

Definition of 'Dowry'

'A dowry is the property which a wife brings to her husband.'

(*The Cassell Dictionary*, 1997)

The converse of bride price is a dowry. The tradition of giving dowries is perhaps most well-known in India where it is still very common, despite being prohibited by law as of 1961.

Traditionally, a dowry consisted of gifts, usually jewellery, given to the bride at the time of her marriage providing her with some financial security. Today, a dowry is negotiated and refers to the wealth that the bride's parents pay the groom and his family as part of the marriage arrangement.

The groom and his family may demand a dowry not only in the form of money, but also in the more modern forms of televisions, videos and DVD recorders, refrigerators, and cars. The amount demanded is often exorbitant. Such demands can continue for months or even years after the wedding.

In addition to being a real financial burden to the parents of the bride, demands for more dowries that cannot be met may result in severe abuse and harassment of the bride. **It is not uncommon for the new bride to be murdered in the first year of a marriage because her dowry is insufficient or for the bride to kill herself to spare her family further hardship.**

Research has highlighted that every day in India 15 women are murdered by their new husbands and/or in-laws for failing to bring a sufficient dowry to the marriage. Dowry deaths are the collective name for these murders (For more details see <http://www.law-lib.utoronto.ca/Diana/fulltext/carl.htm>).

7.3.8 Rape

In the United Kingdom common-law rape has traditionally been described as *a man who forces a woman to have sexual intercourse with him*. Previously it was believed that forced sex by a husband against his wife (marital rape) was not rape, or even a crime, until 1992. Both partners were deemed to have given implicit informed consent in advance to a lifelong sexual relationship as part of their marriage.

Modern criminal law eliminates this exception and includes acts of sexual violence other than vaginal intercourse, such as forced anal intercourse, which were traditionally barred under sodomy laws.

7.3.8.1 Sexual Offences Act 2003 (see Guidance on Investigating Serious Sexual Offences (ACPO, 2005c))

Under the Sexual Offences Act 2003 (which came into force in May 2004) rape in England and Wales was redefined from non-consensual vaginal or anal intercourse and is now defined as 'non-consensual penile penetration of the vagina, anus or mouth of another person'. The changes also made rape punishable by a maximum sentence of life imprisonment.

Although a woman who forces a man to have sex cannot be prosecuted for rape under English law, she can be prosecuted for causing a person to engage in sexual activity without consent, a crime which also carries a maximum life sentence if it involves penetration of a mouth, anus, or vagina.

The statute also includes a new sexual crime called 'assault by penetration', which also has the same punishment as rape and is committed when someone sexually penetrates the anus or vagina with a part of his or her body, or anything else, without that person's consent.

The law puts an onus on all offenders to prove that they did everything possible to obtain consent.

7.3.8.2 Statutory rape

The UK (citing an interest in protecting minors) considers people under 16 years old to be unable to give informed consent. Sexual contact with an individual below the age of consent is considered to be rape even if that person agrees to the sexual activity.

7.3.8.3 Punishment of victims

Some societies punish the victims of rape as well as the perpetrators. They may hold the belief that being raped dishonours the victim and, in some cases, the victim's family and community. This can lead to the victim being murdered or committing suicide due to the social shame and stigma attached to being a rape victim.

7.3.8.4 Rape as punishment

In some cultures rape itself is used as a form of punishment. Usually, the victim of the rape is a female relative of an individual targeted for retaliation. For example in June 2002, a Pakistani woman named Mukhtaran Bibi was gang-raped on the orders of a village council after her brother was (falsely) accused of rape himself. The Pakistani government—along with local religious officials—condemned this action. Of the 14 men charged with the offence, six were sentenced to death (see the report available at <http://www.guardian.co.uk/print/0%2C3858%2C5147201103680%2C00.html>).

In 2005 these rulings were overturned on appeal by the Lahore High Court. However, these overrulings were then suspended by the Pakistani Supreme Court. To this day the case continues as one of the most controversial in Pakistani legal history.

7.3.9 Female genital mutilation (FGM)

Definition of 'Female genital mutilation'

This is 'the term used to refer to the removal of part, or all, of the female genitalia. The procedure consists of a clitoridectomy (where all, or part of, the clitoris is removed), excision and cutting of the 'labia majora' to create raw surfaces, which are then stitched or held together in order to form a cover over the vagina when they heal. A small hole is left to allow urine and menstrual blood to escape'

(Amnesty, 2005)

There are varying reasons why FGM is carried out. In some communities men will not even consider marrying a woman that has not been subjected to FGM while others believe that the clitoris makes a women become over-sexed, putting them at risk of engaging in extra-marital affairs.

The practice has its roots largely in Africa but also in parts of the Middle East and Asia. FGM is practised both within the UK and by taking girls out of the country for the procedure. Many girls are taken out of school for the practice and can suffer physical and mental health consequences as a result. Women who have undergone the procedure tend to come to the attention of health services at the time of, or in the run-up to, childbirth.

FGM is a hidden and under-reported crime. The prohibition of Female Circumcision Act 1985 made FGM a criminal offence in the UK and anyone found guilty of performing the operation is currently liable to a fine or imprisonment. Under the FGM Act 2003 its is illegal for FGM to be performed in the United Kingdom and for any British person to aid, abet, counsel, or procure FGM on any UK national or resident anywhere in the world even if it is not illegal in that country. Parents who allow FGM to be performed on their daughters can be sentenced to 14 years' imprisonment.

7.3.10 **Acid attacks**

Definition of 'Acid attack'

In such an attack 'a man throws acid (the kind found in car batteries) on the face of a girl or woman. Any number of reasons can lead to acid attacks. A delayed meal or the rejection of a marriage proposal is offered as justification for a man to disfigure a woman with acid. Sulphuric acid is ubiquitous, being the basic, inexpensive ingredient for making lead acid batteries in all motorized vehicles all over the world.'

(UNICEF, 2005)

Acid attacks are a recent phenomenon having only been recognized in the past 20 years. They have been documented to occur in Asia, most notably in Bangladesh. The majority of incidents involve female victims and male perpetrators with motives ranging from jilted lovers, spurned sexual advances, rejected marriage proposals, inadequate dowries, as well as land or family disputes.

It is believed that the intention of the acid attacks is to disfigure the woman's looks, so that no other man will want her. The woman's family may suffer as well, because an unmarried daughter is an economic burden. It can also be seen as an attack on a father or husband's *property*.

7.3.11 **Blood feuds**

Definition of 'Blood feuds'

'The custom of blood feuds derives from age-old tribal laws that proclaim that blood must be avenged with blood. These feuds are particularly prevalent in the Balkans, Caucasus region and South Asia.

What lies at the heart of blood feuds is not punishment, but satisfaction that the honour and the reputation of the individual or family has been restored.'

(Gendercide, 2004)

It is not just about retribution, as any male member from the family of the original offender can be targeted. Traditionally the blood feud ideology grants exemption to the murder of females. However, this is not always the case. Blood feuds can last for generations, passed down family lineages, creating a cycle of revenge and murder that can, and have, been transferred to the UK. It has been estimated that every year, at least a thousand men and boys die in blood feud killings in Albania alone and the lives of tens of thousands more are spent in isolation and continuous fear (for more details see <http://www.gendercide.org/case_honour.html?FACTNet>).

7.3.11.1 Vani

Traditionally a blood feud can be settled if the murderer or his family agree to pay compensation to the aggrieved family, usually in the form of money or land. In other instances the exchange of a girl is not decided by her own family but by the decision of an informal court. In parts of Pakistan and South Asia it has been known for females to be given away in marriage as compensation, in a practice called 'Vani' or 'Swara'. According to this custom, female members from the offending male's family are married/given to the victim's family as a reparation or penance. Females are seen as a commodity and the method effective in putting an end to blood feuds, as the link of marriage binds the families together and diverts them away from further fighting. However, these women may remain stigmatized, bearing the brunt of a crime they did not commit.

7.3.12 **Male-child preference**

Male-child preference occurs in societies that value male children above females, emanating from their perceived higher worth. Fundamentally a son is deemed vital in order to continue a family's lineage.

The reasons behind this are that the female gender is perceived as a liability and the male gender an asset. For instance, sons are more likely than daughters to provide family-farm labour or continue a family business, earn wages, and give support to parents. When a son marries, a daughter-in-law is added to the family—providing assistance in household work and also by her dowry. Daughters, however, will eventually leave the family on marriage and require finances for dowry payments.

7.3.13 Female infanticide

Definition of 'Infanticide'

'Infanticide is deemed to be the killing of a child less than twelve months, generally the killing of a new born.'

(Infanticide Act 1938)

It is by far the most prevalent form of infanticide. While there are no reliable infanticide statistics, there are substantial disparities in gender population figures, especially in parts of South Asia. Sex-selective abortion or abandonment are more common methods of disposing of unwanted girls.

7.3.14 Sex-selective abortion

This is the practice of aborting a foetus after a determination of its gender. Again it usually occurs in societies that value male children above females. The practice has escalated since the invention of ultrasound and is believed to be responsible for at least part of the skewed birth statistics in favour of males in China, India, Taiwan, South Korea, Pakistan, and certain Arab states such as Egypt and Saudi Arabia.

Although the practice is illegal in the UK, laws against it are extremely difficult to enforce as parents may hide their true motivation for seeking an abortion or travel to countries where the practice is not illegal and obtaining an abortion is much simpler.

The impact of this practice, along with female infanticide, on gender ratios will be immense. It has been estimated that by 2020 there could be more than 35 million young 'surplus males' in China, 25 million in India, and four million in Pakistan, unable to find girlfriends or wives (for more details see <http://www.nationmaster.com/encyclopedia/Sex-selective-abortion>).

7.3.15 Sex-selective child abandonment

This is the practice of giving away an infant of an undesired sex. Again this practice is more common in societies that value male children above females.

7.3.16 Self-harm

Self-harm is the deliberate injury to one's own body. The injury may be aimed at relieving otherwise unbearable emotions, sensations of unreality, or numbness. It can be associated with mental illnesses, pressure, trauma, abuse, and with characteristics such as perfectionism. Although self-harm may be seen by some as attention-seeking behaviour, many conceal their actions from others.

Studies show that more women than men self-harm (see the BBC news report available at <http://news.bbc.co.uk/1/hi/health/medical_notes/4067129.stm>). In the UK it has been found that **the prevalence of self-harm is disproportionately high among young Asian women** (Bhardwaj, 2001). It is likely that the reasons behind this stem from a lack of support and the clash that can occur when an individual has to conform to differing cultural ideals, some of which are directly associated with HBV, for example forced marriage.

There are many ways that an individual may self-harm. For instance, cutting their body with knives, razor blades or glass, burning their body, biting their body, hitting themselves, hair pulling, starving themselves, or ingesting objects or noxious substances. **Self-harm is a strong predictor for future suicide or suicide attempts** (<http://www.selfharm.org/what/overview.html>).

7.3.17 **Suicide**

HBV and the emotional and the physical abuse associated with it can play an important role in the circumstances of suicide. This is why it is important to look at the factors and antecedents leading up to an individual's suicide as they may have been explicitly pressurized into committing the act.

There is no definitive evidence on how many 'forced' suicides occur in the UK. However, research has unearthed some interesting data suggesting that **young, married South Asian women are a high-risk group for suicide** (Bhugra, Desai and Baldwin, 1999).

The *NHS National Service Framework for Mental Health* (Department of Health, 1999) identified that among women living in England, those born in India and East Africa have a 40 per cent higher suicide rate than those born in England and Wales.

Young women born in the Indian subcontinent also show higher rates of attempted suicide where culture conflict, family, and marital difficulties are commonly cited problems (Merrill and Owens, 1986).

UK law states that an individual who aids, abets, counsels, or procures the suicide of another, or an attempt by another to commit suicide, can be charged with the offence of *complicity in suicide*, carrying a penalty of 14 years in prison.

7.3.17.1 Self-immolation

Self-immolation is the act of setting oneself on fire. Whilst this is suicide, it is unconventional as it is long and extremely painful. It is considered to be among the most powerful symbolic acts of sacrifice (for more detail see <http://www.worldhistory.com/wiki/I/Immolation.htm>).

7.3.17.2 Sati–widow burning

In India the term 'sati' refers to the death, voluntary or involuntary, of widows on the funeral pyre of their husbands and was known to be practised in many different regions of India since medieval times. It was believed that a woman who died in this way was very honourable and went directly to heaven. It was meant to be a voluntary act; however, it is believed to have often been enforced upon the widow by social pressures. Although sati was banned by the British in 1829, instances have continued to occur. Various measures against it now include efforts to stop the 'glorification' of the dead women which often include the erection of shrines, encouragement of pilgrimages to the site, and an income to nearby villagers.

7.3.18 'Murder in the name of so-called honour'

Definition of 'Murders in the name of so-called honour'

These are murders in which victims, predominantly women, are killed for perceived immoral behaviour, which is deemed to have breached the honour code of a family or community, causing shame. They are sometimes called 'honour killings'. There is, however, no honour in murder.

(Richards and Dhothar, 2007a, ACPO Working Definition)

Evidence from research and analysis shows that where such murders occur, most often wives are killed by their husbands and daughters by their fathers. Males can also be victims, sometimes as a consequence of their involvement in what is deemed to be an inappropriate relationship, if they are gay, or if they are believed to be supporting the victim.

Trigger events can include:

- smoking in public
- inappropriate make up or dress
- truanting
- a relationship not being approved of by family and/or community
- inter-faith relationships
- rejection of religion or religious instruction
- rejection of an arranged marriage
- pre-marital conflict
- pre-marital or extra marital affair
- objection to being removed from education
- reporting domestic abuse
- escalation—threats, violence, restrictions
- running away
- sexual conduct—talking, kissing, intimacy in a public place
- pregnancy outside of marriage
- rape
- being a reluctant immigration sponsor
- attempts to separate/divorce
- sexual orientation (including being gay, lesbian, bisexual, or transgender).

Relatives, including females, may conspire, aid, abet, or participate in the killing. Younger relatives may be selected to undertake the killing, to avoid senior family members being arrested. Sometimes contract killers are employed. Evidence shows that these types of murders are often planned and are sometimes made to look like a suicide or an accident. A decision to kill may be preceded by a family council. There often tends to be a degree of premeditation, family conspiracy, and a belief that the victim deserves to die.

When dealing with HBV, missing person enquiries, or 'murder in the name of so-called honour', it is vital to retain an open mind. Family members and/or individuals from within the community concerned may support the primary offender(s), by seeking to mislead, obstruct, or undermine your investigation.

7.4 **How Prevalent is HBV?**

Hundreds of young people are taken abroad each year and forced into marriage. Currently, some 400 cases of forced marriage are reported to the Forced Marriage Unit at the Foreign and Commonwealth Office (F&CO) each year. They receive approximately 5000 enquiries each year. The majority of victims are 15–24 years old and 30 per cent are minors, some as young as ten years old, and males making up about 15 per cent of their cases (F&CO, presentation at IKRWO Conference on 14 May 2008). Reports have substantially increased in the last couple of years and this issue has received a significant media focus owing to the work conducted by the Honour Killings Strategic Homicide Prevention Working Group at New Scotland Yard, the ACPO Forced Marriage Group, and the high-profile trials of the killers of Heshu Yones (2003), Banaz Mahmod (2007), and Surgit Athwal (2007). However, reporting rates have been low, probably more to do with trust and confidence issues as well as not knowing who/where to report matters to. It has been traditionally challenging to get an understanding of the scale of the problem.

Social care, health, education, and voluntary organizations also deal with cases. However, there is no one central body that collects all the cases. Many cases go unreported. With greater awareness, the number of cases reported is likely to increase. We do know that the majority of cases of forced marriage encountered in the UK involve South Asian families. This is partly a reflection of the fact that there is a large, established South Asian population in the UK.

It is clear that forced marriage is not solely a South Asian problem and there have been cases involving families from East Asia, the Middle East, Europe, and Africa. Some forced marriages take place in the UK with no overseas element, while others involve a partner coming from overseas or a British citizen being sent abroad. We need to know more than just numbers. We need to build up a better picture of the nature of the problem—the reasons behind it, the forms it takes and the variety of tactics that families use. Cases are rarely as simple as they first appear and practitioners need to be prepared for that complexity.

7.4.1 **Profiling HBV**

The Homicide Prevention Unit (HPU) at New Scotland Yard undertook ground-breaking research and analysis in this area to inform the police response, focusing on persistent offenders and prevention of repeat victimization. HBV incidents and murders were analysed to build up a profile of these types of incident and crime to generate a comprehensive picture of the nature and extent of abuse in terms of risk, threat, and dangerousness. Structured debriefs of murders and 'near-misses' (cases that could have resulted in a lethal incident if it were not for a fortunate break in the chain of events) also supplemented the analysis.

This extensive evidence base has been drawn on to inform this chapter. The following headline issues have been identified:

7.4.1.1 Child-protection issues

- In one in four cases the victims were under 18 years of age.
- In two in five cases, 15–24-year-olds have reported a *fear* of forced marriage and being taken abroad by their family.
- There has been an increase in forced abortion and female genital mutilation (FGM).
- There is evidence that children are going missing from the education register. This requires further research.

7.4.1.2 Missing persons

- If there are antecedents of HBV, incidents should be treated as critical incidents.
- Carefully consider third-party missing-person reports. Relatives may seek to mislead, by presenting to you another family member as being the person you are seeking. Equally, when dealing with such reports, consider why the family have not reported the individual missing.
- Further, be aware that a family may report someone missing and an allegation of theft may be made to try and get the police to locate them if they have run away.

7.4.1.3 'Threats to life'

- Reporting to the police increases the risk for many victims.
- In one in four cases there were reported threats to kill.
- Take allegations of threats to kill seriously and assess the credibility of such threats based on the antecedents and victimology.
- Balance respecting the victim's wishes against the need to protect the victim by not speaking to the family or trying to mediate but issue other options (and Osman options, where appropriate) to victims. The use of an Osman warning does not release the police from the obligation to protect; in fact it may highlight that obligation even further.

- There is a positive obligation for police to undertake risk assessments and safety planning with victims.
- Refer to your force's 'Threat to life' policy.
- Bring in safe and trusted agency workers if/when required as safe contacts.

7.4.1.4 Risk identification and assessment

- Use an ACPO-compliant risk identification, assessment, and management model such as the Domestic Abuse, Stalking and Harassment, and Honour-Based Violence Risk Model (DASH, 2008).
- Assess specific risks using HBV risk factors.
- There are different risk issues for the victim who is in *fear* of a forced marriage (FM) and the violence from their own family rather than *actual* forced marriage (trying to escape one) where the violence comes from the partner and the in-laws, ie, the family they have married into.
- Ensure that levels of intervention and prevention tactics are targeted as the risk factors present.

7.4.1.5 Risk management

- The window of opportunity for effective intervention can be limited. It is crucial that the right informed tactics are used at the right time by the right person, otherwise the victim could be placed further at risk.
- Refer to the tactical menu of intervention options listed at 7.8 below. Management plans should be aimed at the risk variables identified.
- If there is a credible threat to life, consult your force's 'Threat to Life' policy.
- When a victim does not want to prosecute, they are unlikely to be eligible for witness protection, but nonetheless the obligation to protect them still exists under Art 2, but may fall to local officers.
- Seek advice from specialist units and specialist advisers, who are listed at 7.8.

The failure to consider risks and apply an appropriate strategy constitutes negligence. Court interpretations of Art 2 ECHR place upon public authorities the positive obligation to protect life. *Osman v UK* (1998) 29 EHRR 245 illustrates this point. A positive obligation was held to exist where the 'authorities knew or ought to have known at the time of the existence of a real and immediate risk to life of an identified individual or individuals from the criminal acts of a third party and that they failed to take measures within the scope of their powers which, judged reasonably, might have been expected to avoid that risk'.

KEY POINT

It is worthy of note that liability for the offence of public malfeasance (wilful neglect to perform duty in a judical/public office) may attract to officers that fail to protect those at risk. It's a common-law offence that can carry life imprisonment.

KEY POINTS

- The actual size and extent of the problem of HBV is unknown and many incidents go unreported.Police services will be required to collate information on HBV incidents as part of the forthcoming ACPO HBV Strategy.
- Forced marriage is not the same as an arranged marriage in which both spouses can choose whether or not to accept the arrangement. In forced marriage one or both the spouses do not consent to the marriage and some element of duress is involved. Duress includes both physical and emotional pressure.
- Forced marriage can involve child and sexual abuse including violence, abduction, rape, forced pregnancy, and enforced abortion.
- Forced marriage is an abuse of human rights.
- Rejection can place a person at risk of murder, also known as 'honour killing'.
- Relatives, including females, may conspire and aid, abet, or participate in the killing.
- Forced marriage is not sanctioned within any culture or religion.
- The majority of cases in the UK involved South Asian families, and a number of cases have arisen in the East Asian, Middle Eastern, European, and African communities.
- In the UK the prevalence of self-harm is three times higher among young Asian females that for young white European females.
- A significant number of incidents are victims reporting that they fear being forced into a marriage or commitment to marry during an up-and-coming family holiday.
- Reporting to the police increases the risk for many victims.
- Many victims report allegations to the police, yet do not want to pursue a prosecution for fear of reprisal and bringing further shame onto their family.

7.5 **The Role of the Police**

For many individuals, turning to a police officer is a last resort. Many people will not even discuss their worries with their friends for fear that their families may find out.

7.5.1 **How can I recognize if a person is a victim or likely to be a victim?**

The police may receive information about a forced marriage or other HBV-related factors from the victim, from a friend or relative, or from a teacher or social worker. HBV may also become apparent through careful questioning in the course of investigating other incidents or crimes such as domestic violence, assault, abduction, or a person reported missing. The victim may present with a variety of problems such as truancy, episodes of depression and/or self-harm, or house arrest, for example. There have also been occasions when forced marriage has come to notice with less common warning signs such as the cutting or shaving of a girl's hair as a form of punishment for disobeying or perhaps 'dishonouring' the family.

In some cases, a girl may report that she has been taken to a doctor to be examined to see if she is a virgin. A forced marriage may take place in the UK or an individual may be taken overseas and forced to marry there. In either situation, the police should be ready to give guidance to the individual about their rights and the choices open to them.

7.5.2 **What can I do to help?**

To gain the confidence of the individual, the police must have a good understanding of the issues surrounding forced marriage and the steps that they can take in order to protect a victim. The police need to be aware that people living within a forced marriage, or those under threat of one, may face significant harm if their families become aware that they have sought assistance from either a statutory agency such as the police and Social Care, or from a voluntary or community-based organization. It is essential that full consideration is given to the person's safety.

In many cases, it may not be in the individual's best interest to remain with the family or even in the immediate vicinity. For these reasons, cases of forced marriage, actual or suspected, should only be handled by a 'qualified officer', that is a police officer specially nominated by his or her police force as being qualified by both relevant experience and specialist training to deal with these complex cases.

HBV cuts across all communities. A joined-up, victim-orientated, intelligence-led approach to policing can make a very specific contribution to the safety of victims. Both criminal and civil proceedings can be used to protect individuals suffering or at risk of suffering significant harm.

7.5.3 **Dealing with victims**

When dealing with potential victims it is important to recognize the seriousness/immediacy of the risk. Consider the possibility of forced marriage, abduction, missing persons, and murder. Shame, and therefore the risk to a victim, may persist long after the incident that brought about the dishonour occurred. Consider whether the victim's partner, children, associates, or their siblings are at risk. They may also suffer family and community pressure not to assist you. Remember that reporting is a brave step and an inappropriate police response could put the victim at further risk. They often have no experience of the police and by seeking assistance could be deemed to have brought further shame on the household.

Authorities in some of the countries from which HBV originates may support this practice. Victims may be concerned that you share this view, or that you may return them to their family. They often carry guilt about their rejection of cultural/family expectations. Their immigration status may be dependant on their spouse and it may be used to dissuade them from seeking assistance.

Young victims sometimes truant from school to obtain relief from being 'policed' at home by relatives. Victims of rape may be perceived by relatives as having brought about the offence and their own family may kill them as a consequence. Women that have fled their marriage are often perceived as bringing shame upon their own blood family. Therefore, they may be at risk not only from their husband and in-laws, but also from their own father, brothers, and sons, resulting in isolation, depression, and, on some occasions, suicide.

When dealing with victims, do not speak with them in the presence of their relatives. Obtain a full historical background, not just of the incident that brought the victim/witness into contact with police, as well as a full history of the immediate and extended family. Ensure that accounts are recorded to prevent the family saying the police made it up.

Victims that return to their families should be offered escape plans. Victims should be given the option to donate their DNA, fingerprints, and photograph to the police. Ensure that you make a full record of what is said, what you have done, and to whom you have referred the case.

The needs of forced-marriage victims may vary widely. They might need help to:

- avoid a threatened forced marriage
- deal with the consequences of a forced marrige
- get their belongings safely from the family home
- find alternative accommodation
- remove them from the family home, if falsely imprisoned or under house arrest
- warn a family member to stop harassing them
- obtain immediate protection and safety.

7.5.4 **Mediation**

Mediation, reconciliation, and family counselling as a response to forced marriage can be extremely dangerous. Police, social workers, and teachers undertaking these activities may unwittingly increase an individual's vulnerability and place them in danger.

KEY POINTS—MEDIATION

- Mediation can be extremely dangerous. There have been cases of individuals being murdered by their families whilst mediation was being undertaken.
- Mediation can place the individual at risk of further emotional and physical abuse.

- Simply arranging a meeting between the individual and their family may lead to undue pressure being placed on the individual to return home.
- If the individual wishes to go home or talk to their family, explain all the risks of this course of action and put in place a strategy to monitor their ongoing safety.
- If the individual insists on meeting with their family, it must take place in a safe location, supervised by the trained/specialist officer with an interpreter present. The individual must never have unsupervised contact—even if they request it.
- Police should not get involved in mediation between the victim and the family.

7.5.5 Dealing with victims abroad

Victims are sometimes persuaded to return to their country of origin under false pretences, when in fact the intention could be to kill them. If a woman is taken abroad, the F&CO may assist in repatriating the woman to the UK. In such circumstances the F&CO will take primacy for such operations.

7.5.6 False allegations of crimes or missing person reports made by families to trace victims

Where a victim has fled, be aware that members of the family may make false allegations of crime against them in an attempt to enlist your support to track them down. This may be in the guise of missing person reports or an alleged theft. On occasions you may be approached by other legitimate agencies or individuals to disclose the whereabouts of the victim as they have been asked by the family to assist them.They may also employ bounty hunters/contract killers to trace, return, and/or kill the victim.

7.5.7 What powers do I have as a police officer to deal with cases?

It is necessary to remove offenders from their offending environment where possible. Section 110 of the Serious Organised Crime and Police Act (SOCPA) 2005 and s 24 of the Police and Criminal Evidence Act (PACE) 1984 lay out appropriate general arrest conditions that can be used.

Section 110 of SOCPA 2005 amended the powers of arrest available to a constable under s 24 of PACE. Prior to the introduction of s 110, the powers of arrest were primarily derived from ss 24 and 25 of PACE based on the application of the concept of seriousness attached to the offence.

The exercise of arrest powers will be subject to a test of necessity based around the nature and circumstances of the offence and the interests of the criminal justice system. An arrest will only be justified if the constable believes it is necessary for any of the reasons set out in the new s 24(5) of PACE.

Officers should *consider* whether the action of arrest is proportionate given the balance between the interests of the alleged offender, the need to prevent further offences, and the need to protect the victim and any children present. Arrest will 'normally' be necessary to allow an investigation to be completed and prevent further offences. Officers 'normally' need time with the victim during the period of arrest to ascertain the risk, evidence of violence past and current, the threat, the precise nature of the offence committed, and the wider context of the relationship. Do not lose sight of the fact that victims can, and do, often minimize the threat/danger to themselves and/or to others.

Ultimately, it is the officer's decision whether or not to arrest, NOT the victim's. In *Osman v UK* (1998) 29 EHRR 245 it was held that the police could be liable for breach of Art 2 (Right to Life, HRA, 1998) if they had not taken 'reasonable' 'preventive operational measures' to avoid a 'real immediate' risk to life which they ought to have known about.

The question to the victim 'What do you want us to do?' is *not* appropriate first off. Questions should relate to the offence in terms of what happened, the history of any violence or previous incidents, and the victim's view of their situation—*not* his/her opinion on the appropriate action for a police officer to take. If there is serious injury or threat to the victim sufficient for a charge, an arrest is clearly an appropriate response (refer to the 'Positive Action' section of *Guidance on Investigating Domestic Abuse* (ACPO, 2008).

The decision to arrest or otherwise can have serious consequences, and whatever decision is taken, it must be properly risk assessed.

KEY POINT

If there is an immediate, real, and credible threat to life, and the perpetrator(s) has been assessed as having the intention and ability to carry out that threat, check your 'Threats to life' policy. This procedure is for threats to life only but it may also apply to certain threats to cause serious injury that may prove fatal (ie a threat to shoot someone in the legs). It may be appropriate and reasonable to follow this procedure when dealing with threats of that nature.

KEY POINT

Do not lose sight of the fact that the basic tenets of your responsibilities as an officer are the:

- preservation of life, and
- prevention and detection crime.

7.5.8 What impact does the Human Rights Act 1998 have on action that I may take? (See Appendix D at end of book)

Officers make frequent mention of the 'perceived lack of powers of arrest', particularly with regards to common assaults, with many citing the Human Rights Act 1998. However, this Act should be seen as an opportunity to facilitate proactive and creative police and multi-agency responses to domestic violence, *not* as a barrier for effective action. Home Office circular 19/00 (Home Office, 2000) states that in a case of domestic violence where there is evidence that supports the power of arrest, the 'alleged offender should normally be arrested'.

Where the power of arrest does not exist, there are still a number of options available, such as referral to other agencies and taking detailed statements for use in future criminal/civil proceedings. Some form of *positive action* must *always* be taken. This is both in terms of options surrounding the offender and safety planning in terms of the victim. At the very least, the victim should feel s/he has the option for protection.

7.5.9 What should I do if a victim does not want to proceed with a prosecution? (See Appendix E, s 116 of the Criminal Justice Act 2003, at end of book)

Where a victim does not want to prosecute, they are unlikely to be eligible for witness protection, but nonetheless the obligation to protect them still exists under Art 2, but may fall to local officers.

Just because a victim does not want to proceed any further with a case, it does not necessarily mean that the case is therefore stopped with regards to the police investigation and the Crown Prosecution Service (CPS). Other available evidence should always be considered. A withdrawal statement should always be taken stating *why* the victim is withdrawing. The CPS will also ask why the victim is withdrawing, why the police *think* the victim is withdrawing, and the level of risk posed to the victim, children, and other persons' safety. The police and CPS should explore *all* options fully. In some cases the violence is so serious, or previous history shows a real and continuing danger to the victim, children or other person, that the public interest in going ahead with a prosecution has to outweigh the victim's wishes.

The CPS will have to decide whether:

- the victim is required to give evidence in person in court
- to use the victim's statement as evidence (Criminal Justice Act 2003).

In both cases, consultation is required between the police and CPS. Cases can be prosecuted on behalf of the public at large and not in the interests of any particular individual. Risk assessment is crucial to the decision-making process.

An early case conference between CPS and the police is crucial in all cases. Consideration has to be afforded to whether the victim's partner, children, associates, or their siblings are at risk along with potential witnesses as well. In some cases it may be necessary to speak with the Criminal Justice Protection Unit (CJPU) to discuss options around witness protection matters.

7.6 Risk Identification, Assessment, and Management of Cases

Risk identification, assessment, and management is a dynamic process. It is essential that all police officers and staff that may investigate incidents of so-called HBV are made aware of these unique risk factors and that every incident is effectively risk managed.

Each incident should be risk-assessed using an ACPO-compliant risk assessment model such as the DASH (2008) and recorded on the force crime reporting system and/or other appropriate databases. Once the assessment has been conducted, the intervention plan must be implemented to manage the risks. The senior investigating officer/investigating officer (SIO/IO) should work with crisis intervention teams and community partners to develop support packages/safety plans for victims.

7.6.1. How do I risk-assess a case?

The DASH (2008) model is ACPO-compliant and is used for risk identification, assessment, and management of domestic-abuse cases. Through the research and analysis several emerging risk factors have been identified, including risk factors for HBV specifically.

7.6.1.1 Risk and HBV violence

Needs may differ amongst community groups. This might be in terms of issues of perceived racism, language, culture, insecure immigration status, and accessing relevant support services. Domestic violence may take on different forms within specific communities. Reduced access to services and social isolation can combine to increase lethal risks. For example, this could apply to newly arrived communities, asylum seekers, older people, people with disabilities, travelling, ethnic minority, and/or gay, lesbian, bisexual, or transgender people. There may be difficulties speaking/reading English, not working outside the home, service access issues—not knowing who, how, or where to go for help.

Evidence from research and analysis shows that where such murders occur, most often wives are killed by their husbands and daughters by their fathers (Richards and Dhothar, 2007b). Males can also be victims, sometimes as a consequence of their involvement in what is deemed to be an inappropriate relationship, if they are gay, or if they are believed to be supporting the victim. Relatives, including females, may conspire, aid, abet or participate in the killing. Younger relatives may be selected to undertake the killing, to avoid senior family members being arrested and prosecuted. Sometimes contract killers (bounty hunters) are employed. HBV cuts across all cultures, nationalities, faith groups, and communities.

Do not underestimate that perpetrators of HBV really do kill their closest relatives and/or others for what might seem a trivial transgression. Just the perception or rumour of immoral behaviour may be sufficient to kill. Such trigger incidents may include (this list is not exhaustive):

- smoking in public
- inappropriate make up or dress
- truanting
- a relationship not being approved of by family and/or community
- inter-faith relationships
- rejection of religion or religious instruction
- rejection of an arranged marriage
- pre-marital conflict
- pre-marital or extra marital affair
- objection to being removed from education
- reporting domestic abuse
- escalation—threats, violence, restrictions
- running away
- sexual conduct—talking, kissing, intimacy in a public place
- pregnancy outside of marriage
- rape
- being a reluctant immigration sponsor
- attempts to separate/divorce
- sexual orientation (including being gay, lesbian, bisexual, or transgender).

7.6.2 What are the risk factors associated with HBV?

Research shows (Richards, 2007) that the risks are different for those who **fear** a forced marriage to those who are **actually in** a forced marriage, particulalry regarding **who** they might be at risk **from**. For those who fear a forced marriage—they will tend to be at risk from their own family. Those who are actually in a forced marriage—and looking to separate—will tend to be at risk from their husband and his family.

The following can combine to raise unique risk factors for HBV:

7.6.2.1 Truanting

This is a risk factor amongst teenage girls, in particular. The reasons for this appear to be twofold. First, if a girl is in a controlling environment, being dropped off and collected from school, she may not have any other opportunities to socialize;

therefore truanting may be the only time for any form of independence. Many girls know that they will not finish their education and once they leave school they may be sent abroad to be married, where a British education may be of little use. Care must be taken to ensure that if girls are truanting, schools or other officials do not inadvertently up the ante by alerting parents to this fact if there are HBV issues to be considered.

7.6.2.2 Self-harm

Studies show that more women than men self-harm (see the news report at <http://news.bbc.co.uk/1/hi/health/medical_notes/4067129.stm>). In the UK it has been found that the prevalence of self-harm is disproportionately high among young Asian women (Bhardwaj, 2001). It is likely that the reasons behind this stem from a lack of support and the clash that can occur when an individual has to conform to differing cultural ideals, some of which are directly associated with HBV, ie forced marriage. Self-harm is a strong predictor for future suicide or suicide attempts (for further details see <http://www.selfharm.org/what/overview.html>).

7.6.2.3 House arrest and being 'policed at home'

This includes not being allowed out, being supervised by family members and escorted to places outside of the home address, and restricted access to telephone, internet, finances, passport, and friends, for example.

7.6.2.4 Fear of being forced into an engagement/marriage

This is a real concern. It might be reported to officials or to friends. The risk tends to elevate if the victim is non-compliant with the family's wishes. This is heightened further if they have a partner that the family does not approve of. Care needs to be taken if the victim believes she will be taken overseas against her will. Forced marriage places individuals at risk of rape and possible physical harm. Some cases have resulted in the reluctant spouse being murdered.

7.6.2.5 Pressure to go abroad

This normally happens just before the summer holidays. Reports to police increase at this time and victims fear they will be taken overseas and forced to marry. If a person holds the nationality of two countries, they are a dual national and will have two passports. Be mindful of this if you believe they will be taken out the country. For many young people it may be their first time travelling overseas. If they are being held against their will and forced to marry there are various difficulties if they want to return to the UK. They may find it impossible to communicate by telephone, letter, and email. They may not have access to their passport and money. Women may not be allowed to leave the house unescorted. They may not be able to speak the local language. Often individuals find themselves in remote areas where even getting to the nearest road can be hazardous. They may not receive the assistance they might expect from the local police, neighbours, family, friends, or taxi drivers.

7.6.2.6 Isolation

Individuals forced into marriage often become estranged from their families. Sometimes they find themselves trapped in a cycle of abuse. Many suffer for many years from domestic violence. They may feel unable to leave because of their children, a lack of family support, economic pressures, and other social circumstances. Isolation is one of the biggest problems facing victims of forced marriage. They may feel they have no one to speak to about their situation. These feelings are very similar to those experienced by victims of domestic violence and child abuse. Isolation is very real for those who have escaped a forced marriage or the threat of one. For many, running away is their first experience of living away from home and they suffer without their family, friends, and usual environment. They often live in fear for being tracked down by their family who may solicit the help of others. In addition to leaving, they may be seen as bringing shame on the honour of the individual and the family in the eyes of the community.

7.6.2.7 Attempts to separate or divorce (child contact issues)

Research and analysis shows that attempts to end a relationship are strongly linked to intimate-partner homicide. Websdale (1999) states that attempts to leave violent men are one of the most significant correlates with domestic death. Notions of 'if I can't have her, then no one can' are recurring features of such cases and the killer frequently intends to kill themselves (Wilson and Daly, 1993; Richards, 2003).

Threats that begin with 'if you were to ever leave me. . . ' must be taken seriously. Victims who stay with the abuser because they are afraid to leave may correctly anticipate that leaving would elevate or spread the risk of lethal assault. The data on time-since-separation further suggest that women are particularly at risk within the first two months (Wilson and Daly, 1993; Richards, 2003).

Further, many incidents happen as a result of discussions around child contact or disputes over custody. Children should also be considered in the assessment process. Unique risks are raised in terms of shame and honour. Those who leave are seen to bring shame on the honour of the family in the eyes of the community. This may lead to social ostracism and harassment by the family.

7.6.2.8 Threats that they will never see the children again

This can have a huge impact on a woman, particularly if she believes she has insecure immigration status where she is concerned about being deported while her children remain in the UK. This is often used as a lever to coerce and gain compliance from the victim.

7.6.2.9 A pre-marital relationship or an extra-marital affair

This could be real or perceived by the perpetrator(s). Consider risk of harm to the new partner also.

7.6.2.10 Threats to kill/harm

These tend to be credible and should be treated as such. Assess the antecedents and victimology further. Care should be taken around networks/organizations being used to track down victims that flee from the family, for example accessing IT networks, minicabs, or employing associates within statutory organizations (police, Benefits Agency, family law solicitors, for example).

7.6.3 Managing high-risk cases

If there is an immediate threat to life—check your force's 'Threats to life' policy.

Refer to the tactical menu of intervention options and compile safety and intervention options aimed at the risk factors identified through the risk-assessment process for immediate single-agency intervention first off. Do not delay in contacting agencies if an immediate repsonse/help is required in safeguarding a victim's safety.

Consider who else may be at risk in terms of siblings, children, partner, and/or other members of the family.

Those **victim(s)** who are high risk and/or require a multi-agency response should be referred to either:

- a child-protection case conference
- a domestic-violence forum
- a risk-management panel (RMP) (such as the risk-assessment management panels (RAMP) being piloted in the MPS or priority offender panels currently being used in West Midlands Police)
- a multi-agency risk-assessment conference (MARAC) for a multi-agency response.

Consider liaison with the local/central Intelligence Unit. An analyst can be tasked to aid and support the investigation by building a profile of the offender. Those **offenders** who are at high risk should be referred to either:

- a risk-management panel (RMP), such as the risk-assessment management panels (RAMP) piloted in the MPS or priority-offender panels currently being used in West Midlands Police
- a multi-agency public-protection panel arrangement (MAPPA) for a multi-agency response.

Cases should be reviewed and a detailed proposed action plan should be compiled using a tactical menu of options at 7.8 below. Agencies should be working together to safeguard victims under s 115 of the Crime and Disorder Act 1998 and the Police and Justice Act 2006.

Section 115 ensures all agencies have a power to disclose information. It does not impose a requirement on them to exchange information, and so control over disclosure remains with the agency that holds the data. When considering a disclosure of personal information, the designated officer must determine whether the public interest would justify disclosure against the normal presumption of confidentiality. Each case must be considered separately and a disclosure must be based on an objective assessment of all the available information. The public interest criteria will include the:

- prevention of crime and disorder
- detection of crime
- apprehension of offenders
- protection of vulnerable members of the community
- maintenance of public safety
- administration of justice
- diversion of young offenders.

The Police and Justice Act 2006 strengthens these powers with respect to information-sharing. It places all the key players in CDRPs under a legal duty to share aggregate, depersonalized data between themselves when doing so would be in the interest of preventing crime. New minimum standards for CDRPs require an information-sharing protocol to be signed by all responsible authorities, and for a designated person in each authority to facilitate information-sharing within the CDRP.

Any action taken must be:

- Proportionate
- Legal
- Appropriate and
- Necessary, based on the
- Best Information/intelligence (PLANBI) available at the time the offence is disclosed. It must also comply with human rights legislation.

KEY POINTS ON ASSESSING THE SITUATIONAL CONTEXT

Remember to include in your assessment:

- the ongoing relationship or connection between the perpetrator and victim which may enhance vulnerability to future abuse and act as a barrier to help-seeking options
- the possibility of other siblings being the subject of similar issues
- the possible threat to boyfriend/girlfriend
- any history of abusing others outside the home
- the strong extended family network
- that the family may seek to locate and pressurize the victim
- that the family may seek to use police and/or other professionals to find the victim

- that the family may make allegations of theft or other crimes in an attempt for to get police to locate victims who have gone into hiding of their own accord
- that the family may seek to remove/abduct the victim
- the overseas threat—consider whether other extended-family members may be used in another country or whether they intend to take the victim abroad.

Checklist for officers dealing with victims of HBV

- Remember reporting is a brave step.

- Recognize and respect the individual's wishes.

- See the individual immediately in a secure and private place.

- See them on their own, even if they attend with others.

- Contact, as soon as possible, a trained/specialist officer.

- If under 18 years of age, refer to the Child Protection Unit.

- Create a crime report/intelligence log.

- Conduct a risk assessment.

- Video interview the victim, achieving best evidence (ABE), at the first opportunity. Records should be taped to avoid the family saying the police made it up.

- Obtain a full historical background as opposed to just the incident that brought the victim/witness to the attention of police.

- Obtain a full account of the family tree, both immediate and extended.

- Reassure the victim of police confidentiality.

- Establish a way of contacting them discreetly in the future.

- Obtain full details to create a report to pass on to a trained/specialist officer.

Do not:

- send the individual away in the belief that is not a police matter

- approach members of the family or community leaders

- share information with anyone without the consent of the individual

- breach confidentiality

- attempt ANY form of mediation.

7.7 **Partnerships with other Agencies and Organizations**

It is unlikely that the police or any single agency will be able to meet all the needs of someone. As with the needs of victims of domestic violence and child abuse, the needs of victims of HBV cut across service providers' boundaries. It is very unlikely that police, or any single agency, will be able to meet all the needs of a person who is affected by HBV.

However, it is likely that the police will play a key role in protecting the interests of the individual. Qualified officers should be ready to use any statutory or voluntary agency that can provide assistance safely. In many cases, the Forced Marriage Unit (FMU) at the F&CO will be an important resource. Police should note that Social Care has a duty to make enquiries into allegations of abuse or neglect against a child under s 47 Children Act 1989 and that forced marriage can amount to sexual and emotional abuse that places children at significant risk of abuse. Each area child protection committee (ACPC) has local child-protection protocols and procedures for helping young people who are facing abuse. Key legislation includes the Children Act 1989, the Family Law Act 1996, the Homelessness Act 2002, and the Sexual Offences Act of 1956 and 2003.

The Children Act 2004 outlines new statutory duties and clarifies account-abilities for children's services. However, the wider process for change is *Every Child Matters: Working together to safeguard children—Change for children* (HM Government, 2006), which sets out the national framework for local change programmes to build services round the needs of children and young people so that we maximize opportunity and minimize risk. Be aware that s 5 of the Domestic Violence, Crime and Victims Act (2004) places an obligation on family members to protect a vulnerable family member from other family members.

7.7.1 **Care orders and supervision orders**

Frequently, an emergency protection order (EPO) is followed by an application from the local authority for an interim care order (ss 31 and 38 of the Children Act 1989). Without such an application, an EPO will lapse and the local authority will no longer have parental responsibility. A court will only make an interim care order under s 38 Children Act 1989 if it is satisfied that there are reasonable grounds to believe that the following threshold criteria are met:

- the young person concerned is suffering, or likely to suffer, significant harm (the term significant harm should be taken to mean all forms of abuse—physical, sexual, and emotional and all forms of ill treatment that are not physical) and

- the harm, or likelihood of harm, is attributable to (amongst other things) the care given to the young person, or likely to be given to them if the order were not made, not being what it would be reasonable to expect a parent to give a young person.

7.7.2 Who else can help?

It is essential that police use a multi-agency approach to the problems faced by victims of forced marriage and develop partnerships with the following:

7.7.2.1 Social care

Social Care can assist police in gathering information about an individual and their family. They may have documented evidence of previous incidents relating to other siblings. They can assist in protecting a young person if they are at risk of significant harm and provide safe, appropriate accommodation for individuals wishing to flee a forced marriage or the threat of one. Family law solicitors can be employed and considerations should be given to making victims Wards of Court and to non-molestation orders and injunctions, where appropriate.

7.7.2.2 Local schools and colleges

Local schools and colleges can alert authorities if they are concerned that an individual may have been taken abroad for the purpose of a forced marriage or are concerned that an individual may be forced into marriage in the UK. They should be encouraged to notify police if a vulnerable young person is missing from school. Schools and colleges may have further detailed information about an individual's family and the area overseas from which they originate.

7.7.2.3 Local support, counselling services and non-government organizations (NGOs)

Community-based organizations, namely black and minority ethnic women's groups, advocacy services, and youth and children's groups have a wealth of expertise and knowledge. These services are widely seen by women to be non-judgemental and understanding, and are often more accessible due to reasons of gender, language, or culture. These organizations can offer victims long-term support, counselling, and advocacy. Care should be taken to ensure that they have a good track record of working with women and young people and acting in their best interests. The police should consider approaching established women's groups who have a history of working with survivors of domestic violence and forced marriage and ask these groups to refer them to reputable agencies.

7.7.2.4 The Forced Marriage Unit (FMU) at the F&CO

The FMU and the F&CO can offer advice and assistance to individuals who:

- fear they may be forced into a marriage overseas
- fear for a friend who has been taken overseas and may be forced to marry
- have already been forced to marry and do not want to support their spouse's visa application
- need assistance in repatriation if they have been taken abroad against their will.

7.7.2.5 Strategic Health Authorities (SHAs), Primary Care Trusts (PCTs), GPs, NHS Trusts, and Mental Health Trusts

Cases of forced marriage may come to the attention of health professionals. They should refer individuals to the police, Social Care or other appropriate agencies, support groups, and counselling services.

7.7.2.6 Housing departments and the Benefits Agency

Housing departments and the Benefits Agency may be able to provide the police and social services with useful information relating to the families of victims. Housing departments can also help victims of forced marriage who are over the age of 18. Housing departments consider forced marriage an aspect of domestic violence and this ensures that victims are given priority when being housed. The Homelessness (Priority Need for Accommodation, England) Order 2002 came into effect in July 2002. It extended the number of homeless people with a 'priority need' for accommodation who are entitled to be re-housed under the homelessness legislation. The aim of these changes is to ensure that the greatest protection is given to the most vulnerable people and to those who historically have been found to be at greatest risk of ending up on the streets.

7.8 Tactical Menu of Intervention Options for Victims and Offenders

Table 7.1 Profiling and targeting of perpetrator

Perpetrator	Details to be recorded on the INTELLIGENCE database
Criminality	Consider that the offender may be involved in other areas of crime. Search for previous intelligence entries, use cross-force intelligence and crime-reporting system for offender, accused, victim, vehicle fields, for example. Check PNC, ViSOR, impact nominal index (INI) and firearms licences. Use information from victim, witnesses, family, etc, as well as considering community intelligence about offender. Outstanding warrants, breach of bail/contact orders or failure to conform to CROs or CPRO, non-payment of fines, etc. Utilize Open Source research checks on offender. Consider referral to TT&CG and/or a risk-management panel such as MARAC.

233

Table 7.1 Profiling and targeting of perpetrator

Perpetrator	Details to be recorded on the INTELLIGENCE database
Address	Details of all known addresses (relatives, friends, etc), alternative place of arrest, location and risk to victim(s).
Children	Child Abuse Investigation Units (CAIU), child abuse coming to notice record, youth offending/action teams (YO/ATs), child-protection register, schools liaison officer. If under 18 consider making ward of court if necessary. Liaise with social services.
Previous partners/siblings	Existing risk to previous partner(s)/siblings, history of abuse, intelligence/statement available from previous partner(s). Are you dealing with a serial offender?
Associates	Criminality known about associates, alternative place of arrest, etc.
Vehicle	All vehicles that the offender(s) has access to (private, relatives', work). To be used for information reports, details of bail restrictions, curfews, information to investigating officer, etc.
Phone numbers	Details of landlines, mobile phones and pagers. Lists of numbers stored within phones, details of associates, etc.
Work	Details of offender's workplace, access to information, relevant skills, alternative place of arrest.
Places frequented	Clubs, group activities, school, college, bars, sport centres, etc.

Table 7.2 Investigation of offences

Investigation	Action
Crime reporting and intelligence databases	Detail a clear investigative strategy. Complete crime report and intelligence reports in as much detail regarding the victim, offender (description, relationship, CRO/PNC, etc), venue, offence behaviour including significant language, children being present at time of assault or in household, for example. Create separate crime reports for separate incidents. Cross-reference all crime reports and intelligence reports. Restrict report if necessary.
Statements/supporting documents/community impact assessment	Police officer's notes and statements should fully detail all aspects of the abuse/violence including previous incidents, levels of violence and injury, damage to property, crime scene, emotional abuse, behaviour of both the offender and victim and other relevant factors including the impact on victim/family.

Investigation	Action
	Use a specialist sexual offences officer where allegations of sexual assault are made. Consider documenting victim's negative statement when they do not want to take a specific course of action and a community impact assessment. Consider deploying an accredited family liaison officer (FLO).
Using 999 tapes	Examine demeanour of caller, background noise including comments from witnesses, suspects, and victims; any first description (*res gestae* or things done) of the incident as provided by the witness or victim.
Risk assessment	Clear and effective risk assessment must be documented. Complete a risk assessment of the threat including risks to the victim and anyone else involved, such as their partner, friends or relatives. The assessment must take account of suicide and self-harm behaviour. Refer it on for action. Use an ACPO-compliant risk model such as the DASH (2008) and the HBV risk-considerations document. Put an appropriate intervention plan into place. Identify dates/times of risk to victim, location for bail objections, etc. If there is an immediate, real, and credible threat to life and the perpetrator is assessed as having the intention and ability to carry out that threat check your 'Threats to life' policy. This procedure is for threats to life only but it may also apply to certain threats to cause serious injury that may prove fatal (ie, a threat to shoot someone in the legs). It may be appropriate and reasonable to follow this procedure when dealing with threats of that nature.
Forensics	Treat victim, suspect, other persons at premises and venue as a crime scene: secure, preserve, and control the scenes to limit any access until sufficient information is available to make an informed assessment of the situation. Request a crime scene investigator (CSI) to attend or record the reasons why one could not attend or was not called. Ensure preservation of all other forensic opportunities such as victim's swabs from injuries (if bite or skin not broken), seize clothing, bedding, objects, or weapons used, taking fingerprints, firearms, and scene preservation. Consider blood or liquid distribution, footwear impressions, DNA, signs of a disturbance, injuries and evidence from the forensic medical examination. Use FME or forensic identification officer. Use Sexual Offences Kit, obtain DNA from offender (buccal swab).

235

Table 7.2 Investigation of offences

Investigation	Action
Photographic/ Video	Use of digital camera instant-evidence capture, photograph victim, scene, damage to property etc. Consideration of use of video evidence at scene and/or body worn video can be used on oficers first deployed. Consider hospital images recorded for internal damage prognosis (X-ray) may also be required to support the investigation.
CCTV	Evidence of offence(s), offender placed at scene, area, verification or elimination of alibi. Existing overt CCTV facilities can be used to monitor and target subjects. In some areas it may be possible to reposition CCTV to cover a subject's address or an area known to be of interest to a subject. The local/central Intelligence Unit should have access to covert video equipment, which can be deployed (subject to directed surveillance authority) to monitor a subject and establish intelligence as to their lifestyle.
Surveillance	Use of level 1 or level 2 and specialist surveillance teams. Covert surveillance is a potential investigative tool to gather evidence in certain domestic-abuse cases, particularly where harassment is an issue. Covert policing techniques should only be contemplated when due consideration has been given to all of the circumstances of the case and conventional policing methods have failed or are likely to fail. Police forces should comply with the Regulation of Investigatory Powers Act 2000 (RIPA) and Home Office (2002) Covert Surveillance Code of Practice.
Proactive targeting	The use of level 1 and or level 2 resources to target offender for all areas of criminality. Use front line officers, targeted patrols, specialist teams. Consider using proactive assets for targeting. Capture of evidence though itemized phone billing, answerphone messages, text messages, email, forensic examination of letters, tracking devices, mobile phone triangulation, for example.
Covert Human Intelligence Sources	There may be circumstances where victims or witnesses of domestic abuse seek to provide intelligence regarding other criminal activities of the suspect. Any victim or witness of domestic abuse providing intelligence to police officers should be subject to further risk assessment and safety-planning measures. Officers should ensure that established risk factors for domestic abuse are identified and monitored. The first priority for the police is to ensure the safety and protection of victims and witnesses. In situations where the domestic-abuse victim or witness provides information about offences, other than domestic abuse, the information should be forwarded to the intelligence unit for evaluation.

Investigation	Action
Seeking evidence from other agencies	Other agencies may hold relevant evidence that could assist in supporting a prosecution. This might be photographic evidence, body maps, witness evidence, items or samples that they are safeguarding on behalf of a victim. Partner agencies might, on occasions, be better placed to obtain evidence from victims. For example, victims may consent to have photographs taken of their injuries, or body maps completed, by medical staff at a time when they are not ready to disclose the abuse formally to the police.
Use of interpreters	General guidance is that interpreters live in close proximity to the interview premises, but in domestic abuse and HBV cases it might be prudent to use interpreters that meet the criteria of the suspect, victim, or witness but who do not live within the immediate community.
Communication	Agree a means of discreet future contact. Ask the victim to keep their passport in a safe place and also inform passport office to flag their details. Airports can be alerted and equally safety-planning advice should be given to victim if they believe they will be taken overseas. Seek specialist advice from other units if required such as the F&CO, the Central Community Safety Unit Service Delivery Team (MPS) or Karma Nirvana, for example.
Special measures	Victims may want to speak to their employers to maximize their safety at work. It may be necessary for the victim to inform child minders, nurseries and schools of who exactly is permitted to pick the children up and what action to take if attempts are made to take the children. Consider meeting with and advising the victim's employers of tactics to adopt should the family contact them trying to locate the victims. The victim's consent to share information would be required. Consider whether the victim's name needs to be removed from computerized agency systems such as the electoral roll, DVLA, DHSS, National Insurance, for example. Consider what other measures need to be in place for protection purposes for the victim, partners, siblings, as well as witness. Speak to the Criminal Justice Protection Unit (CJPU), if appropriate.
Forward planning	Consider contacting non-government organizations (NGOs), such as Iranian and Kurdish Women's Rights Organization (IKWRO), Southall Black Sisters (SBS), Ashiana, Roshini, or Karma Nirvana. Karma Nirvana run a friendship network of survivors to mentor, counsel, and discuss risk assessment and safety-planning issues with the victim.

Table 7.3 Prevention of repeat victimization, providing support to victim and formation of a safety plan

Safety Planning	Action
Target hardening	Crime prevention advice from crime reduction officers and crime prevention design officers, consideration around victim's home address, workplace, schools, other places frequented and other vulnerable areas. Engage neighbourhood policing teams.
Forensics	Take DNA, photograph and fingerprints of the victim (with his/her consent). Obtain IMEI or SIM of the victim's phone for tracking if necessary.
Establish regular safe contact	Provision of mobile phone to maintain 24/7 contact in early stage. Some mobile phones go directly through to the control room. Using covert methods to establish regular contact with the victim use signing on bail book; non-police email and/or provide victim with a 'pay as you go' mobile phone. Use an agreed codeword with victim.
Panic alarm	Panic alarms are available to victims who wish to remain in their own homes and for whom the perpetrator presents a significant risk. They will generally only be suitable where the perpetrator has no legal right of access to the premises concerned.
Alarms/Sanctuary schemes	Use of Mascot or other similar systems to be installed within victim's premises. Update caller-aided despatch around installation of alarms and previous history. Issue of personal attack alarms to victims and witnesses. Consider a sanctuary project or other target-hardening service referral. The sanctuary scheme is a victim-centred and innovative approach to homelessness prevention. DV victims are encouraged to remain in their own homes by installation of additional security measures.
Police Watch/Community Officers	Neighbourhood policing teams are tasked to provide a regular visible presence in close proximity to the victim's address and in some circumstances pay welfare visits to the victim provided that consent is given. Officers may also be tasked in relation to the offending behaviour of the perpetrator.
Cocoon Watch	Similar to Neighbourhood Watch, this scheme engages nominated family, friends, and neighbours to provide a support network for the victim and their children. This has to have the knowledge and consent of the victim as the nominated persons would need to be made aware of their situation.

Safety Planning	Action
Escape plan	Ask victim to contact the investigating officer (IO) at least two/three days in advance if they decide to make any dramatic changes or decisions and return home, for example. Consider a contingency plan for relocation to alternative area if location is discovered. Consider nominated safe contact, access to funds and credit card/bank account numbers, passport, identification, insurance documents, birth certificate, social security cards, driver's licence, lease or mortgage papers, school and medical records, welfare and immigration papers, court documents, transport (spare car keys), a change of clothes. Children need to be included in the safety plan and an alternative escape plan for them may be necessary. Rehearse escape plans with children and ensure children know how to contact police.
Specialist refuge service provider	Refuge/Women's Aid, for example, provide places of safety for women fleeing domestic violence across the UK. They also provide specialist refuge places for women with specific ethnic or cultural backgrounds.
Special schemes/ Warning flags on systems for call outs to address	Implementation of Special Schemes on caller-aided dispatch system relating to victim's and offender address. Detail further action to be taken as the result of further calls to the premises as well as which calls should be treated as emergencies.
Integrated Domestic Abuse Programme (IDAP) / Offender tracking	IDAP is a perpetrator programme aimed at challenging violent and abusive behaviour by men against their female partner/ex-partner. Run by Probation it can be part of the sentence delivered to domestic violence perpetrators under a community order or part of the requirement of a post-custody licence. Liaise with probation officer. Establish whether offender is subject to a community sentence (community rehabilitation order or community and punishment rehabilitation order). Track offender to ensure compliance with order. Keep Probation informed of re-offending behaviour. Ensure order is enforced by executing warrants as soon as possible. Consider using ViSOR.
Independent Domestic Violence Advisers (IDVAs)	IDVAs give personal advice and support direct to high-risk victims to help them make decisions about their future and also help them access the range of services they need. Referrals are normally made at the point of crisis. The role of the advocate is to advise and support victims to help ensure their safety independently of any other organization. Generally, IDVAs provide intervention assistance to victims of domestic abuse, identified as high risk, whose cases are referred to a MARAC and are progressing through the criminal justice system. IDVAs should maintain current information about victims and witnesses in domestic abuse cases. They should also update police officers responsible for the case, and attend and contribute to MARACs, as required.

239

Table 7.3 Prevention of repeat victimization, providing support to victim and formation of a safety plan

Safety Planning	Action
Injunctions/Orders	Liaise with partner agencies re: ward of court, injunctions, etc. Consider a **restraining order** under s 5 of the Protection from Harassment Act 1997, injunctions and a non-molestation order. A **non-molestation injunction** forbids the perpetrator from using or threatening violence, harassing, pestering, or intimidating the victim. The court can attach a power of arrest to the order, which, if breached, will ensure that the perpetrator is arrested and placed before a court. The Domestic Violence, Crime and Victims Act 2007 makes breaches of non-molestation a criminal offence. Note that ss 2, 3, and 4 of the Domestic Violence, Crime and Victims Act 2004 extend the provision of the Family Law Act 1996 to same-sex couples and to those who have had an intimate personal relationship with each other which is, or was, of significant duration, thus allowing those individuals to apply for a non-molestation order. If non-contact or molestation orders exist, speak to neighbours to warn them of this. Advise them to contact victim and/or police if offender or his car is seen in the area. Set up local agreements with housing agencies and local government. An **occupation order** provides a remedy to have the perpetrator removed from the home and to forbid him or her from returning within a specified distance, entering, or attempting to enter. A power of arrest can be attached to the order to ensure that the perpetrator is placed before a court should they breach any part of it. A residence order is an order setting the arrangements made as to the person or people with whom a child is to live. The court will undertake a welfare check and make the order. A **prohibited steps order** is an order that no step, of a kind set out on the order, can be taken by a person in meeting their parental responsibility for a child without the comment of the court, for example, to prevent a child being removed from the country. A **contact order** is an order requiring the person with whom the child lives or is to live to allow the child to visit or stay with the person named in the order, or to otherwise have contact with each other. Consider deportation orders for foreign and EU nationals. **Antisocial behaviour orders** (ASBOs) are civil orders made by a court which prohibit the perpetrator from specific antisocial acts and from entering defined areas on a map (exclusion zones). **Sexual offences prevention orders** (SOPOs). Similar to ASBOs. Need to liaise with CPS and obtain SOPOs on conviction for sexual or violent offences. **Notification orders**—Result in offenders who committed sexual offences abroad having to comply with registration requirements in the UK.

Safety Planning	Action
	Risk of sexual harm orders (RoSHOs)—Minimum of 2 yrs. No need for any conviction. Only for persons over 18 who are deemed to pose a risk of sexual harm to under-16s. Breaching a RoSHO will result in registration. **Disqualification orders** (always for life) can be made under the Criminal Justice and Court Services Act (CJCSA) 2000. Can be obtained on conviction at Crown Court for sexual or violent offences against children.
Forced Marriage (Civil Protection) Act 2007	Under the Act the courts have the power to make forced marriage protection orders to stop someone from forcing another person into marriage. The courts have a wide discretion in the type of injunctions they are able to make to enable them to respond effectively to the individual circumstances of the case and prevent or pre-empt forced marriages from occurring. The courts are able to attach powers of arrest to orders so that if someone breaches an order they can be arrested and brought back to the original court to consider the alleged breach. The Act also: • enables people to apply for an injunction at the county courts, rather than just the high courts • enables third parties to apply for an injunction on behalf of somebody else.
CPS/Court Liaison	Ensure early case conference between the police and CPS. Dedicated officer to update victim and witnesses of case progression for both criminal and civil cases.
Bail objections	Previous convictions of offender, previous history known to police, relevant call-outs/crime/intelligence reports relating to offender, past relations. Highlight bail address if in close proximity to victim's address. All relevant information to be passed to CPS with a view to informing the court. The investigating officer must ensure that objections to bail are comprehensively documented and the CPS effectively briefed (if necessary attend court and support the CPS).
Child access	Formalized agreements, risk assessment, supervised visits, etc.
Victim log	Advise victim to record details of all interactions that take place between the victim and the offender.
The Code of Practice for Victims of Crime	Victims of sexual offences or domestic abuse are eligible for enhanced service under the Code, unless the victim informs the service provider of their wish not to have this.

Table 7.3 Prevention of repeat victimization, providing support to victim and formation of a safety plan

Safety Planning	Action
Travel/abduction precautions	Removal and retention of passport. Check whether victim is on parent(s) passport or has dual nationality—as may have two passports. Could flag their passports at passport office in case applications are made for new ones. Advise them to travel on their British passport if going abroad as easier to repatriate. If they are going overseas they could take: • contact details of Embassy/High Commission/trusted third party or Forced Marriage Unit at the FCO • secret stash of money, mobile • copies of passport and tickets for themselves.

7.8.1 Useful contacts and organziations

Ashiana Project (London)
Tel: 020 8539 0427
Ashiana (Sheffield)
Tel: (0114) 255 5740

'Choice' Helpline
HBV Victim Advice Line
Tel: 0800 5999365 (24 hrs)

Hemat Gryffe Women's Aid (Glasgow)
Tel: 0141 353 0859

National Domestic Violence Helpline
Tel: 0808 2000 247

Newham Asian Women's Project (NAWP) (London)
Tel: 0208 472 0528

Roshni (Nottingham Asian Women's Aid)
Tel: 0115 948 3450 (24 hrs)

Hannana Siddiqui, Southall Black Sisters
Tel: 0208 571 9595
Email: southallblacksisters@btconnect.com

Jasvinder Sanghera, Karma Nirvana
Tel: 01332 604098 (24 hrs)

Diana Nammi, Iranian & Kurdish Women's Rights Organisation
Tel: 0207 490 0303 (24 hrs)
Email: ikwro@yahoo.co.uk

Shahien Taj, Henna Foundation (formerly Saheli, Cardiff)
Tel: 0202 0496920
Mobile: 07915212555
E-mail: shahientaj@yahoo.co.uk

Forced Marriage Unit, Foreign and Commonwealth Office
Tel: 020 7008 0151
Email: fmu@fco.gov.uk
Website: <http://www.fco.gov.uk/forcedmarriage>

DCI Gerry Campbell/DC Yvonne Rhoden and team
Central Service Delivery Team
Violent Crime Directorate, Metropolitan Police Service
Tel: 0207 230 1430 / 2229 / 7362

Laura Richards, Accredited HBV Adviser/Consultant ACPO Violence Adviser
Tel: 07775 821416

DI Brent Hyatt, Specialist Crime Directorate, Metropolitan Police Service
Tel: 07748 704087 (24 hrs)

Philip Balmforth, Bradford District Vulnerable Persons Officer (Asian Females)
Email: philip.balmforth@westyorkshire.pnn.police.uk

Claudia Kinrade, Minorities Support Unit, South Wales
Tel: 07866 787631
Email: Claudia.Kinrade@south-wales.pnn.police.uk

Helen Eustace, HBV Adviser, Cleveland Police
Tel: 07736 085 425
Email: Helen.Eustace@cleveland.pnn.police.uk

Nazir Afzal OBE, Director — West London sector
Crown Prosecution Service
Tel: 0208 901 5803

Further information and reading

ACPO, Foreign and Commonwealth Office and Home Office (2005), *Dealing with Cases of Forced Marriage: Guidance for police officers* (2nd ed, London: ACPO).

Foreign and Commonwealth Office (2004), *Practice Guidance for Social Workers: Young people and vulnerable adults facing forced marriage* (London: Home Office).

HM Government (2006), *Every Child Matters: Working together to safeguard children—A guide to inter-agency working to safeguard and promote the welfare of children* (Norwich: The Stationery Office). Available at <http://www.everychild matters.gov.uk>.

8

Domestic-Homicide Review

8.1 **Introduction**

We know much about the dynamics of domestic violence (DV): that victims experience several incidents before they tell anyone; that several agencies may be approached by victims in the help-seeking process; and that there have been occasions when the response provided by agencies has been inappropriate or inadequate, is all well documented. There are also several established risk factors in relation to some forms of domestic violence with options on how to manage risk.

But how do you ensure that your response is effective and does prevent further incidents? How can agencies work better together to ensure that when you are notified of abusive relationships, whether intimate, ex-partner or intra-familial, appropriate intervention intended to keep victims safe and manage perpetrators is practised by all? What can you do to ensure that your policies, strategies, and practices continue to evolve in-line with ever-changing social, economic, and political demographics?

Although decreasing in recent years, domestic homicide remains at a high level nationally and these are some of the questions that those working in the field of DV often ask themselves when a person loses their life in such tragic circumstances. We must not let this loss of life be in vain and should be committed to learning lessons from their murders to better protect victims and hold perpetrators to account in the future. Domestic-homicide reviews have and continue to answer some of those questions by identifying gaps in service provision and enhancing our knowledge of what needs to be included in our strategies for homicide prevention.

The Home Office is currently working on national guidelines for homicide review and there will be an expectation that these will be used by all agencies once they are published. They are expected to be published in the winter of 2008.

8.2 **What is a Domestic-Homicide Review?**

Under s 9(1) of the Domestic Violence, Crimes and Victims Act 2004 a DV homicide review is defined as:

Definition of 'Domestic-Violence Homicide Review'

'A review of the circumstances in which the death of a person aged 16 or over has, or appears to have, resulted from violence, abuse or neglect by:
- (a) person to whom he/she was related or was or had been in an intimate personal relationship, or;
- (b) a member of the same household as himself /herself

held with a view to identifying the lessons to be learnt from the death.'

A domestic-homicide review is the process whereby local relevant agencies (generally those agencies in the locality where the victim normally resided) examine the background of circumstances leading up to the homicide, to identify and learn lessons from the death. From these reviews the findings, recommendations for change or improvement may be formulated at a local, national, or legislative level.

It is not intended to be a review of the police investigation or coroner's hearing or be part of any internal disciplinary or public review. This needs to be clear from the outset and established in guidance and terms of reference to enable agencies to participate in an open and transparent manner without apportioning blame to any single agency. This will provide a basis of trust where information and intelligence can be shared without prejudice making the whole process of learning as effective as possible.

The statutory purpose of a review, in practice, will include:

- identifying the lessons to be learnt from the death, in particular about how local professionals and agencies work together to safeguard victims
- identifying how those lessons will be acted upon and what is expected to change as a result
- improving inter-agency working and improving protection for domestic violence victims.

The concept of domestic-homicide reviews came from the serious-case reviews (formally known as Part 8 reviews), conducted when a child dies as a result of abuse or neglect under Chapter 8 of *Every Child Matters: Working together to safeguard children* (HM Government, 2006). Good practice and guidance is already in place in relation to these reviews. Section 9 of the Domestic Violence Crimes and Victims Act 2004 (DVCVA) legislates for domestic-homicide reviews. Home Office guidance currently in draft form, in response to the legislation, is expected to be published in the winter of 2008. Nevertheless, several force areas have been conducting multi-agency domestic-homicide reviews for some years and the process has been even longer established in other jurisdictions, particularly North America. This chapter seeks to outline the process and good practice already adopted within those force areas across the UK.

It is likely that the governing body for ensuring the formulation of a domestic-homicide review process within each area will fall to the local Crime and Disorder Reduction Partnership (CDRP) or the area's equivalent body.

8.2.1 Who takes part in the review

The review panel will consist of those local agencies and service providers who have a role to play in the identification and prevention of domestic violence. This will include statutory and voluntary bodies who are involved on a daily basis in keeping victims and their children safe and/or managing perpetrators. The panel members should be in a senior position in their respective roles to be able to advise, make decisions, and ensure implementation of local recommendations relevant to their service. The members may not necessarily be the person(s) who conducts the research required for the review within their respective agency, or the person who examines all the available material to identify lessons learnt and make recommendations. This needs to be someone who has expert knowledge and experience of current policy and practice in domestic violence. Many areas now have established multi-agency risk assessment conferences (MARACs) and blanket coverage of England and Wales is expected by 2010. This could possibly be the most effective group to conduct a homicide review.

Section 9(4) DVCVA 2004 specifies that the following persons and bodies have a duty to establish and participate in domestic homicide reviews:
For England and Wales:

- chief officers of police for police areas in England and Wales
- local authorities—for England that means the council of a district, county, or London borough, the Common Council of the City of London, and the council of the Isles of Scilly; for Wales, that means the council of a county or county borough—may include mental health trusts, social services, etc
- local probation boards
- strategic health authorities
- primary care trusts
- local health boards and
- NHS trusts.

For Northern Ireland:

- The Chief Constable of the Police Service for Northern Ireland
- The Probation Board for Northern Ireland
- health and social services boards
- health and social services trusts.

There are also likely to be a number of other agencies holding information on the parties involved, eg independent domestic violence advocates (IDVAs), victim support services (VSS), drug and alcohol services, black and minority ethnic support services, and refuge projects. These may be asked to be part of the core panel or invited to participate as the need arises.

Early contact should be made with the senior investigating officer (SIO) in charge of the case, to inform them that a homicide review will be taking place. They may wish to be part of the panel or may be satisfied with updates on the progress of the review from the panel.

8.2.2 Inviting family members and/or friends

Consideration may be given to inviting family members or friends where it is established that they hold significant background knowledge of the victim's domestic situation prior to the homicide which may be invaluable to the review;

this may entail identifying the victim's social networks, for example a place of worship or childcare provider. However, in some circumstances this will not be feasible as they may have provided a statement to the investigating team and could be called as witnesses in the trial. Also family members or friends may not wish to engage in the process or may even be suspected to have colluded in the homicide.

Whilst it is important to keep the family informed of the review process it must be remembered that the purpose of the review is for relevant agencies to be able to debate in an open and transparent way, to enable effective identification of lessons learnt. The process may be distressing for family members or friends and could hamper full disclosure. Any decisions on attendance of family or friends at the panel meetings need to take these factors into account.

8.2.3 **What are the considerations for the review panel?**

When a homicide occurs, the following questions need to be considered when deciding whether to conduct a full review:

- Does the homicide fall within the definition?
- When a child is involved in the domestic homicide as a victim or witness or in other circumstances whereby a serious case review in accordance with Chapter 8 would normally be conducted, which panel will take the lead in the review or how will the two reviews run together?
- Do any of the agencies hold information on the victim, the suspect, or other identified family members?
- Do one or more of the agencies or professionals involved consider that its concerns were not taken sufficiently seriously or acted upon appropriately by another agency around these incidents?
- Does the incident appear to have implications for a range of agencies and/or professionals?
- Does the incident identify organizational learning issues around DV for the police and external agencies?
- Was there an indication of a risk of significant harm to the victim, which was:

  a) not recognized by agencies or professionals in contact with the victim, suspect, or family
  b) was identified but not shared with other partners or
  c) if received, was not acted upon appropriately?

- Are there any significant matters evident in relation to mental health, drug or alcohol abuse, immigration, language barriers, or other isolating factors for the victim?
- Does the perpetrator have a significant criminal history?

If the answer to more than one of these questions is yes, a domestic-homicide review is likely to be required.

8.2.4 **If a domestic-homicide review is necessary, what happens next?**

The panel should agree generic terms of reference for the group. The terms of reference will include the purpose of the panel, an agreed information-sharing protocol (ISP), and a confidentiality clause which members should be asked to sign up to when the panel is initially established and when members are replaced by newcomers.

It might also be beneficial to include information regarding the legal position within the terms of reference to enable individuals taking part in the review to feel comfortable with the process. In addition, decisions should be made in relation to the media focus: whether and in what form a statement would be given, and by whom. Guidelines and a suitable reporting template should be compiled and provided to members to ensure consistency across agency involvement.

The review panel should then arrange an inaugural meeting where a chair will need to be elected to facilitate the process and any future meetings. Consideration should be given to electing a person with chairing experience independent of the services represented on the panel to maintain the integrity of the review. Membership for the particular review will be discussed and the decision and reasons for conducting, or not conducting, a review based on the primary evidence, recorded.

8.2.5 **Who will take the lead if the victim did not live in the area where they were killed?**

Where a victim has lived in several areas or is killed in an area away from their home address, the area where the victim was predominantly resident will normally take the lead in the review process, although there will be a requirement for information-sharing from those other areas, to complete the review. However, this will be a matter for discussion within the relevant CDRP or area equivalent body from the outset.

If the review is conducted, terms of reference will then be agreed in writing for the case under review.

8.3 **Scope of the Review**

The review will need to assess the following:

- What appear to be the most important issues in this specific case?
- What timescales should the review consider regarding the events prior to the murder?
- What history is relevant? Although there may be a history spanning in excess of three years, the opportunities for organizational learning and recent changes in local procedures and policies may be invalidated.

- What family history/background information will help to better understand the recent past and present which the review should try and capture? If the victim and/or perpetrator are foreign nationals, the police should contact the relevant police service to establish whether there was a history of abuse abroad.
- What social, economical, welfare, or cultural aspects of the death need to be considered to ensure a thorough consideration of future prevention measures?
- Which agencies, professionals, and local groups should contribute to the review, and who else should be asked to submit reports or otherwise contribute?
- Should family members be invited to contribute to the review?
- Will the case give rise to other investigations of practice?
- How should the review process take account of a coroner's enquiry and (if relevant) any criminal investigations or proceedings related to the case?
- Is there a need to liaise with the coroner and/or the Crown Prosecution Service (CPS)?
- Are there implications in light of internal or public reviews surrounding the case?
- Are there likely to be any disclosure matters arising and should the senior investigating officer (SIO) be engaged with the process from the outset?
- If relevant interests outside the main statutory agencies are identified, eg independent professionals and voluntary organizations, how will this information be requested and incorporated into the review?
- How should any public, family, and media interest be handled, before, during, and after the review?
- Are there any diversity or equality considerations for the review panel or the case under review requiring input from specialists? For example, does it involve honour-based violence, a same-sex relationship, or is either the victim or perpetrator an asylum seeker?
- Does the review panel need to obtain independent legal advice about any aspect of the proposed review and how will this be financed?

8.3.1 How information will be gathered?

Once the scope of the review is established within the terms of reference, agencies or professionals will then be asked to complete their research and report back to the panel on their findings with suggested recommendations, using templates provided. It will be necessary to put a time frame around the process to ensure a prompt response to recommendations. The current practice for those areas conducting reviews is a timescale of one month for the review process to be established and three months for completion of the final report; however there will be occasions when this is not achievable and timescales will need to be extended.

The chair will arrange for the reports to be shared amongst the panel members before arranging the next meeting to discuss and agree recommendations and decide who will compile the summary report. The decision may be for someone unconnected to the review process to be responsible to ensure independence.

8.4 Conducting the Review within Each Agency and Identifying Lessons to be Learnt

Care must be taken when deciding who will conduct the review. It is important that whilst they should have or have access to someone who has a sound knowledge in domestic violence policy and procedure within their own organization and how that interacts within the wider DV service providers, it should not be someone closely involved with the family or the line manager for the practitioners in the case. It must be recognized that this requirement may not be feasible within smaller agencies, for example NGOs, where resources are limited.

The process will vary within each agency. Therefore the report templates should reflect the type of information that will be required to be collected bearing in mind the purpose of the review. For the police service (and probably most other agencies), the following information from databases and case files will be important:

Checklist—Information to be retrieved from files and databases

- details of victim, perpetrator and any children to include: age, gender, race, ethnicity, education, employment, immigration status, disability, mental health, criminal records, police intelligence, and court orders

- incident details including date, time, location, method, weapon used, cause of death, witnesses, and why it may have happened, if known

- details of any police engagement with the victim, perpetrator, and family

- a chronology of the involvement with the police over the agreed period of time

- summary of decisions reached in each case

- service provided/offered

- actions taken, by whom, and outcomes

- whether a risk assessment was undertaken and the risk suitably identified, assessed, recorded, and managed

- whether any criminal or civil proceedings have been taken against any party

- whether officers involved complied with standard operating procedures for the investigation of domestic violence and whether the service provision offered was adequate and appropriate in the circumstances

- whether the officers involved received any training on DV, and if so when

- whether decisions were made in a defensible, informed, and professional way and recorded in a retrievable format

- whether policies and standard operating procedures were adequate.

When the research is complete, the material and information will need to be assessed and analysed. There may be a need to expand on what is contained within the paper review and to speak to individual officers to clarify or establish the full facts. On completion of the review, there may be a need to ensure that officers involved are debriefed in relation to the outcome of the review.

Once all available information is captured as above, then consideration will be given as to what changes are needed. For example, identified lessons might include:

Checklist—Examples of potential identified lessons

- Was there a lack of appropriate safety planning?

- Was the intervention appropriate and sensitive to issues such as race, language barriers, religion, etc?

- Was there adequate and appropriate supervision?

- Were the standard operating procedures (SOPs) or appropriate protocols/procedures followed?

- Was good practice highlighted and shared with relevant agencies?

- Was there evidence of defensible decision-making?

- Was there effective risk assessment and management?

- Was partnership-working engaged and effective in relation to victim safety and perpetrator management?

- Was there adequate police/agency training in place?

- Does there need to be any change or additions to policy or procedure?

8.5 What the Report Should Look Like

The following paragraphs outline a suggested format for the report with sample templates for the recording and reporting of the homicide review.

8.5.1 Introduction

- Summarize the circumstances that led to a review being undertaken in this case.
- State the terms of reference of the review.
- List the contributors to the review and the nature of their contribution.
- List the review-body members and the author of the overview report.

8.5.2 **The facts**

- Describe the membership of the family and household.
- Describe the chronology of the involvement with the victim/perpetrator and their families on the part of agencies, professionals, and others who have contributed to the review process. Note the chronology of each occasion on which the victim or perpetrator was seen and the views and wishes that were sought or expressed.
- Provide an overview that summarizes what information was known to the agencies and professionals involved about the family, perpetrator, and the home circumstances of the victim/perpetrator.

8.5.3 **Analysis**

This part of the overview should examine how and why events occurred, decisions were made, and actions taken or not. This is the part of the report in which reviews can consider, with the benefit of an overview of events and involvement, whether different decisions or actions may have led to a different course of events. The analysis section is also where any examples of good practice should be highlighted.

8.5.4 **Conclusions and recommendations**

This part of the report should summarize what lessons are to be drawn from the case and how those lessons should be translated into recommendations for action. Recommendations should include, but are not limited to, the recommendations made in individual agency reports. Recommendations should be relatively few in number, outcome-focused, specific, and capable of being implemented. They must be carefully considered to avoid erroneous outcomes. (For example, it should not be assumed that increased information-sharing should have taken place to avoid the outcome as this is a process that may have led to the victim or other relevant parties disclosing less!)

Multi-agency Domestic-Homicide Review Working Template

REPORT INTO THE DEATH OF

(Add victim's name)

(Report Produced by   Date   )

Content

Introduction

This report examines agency response and support given to *(victim's name)*, a *(area name)* resident to the point of her death on *(date of death)*.

Essentially this review is to establish whether any or all the agencies involved responded correctly and within their own set procedures and guidelines. Where it is found that agencies could have responded more effectively, the panel will then determine whether an alternative course of action would have prevented the victim's death.

The rationale for the review process is to ensure that agencies are responding appropriately to victims of domestic violence by offering and or setting in place appropriate support mechanisms that can avert future incidences of domestic murder.

Timescales

This review began in *(date)* and was concluded in *(date)*. The agreed timescale for all reviews is three months.

Confidentiality

The findings of each review are confidential. Information is only privy to participating officers/professionals and their immediate superiors and or heads of departments who have a pre-declared interest in the review.

Dissemination

Those who have received copies of the report: *(list)*

Executive Summary

1.   The Review Process

1.1   This summary outlines the process undertaken by *(local area name)* Domestic-Violence Homicide Review panel in reviewing the murder of *(victim's name)*.

1.2   *(Suspect's name)* is currently awaiting trial for *(victim's)* murder.

1.3   The process began with an initial meeting on *(date)* of all agencies who potentially had contact with *(victim's name)* prior to the point of death.

1.4   Agencies participating in this case review:

- *(Area)* Housing (Anti-Nuisance Team)
- *(Area)* Education (Access & Inclusion)
- *(Area)* Social Care (Children Social Care Services)
- *(Area)* Police Domestic Abuse Unit
- *(Area)* Police Child Abuse Investigation Unit
- *(Area)* Victim Support
- *(Area)* Refuge Managers' Support Group
- *etc..............*

1.5   Agencies were asked to give chronological accounts of contact with the victim prior to their death. Where there was no involvement or insignificant involvement, agencies advise accordingly. Each agency's report covers varying degrees of the following:

- chronology of interaction with the victim/family
- what was done/agreed
- whether internal procedures followed
- conclusions and recommendation from the agency's point of view.

1.6   The accounts of involvement with this victim cover different periods of time prior to her death. Some of the accounts have more significance than others. The extent to which the key areas have been covered and the format in which they have been presented varies across agencies.

1.7   *(Number)* of the *(total number)* agencies responded. In total *(number)* agencies have responded as having had no contact with either the victim, suspect, or any children involved. *(Name agencies)*.

1.8　*(Number)* have responded with information indicating some level of involvement with the victim. *(Name agencies).*

1.9　*(Indicate here if an agency's contact is of no relevance to the events that led to the death of the victim and state last record of contact and details)*

1.10　The Police report shows that on a number of occasions between *(dates)* the Police had had contact with *(victim in relation to allegations of …name allegations and who committed by. State what the victim's wishes were at the time in terms of proceeding or withdrawing).*

1.11　*(Name agencies who)* responded as having no trace of the victim, suspect, or any children on their database or general registry. *(State here if information has come to light showing the contrary).*

1.12　*State here any agencies showing contact/interaction with victim/ family:*

2.　Key Issues Arising From the Review.

2.1.　………………………………………………

2.2　………………………………………………

2.3　………………………………………………

3.　Conclusions and Recommendations from the Review

3.1　………………………………………………

3.2　………………………………………………

(Name of Area) Domestic Homicide Review Panel Concluding Report
Introduction

This review report is an anthology of information and facts from *(number Area)* agencies all of which were potential support agencies for *(victim)*. Essentially only *(number)* agencies had records of contact with *(victim)* prior to their death. They are:

- ………………………………
- ………………………………
- ………………………………

(State whether the accounts of involvement with this victim cover different periods of time prior to their death. The extent to which the key areas have been covered and the format in which they have been presented varies across agencies).

(State whether any of the accounts bear any direct relation to victim's murder).

All official records of no contact are attached in the Appendix.

Facts

- *where victim lived, where victim was murdered, synopsis of the murder (what actually happened and how killed)*
- *state who else lived at the address and if children residing there, what their ages are*
- *how long they have been living with partner if cohabiting. How long they have been together as a couple*
- *who has been charged with murder and date of trial (if known)*
- *any other relevant fact/information.*

Analysis

(State agency involvement and who was involved as a result of disturbances between which parties)

(State whether the review panel is of the opinion that all agency intervention was appropriate and that agencies acted within their set procedures and guidelines)

(State whether there is information available to the review panel that would give any clear description of parties' names, relationship, and the events that led to victim's murder. If there is, state what the information is and the source of the information)

Conclusions

(State whether the panel, after thorough consideration, believes that under the circumstances agency intervention potentially could have or would not have prevented victim's death given the information that has come to light through the review)

(State whether the information available to this panel suggests that there were /were no recorded incidences of domestic violence between victim and offender and whether this can/cannot be conclusive)

(State whether there was no input from a particular agency leading to limitations of the review and reason, if specified)

(State anything else that is relevant to conclusions resulting from review)

Recommendations

- ………………………………
- ………………………………
- ………………………………
- ………………………………

(Name of author of report)

(Position in agency)

(Date)

Housing Report

Murder of *(victim's name)*

Of *(address, age, and ethnic appearance)*

Name and address of Housing Office

Tenancy Reference—

Tenancy commenced *(date)* is still *(live)*?

Other occupants—*(Name, date of birth and relationship)*

History of Involvement

- *(When victim applied for housing and any other housing applications listed in chronological order)*
- *(Whether victim is on at risk house file)*
- *(Details of any medical problems)*
- *(Details about relationships and children)*
- *(Details of repairs undertaken in terms of locks being changed, for example)*
- *(Anything else that suggests victim may have been at risk)*

(Name of officer completing report)

(Position in agency)

(Date)

Police Report

Introduction

This report deals with all contact police had with *(victim)* for a period of *(number)* years prior to *(his/her)* murder at *(his/her)* at *(venue address)* on *(date)*.

(State whether there was much contact with victim/family and how many times contact was made)

(State whether any criminal intelligence/message generated by a call for assistance to police)

(Checks should be undertaken on victims(s) and suspect(s) and children)

(Include a copy of intelligence/crime reports/PNC records in the review)

(Contact relevant Police Force if the victim and/or perpetrator lived elsewhere, including abroad, and check what information they held on the victims(s) and suspect(s) and children)

(Then describe events in a chronological order)

Chronology

CALL *(number)* on *(date)*.

For example: Police were called to outside 25, Reinmouth Close, Birmingham by Frank Hope. He alleged that youths had damaged his motor vehicle with a football. He threatened to puncture the ball with a knife if police did not attend. Police attended the venue and reported a minor Criminal Damage to Mr. Bernays's vehicle.

CALL *(number)* on *(date)*.

For example: Frank Bernays requests to meet police at 25 Reinmouth Close, Birmingham, in order that he can give them further information regarding the incident on *(date above)*. Police attend and update original crime report.

CALL *(number)* & CRIME *(number)* on *(date)*.

For example: Police were called to 25 Reinmouth Close, Birmingham, by Mrs Bernays who wished to report an assault. She originally called police at 1052 hrs but stated she would not be home until after 1300 hrs, and a scheduled appointment was made for this time.

Police attended and reported an allegation of Common Assault on Mrs Bernays —CRIME *(number)* refers. The circumstances being, at about 2200 hrs on *(date)* Mrs Bernays's husband, Frank Bernays, returned home to find her on the telephone to a male friend. He became jealous and called her and her sister into the bedroom. He asked her if she wanted in or out of the marriage to which she replied 'out'. He responded by striking her in the face and putting his hands around her throat. Her sister managed to pull Mr Bernays off and he spent that night elsewhere.

The following morning he returned in order to collect his belongings and he told Mrs Bernays that 'this isn't finished yet'.

When she reported this incident to police she stated she did not want to substantiate any allegations.

This matter was allocated to PC Terre at 1949 hrs on the day of reporting for secondary investigation. She spoke with Mrs Bernays's sister on *(date)* who stated that Julie was not there but that she was fine and intended to divorce Mr Bernays. PC Terre left her contact details and asked for Julie to contact her. The VSS (Victim Support Service) were notified of the incident on *(date)*.

On *(date)*, PC Terre spoke with Julie and was told that she was not intending to file for divorce as things were amicable between her and Mr Bernays and they were sorting out arrangements with regards to the children. Mrs Bernays declined the offer of further advice or assistance from PC Terre. She also declined to give PC Terre a contact number for Mr Bernays. PC Terre left her contact details for Mr Bernays to call her if necessary; however Mrs Bernays stated she did not feel it would be.

This enquiry was marked as complete on *(date)*.

CRIME *(number)* on *(date)*.

The above crime report refers to a non-crime book domestic incident whereby Mrs Bernays called police to report the fact that her husband Mr Bernays had been verbally abusive towards her. She stated that he turned up at her home address and asked if he could come in and talk. She let him in and he began talking about them being separated, she made it clear to him that there was no chance of them getting back together. He began swearing at her stating that she was 'messing with his life' and 'that she would be sorry'.

This matter was allocated to PC Terre on *(date)* She tried to contact Mrs Bernays that day but got no reply. She tried again on *(date)* with the same result. PC Terre sent a letter to the victim on *(date)* requesting contact. Having had no reply PC Terre tried to contact Mrs Bernays again on *(date)* by telephone and in person without success.

On *(date)* this matter was shown as complete. Mrs Bernays never replied to PC Terre's requests for contact.

CRIME *(number)* on *(date)*

The above crime report refers to an allegation of harassment made by Mrs Bernays against her estranged husband Mr Bernays. This amounted to him constantly ringing her at work and home and being verbally abusive. She requested police to speak to Mr Bernays regarding his behaviour.

This matter was allocated to PC Rushbrooke on *(date)*. He tried to contact Mrs Bernays. However he received no reply and left a message on her mobile phone asking her to contact him.

PC Rushbrooke tried to contact Mrs Bernays again on *(date)* with the same result as before. Mrs Bernays did return his call later that day. She spoke at length to PC Rushbrooke and decided she did not want to pursue any criminal allegations but did intend to apply for a non-molestation order. PC Rushbrooke offered her advice regarding this and she was referred to ALIVE (Advice and Legal Help in Violent Episodes) and was given the name of Peter Bank who runs that particular agency. There being no further assistance required by Mrs Bernays, this matter was shown as complete on *(date)*.

CALL *(number)* on *(date)*

Police were called by Mr Bernays who stated that two weeks ago his stepdaughter Maria Louis aged 7 years had told him that her mother Mrs Bernays had hit her in the head. He also stated that Mrs Bernays, who is his wife, had a male from Africa staying at the house. He had seen his stepdaughter the previous day and she looked depressed. He also expressed the same concerns for his son Bob who also resides at the same address. He stated he had contacted social services at the time (3 weeks previous) but had not heard anything from them.

Police attended and spoke with Mr Bernays; as a result a report was sent to the social services by way of secure email.

INTELLIGENCE *(log number)* on *(date)*

Intelligence shows that Mr Bernays has a history of violence against an ex-partner and has previously used a weapon.

The Murder Investigation

CRIME *(number)*:   Report dealing with the Murder of *(victim's name)*.

INTELLIGENCE   *(ref number)*: Police intelligence record regarding Murder Investigation.

State:

- *what occurred prior to the murder (events and sequence)*
- *whether there was an argument and what it was about*
- *whether there was alcohol/drugs involved*
- *brief details of murder in terms of how the victim was found*
- *where the victim was found*
- *how the victim was killed (MO and weapons)*
- *injuries sustained by the victim etc*
- *any other relevant details about the history of police involvement with victim/family)*
- *court result, if there is one, and when/where suspect is appearing for trial.*

(Officer completing report)

(Area)

(Date)

Victim Support's Report

CASE OF *(victim's name)*

- *(address)*
- *(age)*
- *(ethnic appearance)*

1. OFFENCE

(*date and crime no*)

Referred to VS (*area*) following (*allegation type*).

ACTION

- (*for example: telephoned by a member of staff on date*)
- (*note observations about victim*)
- (*action taken, for example, situation was discussed, the potential dangers, and the need for further assistance and the offer of a home visit made*)

OUTCOME

- ....
- ....
- ....

2. OFFENCE

(*on date and crime no*)

Referred to VS (*area*) following (*allegation type*).

ACTION

- (*for example, telephoned by volunteer on date*).
- (*action: their situation was discussed again, and any potential dangers, a home visit was offered*).

OUTCOME

- ....
- ....
- ....

(*Name of officer completing report*)

(*Position in agency*)

(*Date*)

Appendix

Confirmation of no record of contact from:

- Agency 1
- Agency 2
- Agency 3
- Agency 4
- Agency 5
- Agency 6

8.6 **What Happens with the Findings**

The findings from the review should be summarized in a final report that will be presented to and agreed by members of the review panel. As part of the findings, the review panel should develop an action plan that will ensure that the recommendations for each agency are implemented and that areas of good practice highlighted are shared amongst the relevant agencies. The action plan will indicate the specific action required and by whom and when this will be taken, what outcome this action should bring about and how the organization will evaluate whether the outcomes have been achieved. The action plan will include a tracking process requiring update on the progress of implementation until the panel is satisfied that the action is complete. This information must be distributed to the relevant senior officer of the identified agencies within the action plan who will oversee and instruct the implementation.

An executive summary should be compiled, ensuring that it is sanitized where appropriate, ie agency individuals, surviving children. Consideration should be given for the sanitized report to be disseminated to other appropriate persons, for example those engaged in strategy and policy writing in all areas of public protection, as there may be learning appropriate to their work. The panel must be mindful that the investigation or trial may still be ongoing and publication of the summary report must be delayed until after the trial.

GOOD PRACTICE

It is recommended that a pan-Area/County Multi-Agency Strategic Homicide Review Panel is set up prior to commencing the review process to oversee the area reviews as well as to decide and assess which recommendations are relevant and should be implemented across the area/county, which need to be raised nationally and which are legislative related recommendations.

8.7 **Implications for Disclosure**

All domestic-homicide review-panel meetings need to be recorded and minutes should be taken. At times this will involve sensitive issues and decisions being taken against the backdrop of heightened community concerns and media interest. With raised public awareness of agency and police obligations under the Freedom of Information Act 2000, requests for reports and reviews are steadily increasing. Clearly, on occasions any such request will be refused due to the topics and information discussed in the meetings, but generally as these reviews are focused towards identifying learning and improving the service to DV victims, disclosure of these reviews should be encouraged.

Some agencies may not wish to disclose relevant information to the review process due to their own disclosure and confidentiality procedures and systems. Sometimes this information can be formally requested via the investigation team (if relevant to the murder) by the coroner, or by the courts. If the information is not made available, then the review will reflect this refusal to disclose in the final report.

There will be some areas within the review that may not be able to be disclosed. Any material generated during a review will be treated as third-party material and must be retained by the relevant agency. The agency retaining the material will need to create a schedule detailing the nature of the document that has been disclosed and the fact that the material may be made public knowledge. The disclosure officer involved in the murder investigation or coroner's inquest will take responsibility to ensure that the relevant leads (CPS or coroner) are aware of the existence of the third-party material so that a proper assessment can be made whether to actually disclose or not. In addition there are some Acts or policies that may mean part of the review (particularly police-generated reports) cannot be disclosed as a matter of course as follows:

8.7.1 Police disclosure regarding the investigations and criminal trials

Some of these incidents may likely be of a sensitive nature and reports should be graded and marked up on an MG6C schedule or MG6D schedule as appropriate.

(i)   non-sensitive
(ii)   sensitive—can be edited
(iii) sensitive.

This is then applicable to disclosure under the Criminal Procedure and Investigations Act 1996 unless public-interest immunity applies under the following examples:

(i)   Code 8 of the Public Interest Immunity (PII) Reveals Techniques and Investigative Methods relied on by the Police.
(ii)   Code 10 of the Public Interest Immunity (PII) states that as this document is an internal Police communication it is exempt from standard disclosure.

Under the Freedom of Information Act (FOIA) 2000 members of the public or any agency may request disclosure from police of material relevant to the review; this includes minutes of meetings. If such a request is received, then contact should be made with the service Public Access Office, or equivalent, to confirm what may be disclosed.

Where information is sought using this avenue, ss 30 and 31 of the FOIA identify key exemptions that could prejudice any disclosure.
Section 30:

(i)   confidential human information source (CHIS)
(ii)   confidential outside agency reports/contacts
(iii) crimestoppers information.

Section 31:

(i) prevention or detection of crime

(ii) apprehension or prosecution of offenders

(iii) disciplinary investigations.

When deciding to disclose under any circumstances the following points should be carefully considered by the review panel:

- the need to maintain confidentiality in respect of personal information within reports on the victim, family members, and others
- the accountability of public services and the importance of maintaining public confidence in the process of internal review
- the need to secure full and open participation from the different agencies and professionals involved
- the need to anticipate requests for information and plan in advance how they should be met
- the responsibility to provide relevant information to those with a legitimate interest
- constraints on sharing information when criminal proceedings are outstanding and the fact that access to the relevant information may not be within the control of the DV homicide review panel.

Any decision regarding disclosure should be documented fully and clearly.

8.8 Findings from Domestic-Homicide Reviews in London

Some police forces and agencies have been conducting homicide reviews for some time. London statutory and voluntary agencies have conducted joint domestic-homicide reviews since 2001. In 2003 an analysis of multi-agency findings from 30 reviews completed between January 2001 and April 2002 was published (Richards, 2003). Below is a selection of those findings as they affected the police service and how those findings were later translated into actions and implemented. This is a limited data-set which cannot be indicative of all trends, patterns, and findings. In fact, analysis of current domestic-homicide reviews would produce different findings, which would be expected in light of how the agencies have learnt from previous reviews and attempted to address the gaps in the police response.

Table 8.1 Findings from domestic-homicide reviews

Findings	Recommendations	Action	Outcome
In only four cases (13%) were risk assessments undertaken by police.	All cases should be risk assessed, whether there is a prosecution or not, using an effective DV risk-assessment model.	Team of researchers and analysts to be employed to develop a DV risk-assessment model	The SPECSS+ DV risk identification, assessment, and management model is now applied at all levels of the investigation in all cases whether crime or non-crime reports
Nine police investigations of offences (30%) prior to the murder lacked positive action and suspects were not arrested where sufficient evidence existed to do so.	Positive action needs to be taken and recorded for all DV incidents. Safety planning must be considered if the suspect is not arrested at the scene.	Positive action policy was stressed throughout the standard operating procedures published in 2005 with accompanying training for all officers up to the rank of Inspector.	Arrest of the perpetrator of DV crime is now a national policing performance indicator which is rigidly measured for compliance in the MPS. Local senior management teams on boroughs check for compliance at daily management meetings. This achieves effective supervision and risk management of those cases where suspect awaits arrest.
Information on children in the relationship is not being routinely obtained and recorded for the information of social services.	Police must ascertain details of all children involved in DV incidents, whether present at the scene, or not.	Requirement is stressed in standard operating procedures and included in form 124d, an investigation booklet used by all response officers and front-counter staff. Included within training packages for DV.	Compliance with this requirement is greatly improved and is monitored at levels of investigations by supervisors. Referral desks have been established to ensure effective information-sharing with children's social care.

Findings	Recommendations	Action	Outcome
Officers are not providing information in case files to CPS. In particular, history of offending, allegations, where offender lives in relation to victim, risk assessment, any intelligence, and so forth.	Case files must include all information that will assist in decisions in relation to charge, bail, sentencing, etc.	Form MG3 has been expanded with various fields to ensure that all relevant history in relation to the case at hand is included at the referral stage.	Preparation of case files has improved in ensuring that information in relation to history and risk factors is provided for the information of the court. District judges in London have received joint CPS/MPS input in relation to their domestic-violence training.
Victims are not being routinely referred or signposted to relevant support agencies.	Cards should be given to victims by front-line officers listing support groups/agencies' details, particularly Refuge/Women's Aid help line.	Form 124d to be completed at all DV incidents by front-line officers has a tear-off slip included with contact details of major support services.	All victims will be supplied with a slip by front-line officers at point of initial contact. Follow-up contact by DV specialists will provide contact details or referral to bespoke agencies according to victims' needs.

8.9 Effectiveness of Reviews

Domestic-homicide reviews have proven to be integral to informing effective intervention methods for what is essentially 'harm reduction and homicide-prevention tactics' practiced by service providers. As we become more professional in our response to domestic violence and ensure that recommendations from reviews are implemented in practice, so the need for homicide reviews should become less and less. In an ideal world domestic homicide will be eradicated. However, homicide cannot always be predicted but much can be done to prevent it. Learning the lessons about the antecedents to homicide is important in terms of informing risk identification, assessment, and management models. With many 'new communities' settling in the UK, their knowledge in relation to accessing and seeking services is limited due to a lack of provision of information and language or cultural barriers. There is still much to be done in this area.

There may, in the future, be scope within organizations to take the review process further into learning lessons from other events connected with domestic violence, for example suicide, attempted homicide, serious injury, and neglect, to enhance our knowledge of possible prevention methods. What will become apparent during reviews is that there may be a lack of compliance with current policies and procedures; agencies need to be prepared for this and comply with sanctions already in place within each organization for how these matters will be dealt with.

What is essential is that we begin to see a reduction in homicide and serious violence as a measure of success and as a result of implementation of recommendations from the reviews and the furthering of a 'joined-up' approach between all agencies working to prevent domestic violence.

Further information and reading

HM Government (2006), *Every Child Matters*: *Working together to safeguard children—A guide to inter-agency working to safeguard and promote the welfare of children* (Norwich: The Stationery Office). Available at <http://www.every-childmatters.gov.uk>.

Richards, L (2003), *Findings from the Multi-Agency Domestic Violence Murder Reviews in London: Prepared for the ACPO Homicide Working Group* (London: Metropolitan Police Service). Available at <http://www.met.police.uk/csu/index.htm>.

Information-Sharing

9.1 **Introduction**

This chapter will provide practical guidance on how and when to lawfully and justifiably share information with partner agencies, whilst remaining within the safeguards and permissions afforded by current legislation, including the Data Protection Act 1998 and the European Convention on Human Rights. Finally it will provide simple information-sharing pathways to ensure information is shared securely, with confidence, and in compliance with policy and the law.

Whilst this chapter provides practical guidance, it cannot cover all the complexities of information-sharing which are covered in more depth in other publications. In complex cases, particularly when drawing up formal written agreements for regular information exchange, you should seek further advice from your own legal or information department.

9.2 **Why Share Information?**

Historically, practitioners have been reluctant to share information citing data-protection or human-rights issues, or more often due to a lack of knowledge and understanding about when they could lawfully and correctly share information with others. We cannot continue to hide behind these excuses any longer. In public enquiries and Independent Police Complaints Commission (IPCC) investigations of domestic homicides, concerns over lack of information-sharing continue to be raised. What is important is that the safety of domestic-violence victims and their children should always come first and that we must work together with the widest possible information if we are to deliver this.

Responsible information-sharing is an essential part of keeping people safe and ensuring the effective investigation of domestic violence. If we are to hold offenders accountable, identify and manage risk, and protect victims and their families, you will need to gather and share information within the service, with partner agencies and the general public.

Case study—Paul O' Neil

In February 2006 Paul O'Neil was jailed for life after he held the face of his three-month-old son Aaron against a gas fire and fractured his skull. O'Neil was jealous of the attention the baby received from his mother, who herself was 'trapped' in a relationship with the domineering O'Neil and was afraid to report what he had done.

Following Aaron's death, the Local Safeguarding Children Board (LSCB) commissioned an independent expert to investigate the case.

The report found information-sharing was insufficient to provide a full picture of the family history and risk to the child. It identified that information was held by health and social services that showed O'Neil as a violent individual who posed a risk to women and children but that this information was not properly shared. As a result, analysis of risk was limited across agencies, engagement of professionals was not strongly maintained, and O'Neil was allowed to continue to offend.

9.2.1 The benefits of sharing information

The benefits to victims and their children are:

- timely action to protect victims and children from further abuse
- effective risk identification, assessment, and management based on the best information and intelligence at that time
- appropriate advice and support from all agencies based on a full and accurate understanding of the individual needs of the victim
- a reduction in the need for victims to repeat details of their experiences to multiple agencies.

The benefits to the police and other agencies are:

- coordinated responses to protect victims and their children
- reduced duplication of effort and clear ownership of issues
- increased confidence that victims and their children will be protected in the future
- enhanced reputation and credibility that the police and other partners can and will deal effectively with cases
- joint responsibility for victim's care and needs—rarely can one agency provide for all the victim's needs.

9.3 The European Convention on Human Rights (ECHR) 1998 and Information-Sharing

ECHR should not be seen as a barrier to effective information-sharing but rather as a means to ensure that the safety and welfare of victims and their children are met at all stages of the police response. In fact both Arts 2 (The Right to Life) and 3 (The Right Not to Be Subjected to Torture or to Inhuman or Degrading Treatment or Punishment) place an obligation on public authorities to protect people's rights. Meeting these obligations may necessitate lawful information-sharing.

9.3.1 Article 8: The right to respect for private and family life, home, and correspondence

Article 8 provides a general right to respect for privacy and applies to all public bodies including the police. There shall be no interference with this right, which includes the sharing of personal data, unless it is:

- in accordance with the law, and
- is necessary in a democratic society in the interests of national security, public safety, or the economic well-being of the country
- for the **prevention of disorder or crime**
- for the protection of health or morals, or
- for the protection of the rights and freedoms of others.

9.3.2 Satisfying Art 8 of ECHR

In order to satisfy Art 8 when sharing information you will need to consider each case separately and show that your actions are:

- **In pursuit of a legitimate aim and in accordance with law**
  This means the interference must have a proper legal basis, such as a piece of legislation, for example s 115 of the Crime and Disorder Act 1998, or contained within common law such as the prevention and detection of crime or to reduce serious crime against vulnerable people. These are clear policing purposes and part of the core functions and duties of police, as founded under common law. In order to fulfil this obligation, the sharing of information is necessary and common law provides the legal power to do so.
- **Proportionate**
  The information supplied should be the minimum necessary, and no more, for the objective you are trying to achieve. You need to identify what is it you are trying to achieve by sharing the information and what is the minimum information you need to disclose to do this.
- **Appropriate and necessary to a democratic society**
  The public rightly expects the police to maintain and uphold the law and to do what they can to ensure public safety. Supporting law and order and working to improve its effectiveness and the public confidence in it is an activity necessary to a democratic society.

Case study— One-off disclosure of information

Victim E approaches the police to say her ex-boyfriend is stalking her at her place of work and demanding they get back together. She has been the victim of previous unreported assaults by him. Intelligence checks on the suspect show he has previous convictions for serious assaults, including domestic violence on a previous partner. At this time police do not know where he is living. Having discussed the risks with the victim, the police decide to provide a photograph and description of the suspect to the employer to brief the front desk and security staff so that if he attends the police are called to the location and he is not allowed entry. This information is legally shared under the common-law duty of the police to protect vulnerable people, is the minimum necessary under the circumstances, and is appropriate and necessary to protect both the victim and the general public.

Case study—Regular sharing of information: Integrated domestic abuse programme (IDAP)

This is a court-mandated sentence given to male domestic violence offenders. Conditions are attached to the IDAP order to protect the victim and to address reoffending by the offender in order to facilitate more effective supervision of domestic-violence offenders; to identify, manage, and reduce the risk to the victim, their families and the public; and to provide information and intelligence to better enable staff (police and probation) to investigate crime and hold offenders accountable. A formal information agreement was signed between the local police and probation to share information about offenders subject to an order. As the objective of the agreement was to reduce serious crime against vulnerable people, the data was lawfully shared using the legal basis of common law. The agreement also covered compliance with the data-protection principles and confidentiality.

9.4 Implications of the Data Protection Act 1998

In addition to the legal requirements of the Human Rights Act, the Data Protection Act (DPA) 1998 gives individuals rights over their personal information and requires anyone who handles personal information, including sharing that information, to comply with a number of important principles, unless certain exemptions apply. These eight principles are listed below.

KEY POINTS—EIGHT DATA-PROTECTION PRINCIPLES

Personal data must be:

I.   fairly and lawfully processed
II.   processed for limited purposes
III. adequate, relevant, and not excessive
IV.   accurate and up to date
V.   not kept for longer than is necessary
VI.   processed in line with your rights
VII. secure
VIII. not transferred to other countries without adequate protection.

9.4.1 **Personal information**

The DPA describes personal information as either personal data or sensitive personal data.

9.4.1.1 **Personal data**

This is information which relates to a living individual who can be identified from that data or any other information held or likely to be held. It does not have to be a name but could include a national insurance number or driving licence number which could easily be linked to an identifiable person.

9.4.1.2 **Sensitive data**

This is personal data which consists of information concerning racial or ethnic origin, political opinions, religious or other similar beliefs, physical or mental health or condition, sexual life, alleged or committed offences, and proceedings, disposal or sentence concerning any alleged or committed offences.

It is likely that any data you wish to share will be contained or incorporated within these definitions and therefore subject to the DPA.

9.4.2 **Does the Data Protection Act 1998 allow for the sharing of personal data?**

Yes, as long as you comply with the eight data-protection principles and in particular principle I which requires 'personal data shall be processed fairly and lawfully and, in particular, shall not be processed unless':

(a) at least one of the conditions in Schedule 2 is met, and
(b) in the case of sensitive personal data, at least one of the conditions in Schedule 3 is also met.

9.4.2.1 Schedule 2 conditions

In terms of sharing information concerning domestic violence the most relevant Sch 2 conditions are likely to be:

- the data subject has given consent to the processing
- the processing is necessary in order to protect the vital interests of the data subject
- the processing is necessary for the administration of justice
- the processing is necessary for the exercise of functions of a public nature exercised in the public interest by any person.

9.4.2.2 Schedule 3 conditions

In terms of sharing information concerning domestic violence, the most relevant Sch 3 conditions are likely to be:

- the data subject has given explicit consent to the processing
- the processing is necessary to protect the vital interests of the data subject or another in cases where it is not possible to get consent
- the processing is necessary for the administration of justice.

9.4.3 'Vital interests'

'Vital interests' cover situations where it is necessary to share information for matters of life and death or for the prevention of serious harm to an individual. This could include immediate threats to life or where there is a clear and identifiable risk of significant harm. An example could include where a victim contacts police to say she has taken an overdose. Quite rightly this information will be shared with the ambulance service. It is important that you consider these on a case-by-case basis and fully document any decision to disclose information.

9.4.4 'Administration of justice'

What is meant by 'administration of justice'? This can cover information-sharing both in relation to the victim and offender and will be useful in situations where the perpetrator is unlikely to give consent to disclosure. This would cover cases where you are undertaking an investigation and the information sought is an integral part of that investigation. For example, during an assault the victim states the offender put his hand through a glass window and as a result had to attend hospital. He denies this and states the victim is lying. This evidence would clearly corroborate the evidence of the victim and is relevant to the matter under investigation—therefore you will need to approach the hospital and both share personal data on the offender. Again you will need to carefully consider any confidentiality issues under ECHR and document your action.

9.4.5 **The 'public interest'**

When considering if the disclosure of information is in the public interest you will need to consider each case on its own merits. Firstly, is your activity lawful, necessary, and proportionate to the matter under investigation? In most cases it will be fairly obvious. An allegation of crime has been reported and you are undertaking an investigation which may necessitate the sharing of personal data with another, for example the protection of life or the prevention or detection of crime. An example of this could include investigations of forced marriage or where concerns have been made that an individual may have been taken abroad to be forced into a marriage. You may need to seek information from other individuals such as education staff, employers or another agency such as the Foreign and Commonwealth Office (F&CO) or Immigration which will necessitate you providing personal data on the subject. Information-sharing in this scenario will be necessary to ensure the safety and well-being of the individual and will clearly be in the public interest.

9.4.6 **Exemptions to the DPA**

There are a number of exemptions within the DPA that allow for the lawful sharing of information. In particular, s 29 covers situations where data is shared for the pupose of:

- prevention or detection of crime
- apprehension or prosecution of offenders
- assessment or collection of any tax or duty.

It is important to note that disclosure under this section does not exempt you from the requirement to comply with Schs 2 and 3 concerning processing personal and sensitive data. The Information Commissioner has given clear guidance in relation to s 29 DPA requests that when relying on this exemption you will need to show that there would be a substantial chance, rather than a mere risk, that in the particular circumstances the purpose of the disclosure, eg prevention/detection of crime, would be noticeably damaged by a failure to process the information.

Other sections which may also be relevant are ss 28 (national security), 33 (research and statistics), and 35 (legal proceedings).

In all cases a decision to share information under the DPA must be made on a case-by-case basis and cannot be used to justify routine information-sharing.

9.5 Does the Crime and Disorder Act 1998 allow for the Sharing of Information?

The Crime and Disorder Act 1998 places a statutory responsibility upon the local authority, the police, and the county council to conduct crime and disorder audits and consultations in their local boroughs and then, based on the findings, draw up three-year community-safety strategies with clear targets to reduce crime and disorder in the local areas.

Section 115 of the Act provides a power for information-sharing between responsible public bodies (namely the police, local authority, probation or health authority), as well as cooperating bodies (for example Victim Support or domestic-violence support groups) where the disclosure is necessary or expedient for the purposes of any provision of the Crime and Disorder Act. The sharing of information within this section must be to pursue a specific objective within the strategy and be subject to a written agreement. Any disclosures must also be conducted in accordance with any other relevant legislation, including the Human Rights Act and the Data Protection Act.

9.6 Common-Law Powers concerning Confidentiality and Disclosure

Any information collected from individuals where it is given with an expectation of confidentiality, for example between a patient and doctor or during a police investigation attracts a legal duty of confidence. This legal duty, established under common law, prohibits information use or disclosure without the consent of the individual.

Any further disclosure can only be overridden where:

- the person to whom the duty of confidentiality is owed consents to the disclosure
- it is required by a court order or other legal obligation
- there is a strong public interest justification
- the information is not confidential in nature.

9.6.1 Can I use common law to lawfully share information?

In situations where there is no express or implied statutory gateway available that allows the sharing of information, then you will need to consider sharing information for purposes relating to the common-law duties and functions of the police, namely:

> The prevention and detection of crime, apprehension and prosecution of offenders, protection of life and property, maintenance of law and order, reducing

unwarranted fear of crime and rendering assistance to the public in accordance with policy and procedures.

Therefore, the primary legal power that will allow lawful information-sharing, in this context, will be common law because this is where the legal basis can be found for the policing purposes above.

If you decide to share information using this common-law power, then you will still need to demonstrate compliance with Art 8 ECHR, the Data Protection Act principles, and common-law obligations of confidence.

9.7 Sharing Information with Consent of the Victim

It is good practice to discuss with victims at an early the range of different domestic-violence specialists who can provide support and advice to them and to seek the consent of the victim to share information with these agencies.

9.7.1 What is meant by consent

There is no single definition of consent. The Information Commissioner defines consent as:

Definition of 'Consent'

'. . . any freely given specific and informed indication of his wishes by which the data subject signifies his agreement to personal data relating to him being processed'.

In considering the common-law duty on disclosure, the Information Commissioner has provided further guidance on what consent requires:

- **Consent must be informed**
  The victim must know what are the proposed uses or disclosures of personal data. The use of information sheets/cards given to victims, explaining the agencies police will work with as part of a multi-agency response, is helpful.
- **The person giving consent must have some degree of choice**
  It cannot be given under duress or coercion and must be entirely optional. The victim must always be given the choice as to whether they wish the police to share information. It is inappropriate to operate a system where the information will be shared unless the victim decides to opt out. Consent can be withdrawn at any stage.
- **There must be some indication that the individual has given his or her consent**
  It is good practice to gain explicit consent from the victim at the initial investigation stage.

GOOD PRACTICE

A number of forces use a detachable or perforated form incorporated within their domestic violence reporting packs which includes the officers details, contact numbers of support agencies, what and how information will be shared, and that the victim can withdraw consent at any stage. The victim is asked to sign this form and is provided with a copy at the scene.

9.7.2 **What if consent is refused?**

If a consent-based approach is initially pursued and consent is refused, officers should not seek to override this unless there is an overriding public interest to disclose—such as where there is a real and imminent risk of serious harm or threat to life. In these cases you have an explicit duty of care to take all reasonable actions to protect individuals that will outweigh any data-protection or confidentiality issues. In these situations, advice should be sought from specialist domestic-violence investigators and where the decision is made to disclose information, this should be recorded and the victim informed of the disclosure and the reasons for doing so.

9.8 **Sharing Information relating to Children at Risk or Witnessing Domestic Violence**

There is much academic evidence to show the links between child-protection issues and domestic violence. It is essential that when children are witnesses to domestic violence or live in the same household this information MUST be shared with other child-protection agencies in accordance with your own force policy and guidance. The government has published further guidance on information-sharing relating to children and young persons as part of *Every Child Matters: Information sharing—Practitioners' guide—Integrated working to improve outcomes for children and young people* (HM Government, 2006).

9.9 **Guidance on the Management of Police Information**

In 2006 the Home Secretary introduced a national code of practice and guidance for the management of police information (MoPI). This statutory code was part of the government's response to the recommendations of the Bichard Inquiry into the circumstances surrounding the tragic murders of Holly Wells and Jessica Chapman in Soham. The guidance covers the collection, recording, evaluation, and sharing of police information, as well as its review, retention, and disposal. The management of all police information, including information-sharing, must be done in accordance with this code. Further guidance on MoPI can be found in *ACPO Guidance on the Management of Police Information* (ACPO, 2006a).

9.9.1 **What is police information?**

Police information is defined in MoPI as information that is required for a policing purpose. In order to operate effectively, police forces need to be able to share such information within the service, with partner agencies, and the general public. The code defines policing purpose as:

- protecting life and property
- preserving order
- preventing the commission of offences
- bringing offenders to justice
- any duty or responsibility arising from common or statute law.

These five policing purposes provide the legal basis for collecting, recording, evaluating, sharing, and retaining information. It is important to note that just because information was collected for one purpose does not prevent it being disclosed for another. Only that information which is held for a policing purpose can be lawfully shared.

9.10 **Checklist for Lawful Information-Sharing**

As can be seen from the previous paragraphs there is no single piece of legislation that governs information-sharing. Instead there are a number of different legislative frameworks or gateways through which information can be lawfully shared. The Department for Constitutional Affairs has produced a useful sequence of considerations that should enable a sound judgement to be made about the ability of a public body to share personal data in the public interest, *Public Sector Data Sharing: Guidance on the law* (DCA, 2004).

Checklist for lawful information-sharing

Can I lawfully share this information?

If the answer is 'yes' to all four questions then you can lawfully share the information.

Is it Lawful?   **YES/NO**

Establish whether you have the power to carry out the function to which the data-sharing relates. In doing so it will be important to ascertain whether there are express statutory restrictions (for example, s 115 CDA 1998) on the data-sharing activity proposed, or any restrictions which may be implied by the existence of other statutory, common-law or other provisions (for example, prevention of crime or public interest).

Is it in compliance with Art 8 of ECHR ?   **YES/NO**

Decide whether the sharing of the data would interfere with rights
under Art 8 of the European Convention on Human Rights in a way
which would be disproportionate to the achievement of a legitimate
aim and unnecessary in a democratic society (see 9.3 above).

Is it in compliance with common-law obligations of   **YES/NO**
confidence?

Decide whether the sharing of the data would breach any common-
law obligations of confidence (see 9.6 above).

Is it in compliance with the Data Protection Act?   **YES/NO**

Decide whether the sharing of the data would be in accordance
with the Data Protection Act 1998, in particular the Data Protection
principles (see 9.4 above).

Figure 9.1 Example of information-sharing pathway (Stage 1)—child protection

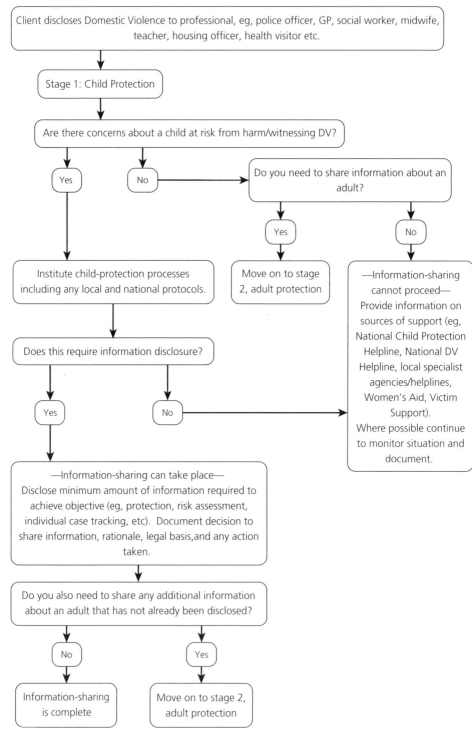

This flowchart in relation to sharing information where children or young persons are involved has been adapted from *Safety and Justice: Sharing personal information in the context of domestic violence—An overview* (Home Office, 2004).

Figure 9.2 Example of information-sharing pathway (Stage 2)—adult protection

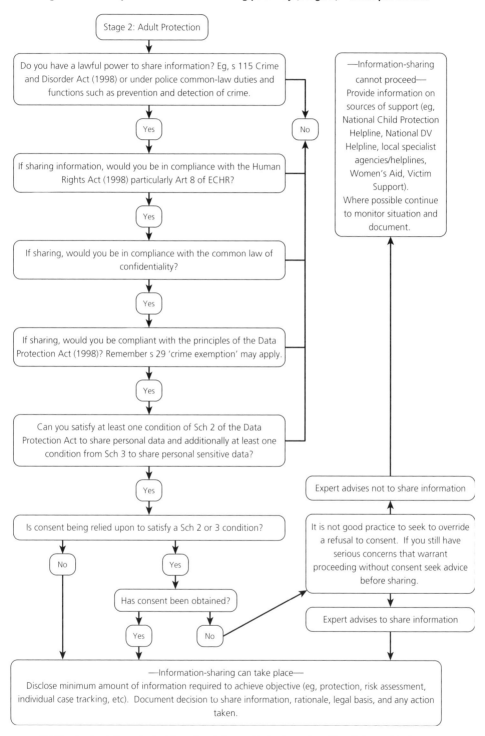

This flowchart in relation to sharing information relating to adults has been adapted from *Safety and Justice: Sharing personal information in the context of domestic violence—An overview* (Home Office, 2004).

Further information and reading

ACPO (2006a), *Guidance on the Management of Police Information* (ACPO, National Police Improvement Agency).

DCA (2003), *Public Sector Data Sharing: Guidance on the law* (London: DCA). Available at <http://www.foi.gov.uk/sharing/toolkit/lawguide.htm#part1>.

HM Government (2006b), *Information Sharing: Practitioners' guide—Integrated working to improve outcomes for children and young people* (London: DfES).

Home Office (2004), *Safety and Justice: Sharing personal information in the context of domestic violence* (London: Home Office).

Civil Law and Other Protective Measures

10.1 **Introduction**

For several years it has been recognized by agencies working specifically in the field of domestic violence, and through the introduction of legislation or other protective services, that there is a need for all agencies that come into contact with victims of domestic violence to be engaged in their protection and the management of those that perpetrate the violence. What must remain paramount throughout all investigations is the safety of the victim and their children.

For many reasons, the criminal-justice route is not always the preferred or feasible option for victims. This can leave the police service with less access to protective measures for keeping victims and their children safe. This chapter outlines what is available to the victim, police, and other agencies in terms of legislation and other protective measures for safeguarding victims and managing perpetrators. This knowledge will enable the police to consider what options they can offer to the victim to enhance their safety, or what actions the police can take to assist in risk management, in addition to any powers available through the criminal-justice process, to ensure positive outcomes for victims in relation to safety and protection. It expands on those options outlined in the tactical menu attached to the domestic-violence risk model. Each option might be implemented as part of a package of measures dependent on the circumstances of the individuals concerned and identified risks.

10.2 **Family Law Civil Injunctions**

The following orders issued under Part IV of the Family Law Act 1996 can be applied for in the magistrates' Family Proceedings Court (FPC), County Court, or High Court for family members experiencing domestic violence.

10.2.1 **Non-molestation orders**

A non-molestation order is used to restrain someone from causing or threatening violence to the victim or to any children, or from molesting them. The Act does not define molestation but it can include intimidation, pestering, threats, and harassment. The actual wording of non-molestation orders forbids the perpetrator from using or threatening violence against the victim and instructing, encouraging, or in any way suggesting that any other person should do so. It can also forbid the respondent from intimidating, harassing, or pestering the victim and instructing, encouraging, or in any way suggesting that any other person should do so. This wording is also used to protect any children named in the application from the perpetrator.

Victims will need to make a sworn statement in the form of an affidavit and complete the application form. Victims can self-apply and represent themselves if they are confident to do so. This process may be free of charge in some magistrates' FPC or require payment of a court fee of £40.00 in the High Court with other fees payable for process servers, etc. Alternatively they can seek the services of a family-law solicitor and may be eligible for community legal service funding if they do not work. A contribution may be required from those who have an income, dependent on a means test.

The National Centre for Domestic Violence is an agency that will provide advocacy and assistance for victims applying for injunctions, including those with no recourse to public funding.

Emergency applications can be made 'without notice' (without the presence of the perpetrator in the first instance) pending a full hearing.

Once issued, a copy of the non-molestation order must be served on the perpetrator and a copy lodged at the police station local to the victim's address. An s 9 Criminal Justice Act 1967 statement of proof of service must be attached to the copy as in the event of a breach this evidence will be required by the Crown Prosecution Service.

Section 1 of the Domestic Violence, Crimes and Victims Act 2004 which came into force in July 2007 makes breach of a non-molestation order an arrestable criminal offence punishable with a maximum of five years' imprisonment. Orders granted in the civil court after July 2007 will therefore not have a power of arrest attached and breaches will be brought before the magistrates' court.

10.2.2 Occupation orders

To apply for an occupation order the victim either has to have a legal right to occupy the home (as joint or sole tenant or owner of that home) or to have been married to, or cohabiting with, a partner who is the owner or tenant. The court will apply a 'balance of harm' test when deciding whether to make the order. When making an occupation order, the court may make other related orders imposing obligations on the victim or the perpetrator, for example relating to repair and maintenance of the home, or to payment of rent or mortgage.

An occupation order regulates the occupation of the home shared by the couple and their children to protect any party or children from domestic violence. The order can exclude a perpetrator from the property altogether, or divide the property to exclude them from part of the accommodation. If a perpetrator has already left the property, an occupation order may, therefore, be used to prevent them from re-entering and/or coming within a certain area of the property.

A power of arrest may be attached in some circumstances, but a breach of an occupation order is not a criminal offence; therefore, any breach will be brought before the civil court by means of an arrest, application for an arrest warrant, or committal proceedings.

10.3 **Restraining Orders and Antisocial Behaviour Orders (ASBOs)**

10.3.1 **Restraining orders**

Section 5 of the Protection from Harassment Act 1997 provides power for the court to impose a restraining order on conviction of an offence under the act as follows:

(1) A court sentencing or otherwise dealing with a person ('the defendant') convicted of an offence under section 2 or 4 may (as well as sentencing him or dealing with him in any other way) make an order under this section.

(2) The order may prohibit the defendant from doing anything described in the order, for the purpose of protecting the victim of the offence, or any other person mentioned in the order, from further conduct which—
    (a) amounts to harassment, or
    (b) will cause a fear of violence,
prohibit the defendant from doing anything described in the order.

(3) The order may have effect for a specified period or until further order.

(4) The prosecutor, the defendant or any other person mentioned in the order may apply to the court which made the order for it to be varied or discharged by a further order.

(5) If without reasonable excuse the defendant does anything which he is prohibited from doing by an order under this section, he is guilty of an offence.

(6) A person guilty of an offence under this section is liable—
    (a) on conviction on indictment, to imprisonment for a term not exceeding five years, or a fine, or both, or
    (b) on summary conviction, to imprisonment for a term not exceeding six months, or a fine not exceeding the statutory maximum, or both.

A restraining order can prohibit the perpetrator from contacting directly or indirectly any named person, retaining, recording, or researching details about any named person, or entering a given area. They can also be required to notify the court if they use a different name or change address. A copy of the order should be handed to the victim and a copy lodged at the police station and recorded in the same way as civil injunctions. Service on the perpetrator should take place at court.

In addition, under s 3 of the Act, application may be made for a restraining order in the County Court or the High Court. The standard of proof will be 'on the balance of probabilities'. A power of arrest cannot be attached to the order and it will be necessary to return to court to obtain a warrant of arrest if the order is breached.

Section 12 of the Domestic Violence, Crimes and Victims Act 2004 will add an additional s 5A which enables courts to impose a restraining order, on conviction for any offence and on acquittal, if it is apparent from the circumstances of the case that the victim needs continuing protection. This section is yet to be enacted.

10.3.2 **Antisocial behaviour orders (ASBOs)**

An ASBO is an order that prevents people from causing harassment, alarm, and distress to persons not of the same household as themselves. They are for dealing with persistent offenders, to protect persons in the local government area from antisocial acts.

The police or the local authority may apply to the magistrates' court for an order that prevents the person from doing anything described in the order; this may be not to go to certain areas outlined in the order.

The standard of proof is to the civil courts 'on the balance of probabilities' not the criminal courts' 'beyond reasonable doubt'. Good practice indicates that the evidence is obtained from reliable sources, for example:

* statements—including withdrawal statements
* crime reports or other domestic violence records
* convictions for like offences
* hearsay evidence recorded appropriately
* sanitized (corroborative) intelligence
* victims' logs.

10.4 **Civil Orders under the Sexual Offences Act 2003**

Orders can be useful tools for the purposes of restricting the behaviour of domestic-violence perpetrators. Four new civil orders created by the Sexual Offences Act 2003 can only be used for controlling sexual, and in some circumstances, violent offending.

The Sexual Offences Act (SOA) 2003 came into force on 1 May 2004; it created four civil orders which are:

* Sexual Offences Prevention Orders (SOPOs)—restrict behaviour of convicted/ cautioned offenders or those found not guilty due to insanity who pose a risk of serious harm. Can be applied for on conviction of Sch 3 (listed sexual) offences and Sch 5 (listed violent) offences.
* Risk of Sexual Harm Orders (RoSHOs)—restrict behaviour of unconvicted offenders who pose a risk of harm to children. The police may apply for these orders through the force legal services department.
* Foreign Travel Orders (FTOs)—restrict foreign travel of offenders who pose a risk of harm to children abroad. May be ordered by the court or applied for by CPS.
* Notification Orders (NOs)—places a requirement on offenders to comply with the notification requirements when convicted of equivalent offences abroad.

This is a brief outline of orders available under the Act and further information and assistance should be sought from the force Public Protection Unit, with early consultation with the CPS.

10.5 Forced Marriage (Civil Protection) Act 2007

This Act is expected to come into force in November 2008. Under the Act the courts will have the power to make forced marriage protection orders to stop someone from forcing another person into marriage. The courts will have a wide discretion in the type of injunctions they will be able to make to enable them to respond effectively to the individual circumstances of the case and prevent or pre-empt forced marriages from occurring.

Furthermore, courts will be able to attach powers of arrest to orders so that if someone breaches an order they can be arrested and brought back to the original court to consider the alleged breach.

The Act will also:

- enable people to apply for an injunction at the County Court rather than just the High Court
- enable third parties to apply for an injunction on behalf of somebody else.

10.6 Extended and Indeterminate Public Protection Sentence

Sections 225 and 227 of the Criminal Justice Act 2003 provide for a sentence of imprisonment for public protection, which is an extended or indeterminate sentence. This sentence may only be passed by a court if the offender is convicted of a specified sexual or violent offence (listed in Sch 15) carrying a maximum sentence of ten years or more and the court considers that the offender poses a significant risk of serious harm. These sentences therefore provide for the extended or indeterminate detention of those dangerous offenders who continue to pose a significant risk of harm to the public. Early consultation with the CPS will be required and form MG16 completed accordingly.

10.7 Integrated Domestic Abuse Programme (IDAP)

This is a perpetrator programme aimed at challenging violent and abusive behaviour by men against their female partner/ex-partner. Run by probation services, it can be part of the sentence delivered to domestic-violence perpetrators under a community order or part of the requirement of a post-custody licence. The programme generally runs for six to eight months under the supervision of the perpetrator's probation officer. If they do not comply with the requirements of the order or licence, they risk being taken back to court or recalled to prison.

In every case where a man is sentenced to an IDAP, the partner/ex-partner will be offered support by a women's safety worker (WSW), to ensure that she is kept informed of the progress of the perpetrator and to ensure effective monitoring of the perpetrator's behaviour.

There are now many independent perpetrators' programmes, running across the UK and managed locally, whereby perpetrators can self-refer or be referred outside of the criminal-justice process. Only those accredited by RespectUK are recommended.

10.8 Orders in Relation to Children

The following orders are available and will be relevant to decisions and outcomes of child-protection conferencing. The lead agency for application will generally be the local authority, children's social care, or the police.

10.8.1 Care order

A local authority or other authorized body (but not the police) may apply for a care order that places the child in the care of the local authority. When court proceedings to decide upon a care order are adjourned, the court may make an interim care order. This specifies the period for which it is in force but may not last longer than eight weeks. The court may make an exclusion requirement and may attach a power for the police to arrest any person suspected of being in breach of it. Officers should check the terms and timescale of any power of arrest.

10.8.2 Contact order

This order requires the person with whom the child is living to allow the child to visit or to stay with the person named in the order, or otherwise allow for that person and the child to have contact with each other. Normally such orders expire when the child attains the age of 16 years.

10.8.3 Child assessment order

The local authority and other authorized bodies (but not the police) may apply for a child assessment order. This directs the person who is in a position to produce the child to comply with the directions of the court to ensure that a medical examination, psychiatric assessment, or other assessment of the child takes place. If the child is of sufficient understanding to make an informed decision, he or she is entitled to refuse to undergo any assessment.

10.8.4 Emergency protection order (EPO)

An EPO allows a child to be placed in the temporary care of the local authority. It has effect for a maximum of eight days (or for a shorter period if the court requires). Anyone, including police officers, may apply for an EPO and an application should be made in preference to using police protection powers wherever possible. Before the court may grant the application it must be satisfied that the child is likely to suffer significant harm if not removed to accommodation provided by the applicant or if the child does not remain in the place where he or she is being accommodated. An EPO may also be made if enquiries under s 47 of the Children Act 1989 are being frustrated such as access to the child being unreasonably refused to a person authorized to seek access, and the applicant has reasonable cause to believe that access is needed as a matter of urgency. Where a police officer considers making such an application, it should be made following consultation with social services.

10.8.5 Exclusion order or exclusion requirement

The care order and EPO may, subject to conditions, specify certain people who should be excluded from living where the child is resident. This is known as an exclusion order or exclusion requirement. The court may attach a power for the police to arrest anyone suspected to be in breach of an exclusion requirement.

10.8.6 Wards of court

A child may be declared a ward of court if his or her parents are dead or unfit, and no other competent person requests guardianship. The court will appoint a guardian to take care of the child, under the supervision of the court.

10.8.7 Prohibited steps order

This order can only be granted to someone with parental responsibility and prohibits certain steps being taken without the consent of the court. These steps could ordinarily be taken by a parent in meeting their parental responsibilities to the child. The order applies to any person, not just the parents. Normally such orders expire when the child attains the age of 16 years. Such orders may be useful in preventing offences such as planned FGM or forced marriage by a parent or carer.

10.8.8 Recovery order

This order authorizes the recovery of a child in a variety of circumstances including where a child is in police protection. The order can require a person who has information about a child's whereabouts to disclose that information to a police officer or an officer of the court. It can also authorize entry to particular premises to search for a child, using reasonable force if necessary.

10.8.9 Residence order

The court may make an order which determines the place of residence of a child and with whom the child is to live. Such orders usually expire when the child attains the age of 16 years.

10.8.10 **Specific issue order**

This order gives directions for determining a specific question which has arisen or which may arise in connection with any aspect of parental responsibility for a child. In effect, the order attempts to reduce the number of occasions when the court needs to be referred to by anticipating and setting out the means by which a particular question may be answered. These orders usually expire when the child attains the age of 16 years. They may be useful in preventing offences such as planned FGM or forced marriage by a parent or carer.

10.8.11 **Undertakings**

Where the court has power to make an exclusion requirement to an EPO, it may accept an undertaking from the relevant person. There is no power of arrest in respect of any breach of the undertaking but it can be enforced as if it were an order of the court.

10.9 **Sanctuary Scheme**

The sanctuary scheme is a victim-centred and innovative approach to homelessness prevention. It provides professionally installed security measures to allow those experiencing domestic violence to remain in their own accommodation where it is safe for them to do so, **where it is their choice**, where the perpetrator no longer lives within the accommodation, and when they would otherwise become homeless and the local authority would have a duty to accommodate. The type of tenure is not a qualifying factor although in the case of private rented accommodation, permission will be needed from the landlord.

Many victims prefer to remain in their own homes; therefore the safety aspects and social benefits provided by the scheme are numerous. In addition, the installation of a sanctuary is likely to be considerably less expensive than placing victims and their children in temporary accommodation.

The main feature of the scheme is the creation of a 'sanctuary room' providing a safe room or sanctuary from where the victim can call and wait for the arrival of police. Additional external security can also be provided, for example locks on windows and doors, gated security to the outside of a property, fire hammers, fire blankets, and emergency lighting.

The main partner agencies will include the police, the fire brigade, and a specialist domestic-violence support service and will be fully integrated with local risk-assessment processes focused on safety, together with information-sharing protocols (particularly pertinent in relation to providing information on premises included in the scheme to local fire stations).

The Department for Communities and Local Government has published options and minimum standards for setting up a sanctuary scheme.

Responsibility for implementing the scheme falls to the local authority including funding considerations.

10.10 Alarms and Mobile Phones

10.10.1 Panic alarms

Panic alarms are available to those victims of domestic violence who wish to remain in their own homes and for whom the perpetrator presents a significant risk. They will generally only be suitable where the perpetrator has no legal right of access to the premises concerned. Alarms may be connected to the force radio system or to a locally operated emergency system for contacting the police. It is important that the presence of a panic alarm is recorded on the force call receipt and dispatching system and systematically risk-assessed and reviewed.

In addition to safety in the home, consideration might be given to providing the victim with a personal attack alarm for outside of the home.

10.10.2 Mobile Phones

There are several schemes across the UK that will provide police with re-cycled mobile phones that can be given to victims of domestic violence. This will enable quick and confidential access to emergency services.

10.11 Neighbourhood Policing and Cocoon Watch

Safer-neighbourhood-policing teams may be tasked to provide a regular visible presence in close proximity to the victim's address and in some circumstances pay welfare visits to the victim provided that consent is given. Officers may also be tasked in relation to the offending behaviour of the perpetrator. It is important that beat officers are aware of those addresses where injunctions are in force, panic alarms are installed, bail conditions apply in relation to keeping the perpetrator away from the address, a sanctuary scheme has been applied, etc.

10.11.1 Cocoon watch

Similar to neighbourhood watch, this scheme engages nominated family, friends, and neighbours to provide a support network for the victim and their children. This has to have the knowledge and consent of the victim as the nominated persons would need to be made aware of their situation. Those nominated would then be expected to look out for the victim and report any suspicious activity to the police or other identified agency or individual. Care will need to be taken that none of the nominated persons is allied to the perpetrator.

10.12 **Safety Plans**

There are many domestic-violence support agencies that will engage with victims to discuss the options for keeping victims and their children safe and compile unique safety plans with them based on their actual or perceived dangers.

10.12.1 **Safety tips**

Examples of safety tips can be downloaded from some DV agency websites or obtained in hard copy direct from the agencies. The following templates outline safety tips that have been reproduced in the *Guidance on Investigating Domestic Abuse* (ACPO, 2008).

Checklist—For those staying with their abuser

- Seek professional advice and support from local support and outreach organizations, domestic abuse services, and helplines.
- Consider how agencies can make contact safely, eg through a work number or at a friend's address.
- Consider where you can quickly and easily use a telephone and who are safe people to contact—memorize a list of numbers for use in an emergency, like friends, police, and support organizations.
- Consider a signal (such as a codeword) with children, family, neighbours, friends, or colleagues, which will alert them to call the police when help is needed.
- Think through escape routes in advance, avoiding rooms with no exit or with weapons in (eg, bathroom or kitchen) where possible.
- Try to put by some money for fares and other expenses.
- Receive medical help for any injuries ensuring that they are recorded and if possible photographed. These may be used at a later date to support court cases or rehousing applications.

Checklist—For those planning to leave their abuser

- Take care over whom to trust with any plans that you are making to leave.
- Consider whether or not a civil order is a viable option—seek legal advice.
- Make an extra set of keys for home and/or car and store them somewhere safe.
- Make up a bag with spare clothes, telephone numbers, keys, and money and keep it safe so you can take it quickly, or keep it with a trusted friend.

- Have the following available in case you have to leave quickly: important papers such as birth certificates, social security cards, driver's licence, divorce papers, lease or mortgage papers, passports, insurance information,school and medical records, welfare and immigration documents, court documents; credit cards, bank account number, and some money; an extra sets of keys for the car, house and work; medications and prescriptions including those for children; telephone numbers and addresses for family, friends, doctors, lawyers and community agencies; clothing and comfort items for you and the children; photographs and other items of sentimental value such as jewellery.

- Take identification that might help others to protect you from the abuser, such as a recent photo of the abuser and their car details.

- Talk to children about the possibility of leaving and try to take all the children, whatever long-term arrangements might be.

Checklist—For those living without their abuser after separation (in their own home or after moving)

- Seek expert legal advice on child contact and residence applications, and about options for injunctions.

- Change telephone numbers to ex-directory, screen calls, and pre-programme emergency numbers into the telephone.

- Change the locks and install a security system, smoke alarms, and an outside lighting system.

- Notify neighbours, employers, and schools about any injunction, and ask them to call the police immediately if they see the abuser nearby.

- Make sure that schools and those who care for your children know who has authorization to collect them.

- Employ safety measures before, during, and after contact visits with children.

- Consider changing children's schools, work patterns—hours and route taken—and the route taken to transport the children to school.

- Avoid banks, shops, and other places frequented when living with the abuser.

- Make up a codeword for family, colleagues, teachers, or friends so that they know when to call the police for help.

- Keep copies of all relevant paperwork (including civil injunctions) and make written records of any further incidents.

10.12.2 **Electoral roll and other databases**

There have been many occasions where perpetrators have used government databases to track down victims who have fled domestic violence.

The Electoral Administration Act 2006 allows victims who can prove domestic violence to register for the electoral roll anonymously without losing their right to vote. The evidence has to be either a relevant current court order or injunction, or an attestation by a qualifying officer, such as a chief constable or a director of social services. Application will be made to the Electoral Services Section at the local authority. Similarly, application may be made to other agencies, for example the Driver and Vehicle Licensing Centre or the Benefits Agency, to have victims' details maintained clerically.

Advice will also need to be provided to the victim who may be engaging with others on social networking websites, for example Facebook or YouTube, as this may identify the whereabouts of the victim.

10.13 **Specialist Refuge Service Providers and Emergency Accommodation**

Refuge and Women's Aid, for example, have been working to protect domestic-violence victims and their children for many years. They provide places of safety for women fleeing domestic violence across the UK. They also provide specialist refuge places for women with specific ethnic or cultural backgrounds. Victims living in refuge places are provided support and counselling to enable them to make decisions for the future. Refuge space is temporary until permanent accommodation can be found for them; once they are placed in permanent accommodation, Refuge/Women's Aid provides outreach services to assist resettlement.

10.13.1 **Refuge helpline**

Refuge, in partnership with Women's Aid, run a 24-hour domestic-violence helpline. Local refuge-service contact details can be found in the Gold Book published by Women's Aid, or on the Refuge and Women's Aid website.

In London, Refuge provide an independent advocacy service who work to protect women at very high risk of harm and this is likely to be introduced in other areas nationally.

10.13.2 **Emergency accommodation**

Part VII of the Housing Act 1996 and the Homelessness Act 2002 outline the duty of the local authority in relation to providing emergency or temporary accommodation. The following criteria are relevant to decisions relating to victims and their children fleeing their homes on account of experiencing domestic violence:

- They are unintentionally homeless.
- They are a priority need.
- They are eligible, ie, have recourse to public funds and are habitually resident in the UK.

Whilst victims do not have to prove violence against them, it is likely that the local authority will contact police as part of their enquiries to verify the situation. Priority will be given to those who are pregnant or have dependent children or are vulnerable through mental illness or disability.

Asylum seekers or refugees may not be eligible, dependent on their immigration status. Victims should be referred or taken to the local homeless persons unit or housing department.

10.13.3 **Witness mobility scheme**

This is a scheme aimed at providing safe housing for intimidated witnesses. It gives police, local authorities, and social landlords access to fast-track relocation and support services. Each area will have a designated housing officer within the local authority for the scheme and decisions will be based on criteria and risk affecting the witness.

10.14 **Independent Domestic Violence Advisers (IDVA)**

Police officers are able to provide support and advice to victims to a limited extent, but victims' needs might be varied and complex beyond the knowledge of officers. This often results in victims being referred to, or having to approach, a range of agencies to obtain the appropriate help. Under the government's National Action Plan for domestic violence, funding has been made available to provide dedicated advice and assistance from an independent source, available to those both inside and outside the criminal justice system.

The role of the IDVA is to advise and support victims who are high/very high risk, referred by the police, or occasionally health professionals, to help ensure their safety, independently of any other organization. They give personal advice and support direct to victims to help them make decisions about their future and also help them access the range of services they need. IDVAs are specially trained under the Coordinated Action Against Domestic Abuse (CAADA) accredited programme to understand the full range of remedies and resources available in the civil and criminal justice systems, as well as the physical safety options available to a victim through other statutory and voluntary sector services, and to be able to assess their suitability in each case. They work from the point of crisis with a victim and offer intensive support to help assure their short- and medium-term safety. Advisers must understand the assessment of risk as it relates to domestic violence victims and how to manage it.

IDVAs will be a member of the local MARAC (multi-agency risk-assessment conference) and will work in partnership with all relevant agencies. It is vital that they are engaged in supporting victims who report to police.

CAADA is a charity established to encourage the use of independent advocacy as a way to increase the safety of survivors. As part of the government's initiative in designating new specialist domestic violence court areas, they run training on MARACs and provide toolkits and information on their website.

10.15 **Domestic-Violence Support Agencies**

There are many non-government and voluntary-sector organizations that provide services for women and children who are victims of domestic violence; there are some that provide specialist support for minority groups including black and other ethnicity, sexual orientation, and men. Their services are key to early and effective intervention and it is important that police engage local service provision in their prevention and repeat-victimization strategies. The Women's Aid website (<http://www.womensaid.org.uk>) provides a list of agencies, generally engaged in refuge services, across the UK.

10.15.1 **Multi-agency risk-assessment conferences (MARACs)**

The MARAC is a formal conference to facilitate the risk-assessment and management process for high-risk victims of domestic violence. The purpose is for agencies to share information with a view to identifying those at high and very high risk and thereafter jointly constructing a management plan to provide professional bespoke support to all those at risk. Such meetings are usually held on a fortnightly or monthly basis (or sooner if a case requires urgent attention) and any agency may refer into the MARAC provided the victim meets the appropriate threshold of risk identified, using the accredited risk model.

The following agencies will always be invited to a MARAC meeting: the police, social care, probation, health, housing, IDVAs, and education (where relevant). Representatives of other statutory or voluntary agencies may also be invited to the meeting depending on whether those agencies have (or may have) any specific involvement with any of the subjects, for example youth offending teams, the community psychiatric nurse, housing associations, NSPCC, Women's Aid, etc. The CPS are not involved because of disclosure rules.

This ensures that agencies can build up a more comprehensive picture of the abuse and agree action to best support and protect a domestic-violence victim and their family and manage the risk posed by the perpetrator.

10.15.2 **Multi-agency public-protection arrangements (MAPPAs)**

MAPPAs are the means by which local agencies work together to best protect the community from the serious harm that some offenders may still present after being convicted. Those offenders are categorized as follows:

Category 1: registered sex offenders for the period of their registration.

Category 2: violent and other sex offenders; often summarized as violent offenders imprisoned for 12 months or more and includes those detained under hospital or guardianship orders. They usually exit MAPPA when statutory supervision ceases.

Category 3: other offenders who have been convicted of an offence which indicates that he/she is capable of causing serious harm to the public and the responsible authority reasonably considers that the offender may cause serious harm to the public.

They are managed as follows:

MAPPA Level 1: used in cases where the risk posed by the offender can be managed by one agency without actively or significantly involving other agencies.

MAPPA Level 2: used where the **active** involvement of more than one agency is required but where either the level of risk or complexity of managing the risk is not so great as to require referral to level 3.

MAPPA Level 3: used for the management of the 'critical few'. This would apply where the offender is assessed under OASys (the system for assessing risk used by prison and probation services) as being a high or very high risk of causing serious harm **and** presents risks that can only be managed by a plan that requires close cooperation at a senior level due to the complexity of the case and/or because of the unusual resource commitments it requires, **or** although not assessed as a high or very high risk, the case is exceptional because of the likelihood of media scrutiny and/or public interest in the management of the case is very high.

10.15.2.1 MAPPA agencies

The responsible authorities are:

- the police
- probation
- the prison service.

The following organizations have a legal duty (set out in the Criminal Justice Act 2003) to work together to protect the public:

- youth offending teams
- Jobcentre Plus
- local education authorities
- local housing authorities
- registered social landlords

- social services
- strategic health authorities, primary care trusts and NHS trusts
- electronic monitoring providers.

10.15.3 Child-protection conferencing

A child-protection conference should be convened by the Local Authority Children's Social Care if concerns about a child are substantiated (after careful assessment based on best information and strategy discussions) and the child is judged to be at continuing risk of significant harm. If the conference is to reach well-informed decisions based on evidence, it should take place following adequate preparation and assessment of the child's needs and circumstances.

10.16 Domestic Violence and the Immigration Rule

For women who enter the UK to marry or join their partner who is already settled in the country, they must remain with them for two years before they can apply for indefinite leave to remain. However, victims of domestic violence who can produce evidence of abuse against set criteria may make an application to allow them to apply for indefinite leave to remain in the UK in their own right. This may then entitle them to access public funds normally denied them. To qualify for leave to remain in the UK under Immigration Rules 2002, as a victim of domestic violence, you have to show all the following:

- limited leave to enter or remain in the UK as the spouse or partner of someone already settled here
- subject to the two-year probationary period
- domestic violence occurred during this probationary period
- no longer living with the perpetrator
- domestic violence was the reason for the breakdown of this relationship
- evidence of domestic violence supported by one of the following forms of 'proof':
  1. a non-molestation order or other protection order
  2. a relevant court conviction against the perpetrator
  3. full details of a relevant police caution.

If none of the above is available, however, then **two or more** of the following:

1. a letter from a refuge organization or other domestic violence service confirming experience of domestic violence
2. a medical report from a hospital doctor confirming that injuries are consistent with being the victim of domestic violence

3. a letter from a GP who has carried out an examination and is satisfied that injuries are consistent with being the victim of domestic violence

4. an undertaking given to a court from the perpetrator to not approach the victim

5. a police report confirming their attendance at the victim's address due to domestic violence

6. a letter from social services confirming their involvement in connection with domestic violence.

Useful contacts

Coordinated Action Against Domestic Violence
Website: <http://www.caada.org.uk>

National Centre for Domestic Violence
Website: <http://www.ncdv.org.uk>
Telephone number 08009 70 20 70

RespectUK
Website: <http://www.respect.uk.net>
Telephone number: 0845 1228609

Refuge
Website: <http://www.refuge.org.uk>
Telephone number: 0808 200 247

Women's Aid
Website: <http://www.womensaid.org.uk>
Telephone number: 0808 200 247

Domestic-violence helplines

The following helplines can offer you practical help and advice including:

- emergency refuge accommodation
- safety planning and advice
- translation facilities if you have difficulty communicating in English.

English National Domestic Violence helpline
Telephone number: 0808 2000 247

Northern Ireland Women's Aid 24 Hour Domestic Violence Helpline
Telephone number: 028 9033 1818

Scottish Domestic Abuse Helpline
Telephone number: 0800 027 1234

Wales Domestic Abuse Helpline
Website: <http://www.wdah.org>
Telephone number: 0808 80 10 800

Male Advice & Enquiry Line
Telephone number: 0845 064 6800

The Dyn Wales/Dyn Cymru Helpline
Telephone number: 0808 801 0321

Appendix A
Risk: Considerations of risk for victims

The analysis highlighted that certain victims may be more at risk of forced marriage. Other factors can compound to elevate the risk posed to a victim. Advanced analysis is to be conducted in this area to ascertain the links and continuum of violence that can lead to murder. In some cases the chain reaction from forced marriage to murder can be rapid and therefore all risks must be identified, assessed, and managed—'first time, right time'.

Figure A1: Risk identification factors for victims of forced marriage

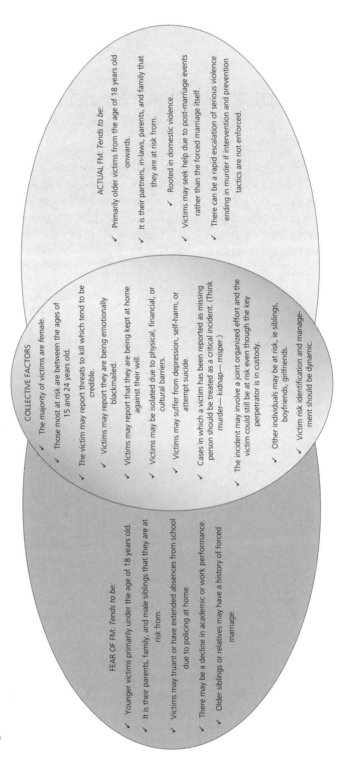

COLLECTIVE FACTORS

✓ The majority of victims are *female*.

✓ Those most at risk are between the ages of 15 and 24 years old.

✓ The victim may report threats to kill which tend to be credible.

✓ Victims may report they are being emotionally blackmailed.

✓ Victims may report that they are being kept at home against their will.

✓ Victims may be isolated due to physical, financial, or cultural barriers.

✓ Victims may suffer from depression, self-harm, or attempt suicide.

✓ Cases in which a victim has been reported as missing person should be treated as a critical incident. (Think murder— kidnap— misper.)

✓ The incident may involve a joint organized effort and the victim could still be at risk even though the key perpetrator is in custody.

✓ Other individuals may be at risk, ie siblings, boyfriends, girlfriends.

✓ Victim risk identification and management should be dynamic.

ACTUAL FM: *Tends to be:*

✓ Primarily older victims from the age of 18 years old onwards.

✓ It is their partners, in-laws, parents, and family that they are at risk from.

✓ Rooted in domestic violence.

✓ Victims may seek help due to post-marriage events rather than the forced marriage itself.

✓ There can be a rapid escalation of serious violence ending in murder if intervention and prevention tactics are not enforced.

FEAR OF FM: *Tends to be:*

✓ Younger victims primarily under the age of 18 years old.

✓ It is their parents, family, and male siblings that they are at risk from.

✓ Victims may truant or have extended absences from school due to policing at home.

✓ There may be a decline in academic or work performance.

✓ Older siblings or relatives may have a history of forced marriage.

Appendix B

The Crime and Disorder Act 1998 and Police and Justice Act 2006: Exchange of Personal Information

The following guidance on information sharing between agencies under s 115 of the Crime and Disorder Act 1998 was issued in November 1998 in a joint statement by the Home Office and Data Protection Registrar.

Before public or statutory bodies can disclose information, they must first establish whether they have power to do so and/or whether they have a responsibility to do so. Once the question of power is resolved, they must carry out the disclosure in a lawful manner.

Section 115 ensures all agencies have a power to disclose. It does not impose a requirement on them to exchange information, and so control over disclosure remains with the agency that holds the data. Information exchange, whether carried out under the power in s 115 or under any other common law or statutory power, is therefore controlled by the normal data protection regime and common law. The public rightly expects that personal information known to public bodies will be properly protected. However, the public also expects the proper sharing of information, as this can be an important weapon against crime. Agencies should, therefore, seek to share information where this would be in the public interest.

An underlying principle of the protocol is that an agency will always retain ownership of the personal information it discloses to another member of the partnership. A recipient of such information must, therefore, obtain the consent of the original data owner before making a further disclosure. For the purposes of this requirement, each local authority department will be treated as a separate agency.

This provision will also apply when it is intended to disclose information to voluntary groups or other organisations who are not signatories to the protocol. In such cases the disclosure must be to support action under the Act. Section 116 of the Crime and Disorder Act provides a lawful power to exchange personal information. This must be for the purpose of implementing the provisions of the Act. However, although the Act creates a situation where the exchange of information may be lawful, the presumption of confidentiality will still apply. This means that designated officers must make an objective assessment of all the available information to determine whether the public interest justifies disclosure.

When considering a disclosure of personal information, the designated officer must determine whether the public interest would justify disclosure against the normal presumption of confidentiality. Each case must be considered separately and a disclosure must be based on an objective assessment of all the available information. The public interest criteria will include the:

- prevention of crime and disorder
- detection of crime
- apprehension of offenders
- protection of vulnerable members of the community
- maintenance of public safety
- administration of justice
- diversion of young offenders.

The designated officers must assess, on a case-by-case basis, whether a disclosure is necessary to support action under the Crime and Disorder Act and the public interest is of sufficient weight to override the presumption of confidentiality.

Example
A designated officer may disclose personal information relating to a perpetrator on the grounds that this will **prevent** crime.

In such a case, the designated officer must:

- identify why there is an obvious **risk** of a crime occurring
- examine how a disclosure may prevent a further crime being committed
- consider how the disclosure will support action under the Crime and Disorder Act
- adopt a common-sense approach which identifies the public interest, and
- recognise any duty of confidentiality to a witness, informant, victim or perpetrator.

The personal details of a victim, informant or witness should be provided to another agency with the prior written consent of the person concerned. Such details can only be released without the consent of the relevant person in the most serious circumstances where the public interest would otherwise be profoundly and adversely affected.

Witness statements that will support action under the Crime and Disorder Act may also be passed to another agency with the written consent of the person concerned. If the statements' content identifies another individual, the disclosure of *their* details must also be based upon their written consent or upon the grounds of public interest. The requirement to weigh the public interest against the duty of confidentiality applies to all aspects of the Crime and Disorder Act. It must be fully compliant with the Human Rights Act, which requires public agencies to act within their powers and respect an individual's right to privacy. Designated officers must always make an objective assessment of the facts to ensure that a disclosure is both lawful and fair. The requirement will, therefore, be relevant to specific measures which are intended to support action in the following areas:

- the reduction of crime and disorder
- crime displacement
- drug action team work
- the reduction of fear of crime
- the tackling of crime on housing estates
- cross-border analysis
- the relocation of newly-released prisoners to safer living areas
- public safety risk assessments in relation to the supervision, treatment or placement of mentally disordered offenders or those who have been detained under the Mental Health Act
- **repeat victimisation studies, including those relating to hate crime, domestic violence or the mentally ill**
- street crime activity
- truancy and youth crime (including youth offending team work) and
- dealing with anti-social behaviour.

Before making a disclosure, the designated officer must be satisfied that the recipient has made proper arrangements for the safekeeping of the information. The local protocol should also specify how personal information will be destroyed when it is no longer required for the purpose for which it was provided.

Only once all these factors have been considered will the designated officer be able to decide whether a disclosure can be justified. Copies of police documents and printouts from the PNC or other databases will not be supplied to other agencies. Relevant information from a police database should be transcribed onto plain paper before being exchanged.

The Police and Justice Act 2006 strengthens these powers with respect to information sharing. It places all the key players in CDRPs under a legal duty to share aggregate, depersonalised data between themselves, when doing so would be in the interest of preventing crime. New minimum standards for CDRPs require an information sharing protocol to be signed by all responsible authorities, and for a designated person in each authority to facilitate information sharing within the CDRP.

Appendix C
SOCPA 2005 s 110: Reminder of general powers for arrest

Section 110 of the Serious Organised Crime and Police Act 2005 amended the powers of arrest available to a constable under s 24 of the Police and Criminal Evidence Act 1984. Prior to the introduction of s 110, the powers of arrest were primarily derived from ss 24 and 25 of PACE based on the application of the concept of seriousness attached to the offence.

The exercise of arrest powers will be subject to a test of necessity based around the nature and circumstances of the offence and the interests of the criminal justice system. An arrest will only be justified if the constable believes it is necessary for any of the reasons set out in the new s 24(5).

Section 24—Arrest without warrant: constables (and designated persons)

24(1) A constable [or designated person] may arrest without a warrant:-
   (a) anyone who is about to commit an offence;
   (b) anyone who is in the act of committing an offence;
   (c) anyone whom he has reasonable grounds for suspecting to be about to commit an offence;
   (d) anyone whom he has reasonable grounds for suspecting to be committing an offence.

(2) If a constable [or designated person] has reasonable grounds for suspecting that an offence has been committed, he may arrest without a warrant anyone whom he has reasonable grounds to suspect of being guilty of it.

(3) If an offence has been committed, a constable [or designated person] may arrest without a warrant:-
   (a) anyone who is guilty of the offence;
   (b) anyone whom he has reasonable grounds for suspecting to be guilty of it.

(4) But the power of summary arrest conferred by subsection (1), (2) or (3) is exercisable only if the constable [or designated person] has reasonable grounds for believing that for any of the reasons mentioned in subsection (5) it is necessary to arrest the person in question.

(5) The reasons are:-
   (a) to enable the name of the person in question to be ascertained (in the case where the constable does not know, and cannot readily ascertain, the person's name, or has reasonable grounds for doubting whether a name given by the person as his name is his real name);
   (b) correspondingly as regards the person's address;

(c) to prevent the person in question:-
   (i) causing physical injury to himself or any other person;
   (ii) suffering physical injury;
   (iii) causing loss of or damage to property;
   (iv) committing an offence against public decency (subject to subsection (6)); or
   (v) causing an unlawful obstruction of the highway;
(d) to protect a child or other vulnerable person from the person in question;
(e) to allow the prompt and effective investigation of the offence or of the conduct of the person in question;
(f) to prevent any prosecution for the offence from being hindered by the disappearance of the person in question.

Appendix D
Human Rights Act 1998

The Human Rights Act 1998 incorporates the rights and freedoms set out in the European Convention on Human Rights into UK law.

Convention Rights

Absolute rights (with no exceptions)

- Article 2:   right to life
- Article 3:   right not to be subjected to torture, inhuman or degrading treatment
- Article 4.1:   right not to be held in slavery or servitude
- Article 7:   no retrospective criminal laws or sentences

Strong rights (limited rights)

- Article 5:   the right to liberty and security of person
- Article 6:   the right to a fair trial
- Article 14:   no discrimination in the enjoyment of Convention rights

There is a presumption of the right but there are stated exceptions to those rights, ie Art 5 states that everyone has the right to liberty and security of person. No one shall be deprived of his liberty save in the following cases and in accordance with a procedure prescribed by law:

Prima Facie rights (qualified rights)

- Article 8:   the right to respect for private and family life
- Article 9:   the right to freedom of thought, conscience and religion
- Article 10:   the right to freedom of expression
- Article 11:   the right to freedom of assembly and association

The *qualified rights* are still rights but there has to be a balance drawn between the right of the individual and that of the democratic society (proportionality). The authority will only be acting lawfully if the act committed was necessary for:

- national security
- public safety
- economic well-being of the country
- prevention of disorder or crime
- the protection of health or morals
- the protection of the rights and freedoms of others.

Appendix E
Criminal Justice Act 2003—hearsay—cases where witness unavailable

Section 116 of the Criminal Justice Act sets out a series of categories under which first-hand hearsay evidence, whether oral or documentary, will be admissible, provided that the witness is unavailable to testify for a specified reason. The new provisions will be available to the prosecution and the defence.

Cases where a witness is unavailable

116(1) In criminal proceedings a statement not made in oral evidence in the proceedings is admissible of any matter stated if:

(a) oral evidence given in the proceedings by the person who made the statement would be admissible as evidence of that matter,

(b) the person who made the statement (relevant person) is identified to the court's satisfaction, and

(c) any of the five conditions mentioned in the subsection (2) is satisfied.

(2) The conditions are:

(a) that the relevant person is dead;

(b) that the relevant person is unfit to be a witness because of his bodily or mental condition;

(c) that the relevant person is outside the United Kingdom and it is not reasonably practicable to secure his attendance

(d) that the relevant person cannot be found although such steps as it is reasonably practicable to take to find him have been taken;

(e) that through fear the relevant person does not give (or does not continue to give) oral evidence in the proceedings, either at all or in conjunction with the subject matter of the statement, and the court gives leave for the statement to be given in evidence.

(3) For the purposes of subsection (2)(e) 'fear' is to be widely construed and (for example) includes fear of the death or injury of another person or of financial loss.

Domestic violence cases

Consider using s 116(2) if a battered partner is too frightened to give evidence, too ill or cannot be traced. It has been successfully used in assault cases, even in common assault. An example was circulated by the CPS after a successful application to include the evidence of more than one officer that an assaulted wife said

'Michael, he has hit me' at the time of the assault. She was too frightened to make a complaint and could not be traced at the time of her husband's trial (for common assault) ay Bradford Magistrates' Court in March 2006. An application was made to the district judge to include the hearsay evidence from the officers and the trial that followed led to a successful conviction.

116(4) Leave may be given under subsection (2)(e) only if the court considers that the statement ought to be admitted in the interests of justice, having regard:

    (a) to the statement's contents

    (b) to any risk that its admission or exclusion will result in the unfairness to any party to the proceedings (and in particular to how difficult it will be to challenge the statement if the relevant person does not give oral evidence),

    (c) in appropriate cases, to the fact that a direction under section 19 of the Youth Justice and Criminal Evidence Act 1999 (special measures for giving of evidence by fearful witnesses etc) could be made in relation to the relevant person, and

    (d) to any other relevant circumstances

(5) A condition set out in any paragraph of the subsection (2) which is in fact satisfied is to be treated as not satisfied if it is shown that the circumstances described in the paragraph are caused:

    (a) by the person in support of whose case it is sought to give the statement in evidence, or

    (b) by the person acting on his behalf,

        in order to prevent the relevant person giving oral evidence in the proceedings (whether at all or in connection with the subject matter of the statement).

Appendix F
Special Schemes Topics

These are schemes that can be placed on caller aided despatch. In *ALL* assault cases:

- Seize and secure all forensic opportunities, ie offender's DNA, fingerprint evidence, and objects used.
- Always seek to obtain corroborative evidence, ie digital photographs, witness evidence, forensics, and so forth.
- Photograph the victim's injuries and consider examination by a forensic medical examiner.
- Consider powers of arrest. Police action must be necessary and proportionate in response to the seriousness of the offence in accordance with the Human Rights Act (PLANBI).
- Consider the Protection from Harassment Act 1997.
- A risk assessment must be conducted. If victim is at high risk and/or the offender has not been arrested, inform a supervising officer.
- During office hours, 0800–2000 hours, a specialist domestic violence officer **should** be informed.

References and Websites

ACPO (2004), *Investigative Interviewing Strategy* (London: NPIA).

(2005a), *Guidance on Investigating Child Abuse and Safeguarding Children* (London: NPIA).

(2005b), *Guidance on Identifying, Assessing and Managing Risk in the Context of Policing Domestic Violence* (London: NPIA).

(2005c), *Guidance on Investigating Serious Sexual Offences* (London: NPIA).

(2005d), *Guidance on the National Intelligence Model*, available at <http://www.acpo. police.uk/asp/policies/Data/nim2005.pdf>.

(2005e), *Responses to Domestic Violence Modular Training Programme* (London: NPIA).

(2006a) *Guidance on the Management of Police Information* (Wyboston: NCPE).

(2006b), NCPE Update Briefing No 1/2006 Domestic Violence, available at <http:// www.genesis.pnn.police.uk>.

(2006c), *Practice Advice on Professionalising the Business of Neighbourhood Policing* (London: NPIA).

(2008a), *Guidance on Investigating Domestic Abuse* (London: NPIA).

(2008b), *Honour-Based Violence Strategy* (London: ACPO).

Andrews, DA (1989), 'Recidivism is predictable and can be influenced: Using risk assessments to reduce recidivism', *Forum on Corrections Research*, 1, 11–17.

Asif, S (2006), *Findings from the HBV Community Engagement Project: Developed by community consultant Dr Salman Asif on behalf of MPS* (London: Metropolitan Police Service).

Bacchus, L, Bewley, S, and Mezey, G (2001), 'Domestic violence and pregnancy review', *The Obstetrician and Gynaecologist*, 3(2), 56–9.

Baker, A, and Richards, L (2005), 'Prevention of homicide and serious violence', *The Journal of Homicide and Major Incident Investigation*, 1(1), 3–14 (erratum in Vol 1 Issue 2).

Barnish, M (2004), *Domestic Violence: A literature review* (London: HM Inspectorate of Probation).

Bennett, L, Goodman, L, and Dutton, M (2000), 'Risk assessment among batterers arrested for domestic assault: The salience of psychological abuse', *Violence Against Women*, 6(11), 1190–203.

Bewley, S, Friend, J, and Mezey, G (eds) (1997), *Violence Against Women* (London: Royal College of Obstetricians and Gynaecologists).

Bhardwaj, A (2001), 'Growing up young Asian and female in Britain: a report on self-harm and suicide', *Feminist Review*, 68(1), 52–67.

Bhugra, D, Desai, M, and Baldwin D (1999), 'Suicide and attempted suicide across cultures', in Dinesh Bhugra and Veena Bahl (eds), *Ethnicity: An agenda for mental health* (London: Gaskell).

Bichard, Sir Michael (2004), *The Bichard Inquiry Report* (Norwich: The Stationary Office). Available at <http://www.bichardinquiry.org.uk/10663/report.pdf>.

Blaauw, E, Winkel, FW, Sheridan, L, Malsch, M, and Arensman, E (2002), 'The psychological consequences of stalking victimisation', in J Boon and L Sheridan (eds), *Stalking and Psychosexual Obsession* (New York: John Wiley and Sons Inc), 23–33.

Bowker, L, Artbitell, M, and McFerron, J (1998), Domestic Violence Fact Sheet: Children (Women's Aid Federation of England).

Brookman, F, and Maguire, M (2003), 'Reducing homicide: Summary of a review of the possibilities', RDS Occasional Paper No 84.

Browne, A (1987), *When Battered Women Kill* (New York: Free Press).

Buzawa, E, Hotaling, G, Klein, A, and Byrne, J (2000), *Response to Domestic Violence in a Proactive Court Setting: Executive summary* (US Department of Justice).

Byles, J (1978), 'Violence, alcohol problems and other problems in disintegrating families', *Journal of Studies Alcohol*, 39, 551–3.

Campbell, J (1995), 'Prediction of homicide of and by battered women', in JC Campbell (ed), *Assessing Dangerousness: Violence by sexual offenders, batterers and child abusers* (London: Sage).

(2001), *Danger Assessment*, available at <http://www.ncdsv.org/images/dangerassessment.pdf>.

(2003), 'Risk factors for femicide in abusive relationships: Results from a multisite case control study', *Journal of Public Health*, 93(7).

Campbell, JC (1986), 'Assessing the risk of homicide for battered women', *Advances in Nursing Science*, 8(4), 36–51.

Caspi, A, and Moffitt, TE (1995), 'The continuity of maladaptive behaviour: From description to explanation in the study of antisocial behaviour', in D Cicchetti, K Cavanagh, RP Dobash, R Dobash, and R Lewis (2002), *Homicide in Britain: Risk factors, situational contexts and lethal intentions (interviews with women)*, Research Bulletin No 3 (Manchester: Department of Applied Social Science).

Cavanagh, K, Dobush, RE, and Dobash RP (2007), 'The murder, of children by fathers in the context of child abuse' *Journal of Child Abuse and Neglect*, vol 2, Issue 7, 731–40.

Chan, W (2001), *Women, Murder and Justice* (Basingstoke: Palgrave).

Cohen, D (2006), 'Developmental psychopathology', in D Cicchetti and D Cohen (eds), *Developmental Neuroscience* (2nd ed, New York: Wiley), Vol 2, 472–522.

Cohen, MJ, and Kweller, C (2000), 'Domestic violence and animal abuse: The deadly connection', Physicians Committee for Responsible Medicine, Commentary, as available at <http://www.pcrm.org/issues/commentary>.

Coker, AL, Smith, PH, McKeown, RE, and King, MJ (2000), 'Frequency and correlates of intimate partner violence by type: Physical, sexual and psychological battering', *American Journal of Public Health*, 90, 553–9.

Cope, N (2005), 'The range of issues in crime analysis', in L Alison (ed), *The Forensic Psychologists' Casebook* (Devon: Willan), 90–113.

Criminal Justice System (2005), *The Code of Practice for Victims of Crime* (London: Office for Criminal Justice Reform).

(2006), *Working with Intimidated Witnesses: A manual for police and practitioners responsible for identifying and supporting intimidated witnesses* (London: Office for Criminal Justice Reform).

(2007), *Achieving Best Evidence in Criminal Proceedings* (London: Office for Criminal Justice Reform).

Crisp, D, Stanko, B, and Richards, L (2002), 'Making two plus two equal four', *Safe: The Domestic Abuse Quarterly*, spring ed, 3–5.

Crown Prosecution Service (2004a), *The Code for Crown Prosecutors* (London: Crown Prosecution Service), available at <http://www.cps.gov.uk/victims_witnesses/code.html>.

(2004b), *The Use of Expert Witness Testimony in the Prosecution of Domestic Violence* (London: Crown Prosecution Service), available at <http://www.cps.gov.uk/publications/docs/expertwitnessdv.pdf>.

(2005), *Guidance for Prosecuting Cases of Domestic Violence* (London: Crown Prosecution Service), available at <http://www.cps.gov.uk/publications/prosecution/domestic>.

(2006a), Domestic Violence Monitoring Snapshot December. Available at <http://www.cps.gov.uk/publications/prosecution/domestic/snapshot_2006_12.html>.

Dempsey, M (2004), *The Use of Expert Witness Testimony in the Prosecution of Domestic Violence* (London: CPS).

Department of Health (1998), *Why Mothers Die: Report on confidential enquiries into maternal death in the United Kingdom* (Norwich: The Stationery Office). Available at <http://www.dh.gov.uk/en/Publicationsandstatistics/Publications/PublicationsStatistics/DH_4009520>.

(1999), *National Service Framework for Mental Health* (London: National Health Service).

(2002), *Women's Mental Health: Into the mainstream. Strategic development of mental health care for women* (London: Department of Health).

(2003), *Strategic Development of Mental Health Care for Women* (London: Department of Health).

Department for Constitutional Affairs (2004), *Public Sector Data Sharing: Guidance on the law* (London: DCA).

Dietz, P, Matthews, D, Martell, D, Stewart, T, Hrouda, D, and Warren, J (1991b), 'Threatening and otherwise inappropriate letters to members of the United States Congress', *Journal of Forensic Sciences*, 36, 1445–68.

Dietz, P, Matthews, D, Van Duyne, C, Martell, D, Parry, C, Stewart, T, Warren, J, and Crowder, J (1991a), 'Threatening and otherwise inappropriate letters to Hollywood celebrities', *Journal of Forensic Sciences*, 36, 185–209.

Dobash, RP, Dobash, RE, Cavanagh, K, and Lewis, R (2002), *Homicide in Britain: Risk factors, situational contexts and lethal intentions (focus on male offenders)*, Research Bulletin No 1 (Manchester: Department of Applied Social Science).

(2004), 'Not an ordinary killer—Just an Ordinary Guy: When men murder an intimate woman partner', *Violence Against Women*, 10, 577–605.

Dobash, RP, Dobash, RE, and Medina-Ariza, J (2000), 'Lethal and non lethal violence against an intimate partner: Risks, needs and programmes' (Unpublished).

Donovan, C, Hester, M, Holmes, J, and Mccrary, M (2006), *Comparing Domestic Abuse in Same Sex and Heterosexual Relationships*, initial report from ESRC study, award no RES-000-23-0650. Available at <http://www.bristol.ac.uk/vawrg>.

Dutton, D, and Kropp, R (2000), 'A review of domestic violence instruments', *Trauma, Violence and Abuse*, 1(2), April.

Easteal, P (1993), *Killing the Beloved: Homicide between adult sexual intimates* (Canberra: Australian Institute of Criminology).

Erol, R (2006), *Alcohol Misuse Enforcement Campaign: Guidance on problem profiles* (London: UCL Jill Dando Institute).

Fagan, J (1989), 'Cessation of family violence: Deterrence and dissuasion', in L Ohlin and M Tonry (eds), *Family Violence Vol 11, Crime and Justice: A review of research* (Chicago: University of Chicago Press), 377–425.

319

Fagan, JA, Stewart, DK, and Hansen, KV (1983), 'Violent men or violent husbands? Background factors and situational correlates', in D Finkelhor, R Gelles, G Hotaling, and M Straus (eds), *The Dark Side of Families* (California: Sage Publications).

Farmer, E and Owen, M (1995), *Child Protection Practice: Private risks and public remedies—decision making, intervention and outcome in child protection work* (London: HMSO).

Gelles, RJ (1988), 'Violence and pregnancy: Are pregnant women at greater risk of abuse?', *Journal of Marriage and Family*, 50, 841.

Golding, J (1999), 'Intimate partner violence as a risk factor for mental disorders: A meta-analysis', *Journal of Family Violence*, 14(2), 99–132.

Hall, T and Wright, S (2003), *Making It Count: A practical guide to collecting and managing domestic violence data* (London: NACRO).

Hanmer, J and Griffiths, S (2000), *Reducing Domestic Violence . . . What Works? Policing domestic violence*, Crime Reduction Research Series Briefing Note (London: Home Office).

Hanmer, J, Griffiths, S, and Jerwood, D (1999), *Arresting Evidence: Domestic violence and repeat victimisation*, Police Research Series, Paper 104 (London: Police Reducing Crime Unit).

Harmon, RB, Rosner, R, and Owens, H (1995), 'Obsessional harassment and erotomania in a criminal court population', *Journal of Forensic Sciences*, 40, 188–96.

——— (1998), 'Sex and violence in a forensic population of obsessional harassers', *Psychology, Public Policy, and Law*, 4, 236–49.

Hart, B (1990), *Assessing Whether Batterers Will Kill* (Harrisburg, PA: Pennsylvania Coalition against Domestic Violence).

Hayward, RF (2000), *Breaking the Earthenware Jar: Lessons from South Asia to end violence against women and girls* (Nepal: UNICEF).

Heckert, DA and Gondolf, EW (2004), 'Battered women's perceptions of risk versus risk factors and instruments in predicting repeat reassault', *Journal of Interpersonal Violence*, 19, 778–800.

Heise, L (1993), *Violence Against Women: The hidden health burden* (New York: World Bank).

Hemphill, JF, Hare, RD, and Wong, S (1998), 'Psychopathy and recidivism: A review', *Legal and Criminological Psychology*, 3, 139–70.

Hester, M (2006), 'Making it through the criminal justice system: Attrition and domestic violence', *Social Policy and Society*, 5(1), 79–90.

Hester, M and Westmarland, N (2005), *Tackling Domestic Violence: Effective interventions and approaches*, Home Office Research Study 290 (London: Home Office).

——— (2006), *Service Provision for Perpetrators of Domestic Violence* (Bristol: University of Bristol).

HM Government (2006), *Every Child Matters: Working together to safeguard children: A guide to inter-agency working to safeguard and promote the welfare of children* (Norwich: The Stationery Office). Available at <http://www.everychildmatters.gov.uk>.

HMIC/HMCPSI (2004), *An Inspection of the Investigation and Prosecution of Cases Involving Domestic Violence* (London: Home Office).

Home Office (1999), *Criminal Statistics* (London: Home Office).

——— (2000), *Domestic Violence: Revised circular to the Police*, 19/2000 (London: Home Office).

(2002), *Offender Assessment System (OASys) User Manual* (London: Home Office, revised in 2006).

(2004), *Safety and Justice: Sharing personal information in the context of domestic violence* (London: Home Office).

(2006a), *Lessons Learned from the Domestic Violence Enforcement Campaigns 2006* (London: Home Office).

(2006b), *Use of Interpreters within the Criminal Justice System*, Home Office Circular 17/2006 (London: Home Office).

(2008a), *Crime in England and Wales 2006/2007* (London: Home Office). Available at <http://www.homeoffice.gov.uk/rds/crimeew0607.html>.

(2008b), Home Office Crime Reduction Domestic Violence Mini-Site, <http://www.crimereduction.homeoffice.gov.uk/dv/dv01.htm>.

Home Office and Metropolitan Police Service (2001), *Understanding and Responding to Hate Crime Team Fact Sheets: Domestic and sexual* (London: Home Office).

Home Office Violent Crime Unit (2004), *Developing Domestic Violence Strategies: A guide for partnerships* (London: Home Office).

Horon, I (2003), *Women Murdered Due to Pregnancy*, available at <http://www.thewbalchannel.com/news/2194083/detail.html>.

Hotaling, GT and Sugarman, DB (1986), 'An analysis of risk markers in husband to wife violence: The current state of knowledge', *Violence and Victims*, 1, 101–24.

House of Commons (2004), The UK Parliamentary Select Committee on Health, Minutes of evidence memorandum by Action on Elder Abuse.

Hughes, H (1992), 'Impact of spouse abuse on children of battered women', *Violence Update*, 1 August, 9–11.

Hughes, HM, Parkinson, D, and Vargo, M (1989), 'Witnessing spouse abuse and experiencing physical abuse: A double whammy?', *Journal of Family Violence*, 4(2),197–207.

Huisman, K (1996), 'Wife battering in Asian American communities. Identifying the service needs of an overlooked segment of the US population', *Violence Against Women*, 2(3), 260–83.

Humphreys, C and Thiara, RK (2003), 'Neither justice nor protection: Women's experiences of post-separation violence', *Journal of Social Welfare and Family Law*, 25, 195–214.

Independent Police Complaints Commission (June 2007), 'Domestic Violence', *Learning the Lessons Bulletin 1*.

Jacobs, J (1998), *The Links between Substance Misuse and Domestic Violence: Current knowledge and debates* (London: Alcohol Concern).

James, DV and Farnham, FR (2003), 'Stalking and serious violence', *Journal of the American Academy of Psychiatry and the Law*, 31, 432–9.

Jasinski, JL (2004), 'Pregnancy and domestic violence: A review of the literature', *Journal of Trauma, Violence and Abuse*, 5, 47–64.

Kelly, L (1999), *Violence Against Women: A briefing document on international issues and responses* (Britain: The British Council).

Kelly, Sir Christopher (2004), *Serious Case Review: Ian Huntley* (North East Lincoln-shire: ACPC). Available at <http://www.nelincs.gov.uk/socialcare/childprotection/serious-case-review.htm>.

Kropp, PR (2004), 'Some questions regarding spousal assault risk assessment', *Violence Against Women*, 10(6), 676–97.

Krug, E, Dahlberg, L, Mercy, J, Zwi, A, and Lozano, R (2002), *World Report on Violence and Health* (Geneva: World Health Organisation).

Laming, Lord (2003), *The Victoria Climbie Inquiry*, CM 5730 (London: The Stationery Office).

Lewis, R, Dobash, RP, Dobash, RE, and Cavanagh, K (2002), *Homicide in Britain: Risk factors, situational contexts and lethal intentions (interviews with men)*, Research Bulletin No 2 (Manchester: Department of Applied Social Science).

Macfarlane, JM, Campbell, JC, Wilot, S, Sachs, C, Ulrich, Y, and Xu, X (1999), 'Stalking and intimate partner femicide', *Homicide Studies*, 3(4), 300–17.

Maguire, M, Kemshall, H, Noaks, L, Wincup, E, and Sharpe, K (2001), *Risk Management of Sexual and Violent Offenders: The work of public protection panels* (London: Home Office).

McCann, JT (2000), 'A descriptive study of child and adolescent obsessional followers', *Journal of Forensic Sciences*, 45, 195.

McNeil, M (1987), 'Domestic violence: The skeleton in Tarrasoff's closet', in DJ Sonkin (ed), *Domestic Violence on Trial: Psychological and legal dimensions of family violence* (New York: Springer), 197–212.

McWilliams, M, and McKiernan, J (1993), *Bringing it Out into the Open* (Belfast: HMSO).

Meloy, JR (1996), 'Stalking (Obsessional Following): A review of some preliminary studies', *Aggression and Violent Behavior*, 1, 147–62.

Menzies, RJ, Webster, CD, and Sepejak, DS (1985), 'The dimensions of dangerousness: Evaluating the accuracy of psychometric predictions of violence among forensic patients', *Law and Human Behaviour*, 9, 49–70.

Merrill, J, and Owens, J (1986), 'Ethnic differences in self-poisoning: A comparison of Asian and White groups', *British Journal of Psychiatry*, 148, 708–12.

Mezey, GC (1997), 'Domestic violence in pregnancy', in S Bewley et al (eds), *Violence Against Women* (London: RCOG), 121.

Mezey, G, Bacchus, L, Bewley, S, and Haworth, A (2002), *An Exploration of the Prevalence, Nature and Effects of Domestic Violence in Pregnancy*, ESRC Violence Research Programme Findings (Swindon: ESRC).

Moffitt, TE, and Caspi, A (1998), 'Annotation: Implications of violence between intimate partners for child psychologists and psychiatrists', *Journal of Child Psychology and Psychiatry*, 39(2), 137–44.

Mohandei, K, Meloy, R, McGowan, M, and Williams, J (2006), 'The RECON typology of stalking: Reliability and validity based upon a large sample of North American stalkers', *Journal of Forensic Science*, 51(1), 147–55.

Morris, S, Anderson, S, and Murray, L (2002), *Stalking and Harassment in Scotland*, Crime and Criminal Justice Research Finding No 67 (Edinburgh: Scottish Executive Social Research). Available at <http://www.scotland.gov.uk/Publications/2002/11/15740/12683>.

Mullen, PE, Pathé, M, Purcell, R, and Stuart, GW (1999), 'Study of stalkers', *The American Journal of Psychiatry*, 156, 1244–9.

(2000), *Stalkers and their victims* (Cambridge: Cambridge University Press).

Newham Area Child Protection Committee (2002), *Report of Chapter 8 Review of Death of Ainlee Labonte* (Newham Area Child Protection Committee).

Nicholas, S, Kershaw, C, and Walker, A (2007), *Crime in England and Wales 2006/07*, Home Office Statistical Bulletin 11/07, (London: Home Office).

NSPCC (2003), *Making the Links: Child abuse, animal abuse and domestic violence* (London: NSPCC).

Osattin, A, and Short, L (1998), Intimate partner violence and sexual assault: A guide to training and programs for health care providers, National Centre for Injury Prevention and Control (unpublished).

Palerea, R, Zona, MA, Lane, JC, and Langhinrichsen-Rohling, J (1999), 'The dangerous nature of intimate relationship stalking: Threats, violence and associated risks', *Behavioural Science Law,* 17, 269–83.

Pease, K, and Laycock, G (1999), 'Revictimisation: Reducing the heat on hot victims' trends and issues in crime and criminal justice', Australian Institute of Criminology, paper No 128.

Police and Crime Standards Directorate (2007), *Guidance for the Use of Body-Worn Video Devices* (London: Home Office).

Povey, D (ed) (2005), *Crime in England and Wales 2003/2004: Supplementary Volume 1: Homicide and Gun Crime*, Home Office Statistical Bulletin No 02/05 (London: Home Office).

Nicholas, S, Povey, D, Walker, A, and Kershaw, C (2005), *Crime in England and Wales 2004/2005*, Home Office Statistical Bulletin No 11/05 (London: Home Office).

Richards, L (2003), *Findings From the Multi-Agency Domestic Violence Murder Reviews in London*, prepared for the ACPO Homicide Working Group (London: Metropolitan Police Service). Available at <http://www.met.police.uk/csu/index.htm>.

(2004), 'Getting away with it: A profile of the domestic violence sexual and serious offenders' (London: Metropolitan Police Service). Available at <http://www.met.police.uk/csu/index.htm>.

(2006), 'Homicide prevention: Findings from the multi-agency domestic violence homicide review', *The Journal of Homicide and Major Incident Investigation,* 2(2).

(2007), *Tactical Menu of Intervention Options for Honour Based Violence Victims and Offenders* (London: ACPO).

Richards, L and Dhothar, P (2006), *Problem Profile of Forced Marriage Incidents Reported to the MPS between April 2003 and March 2005* (London: Metropolitan Police Service).

(2007a), Honour Based Violence fact sheets—April 2007, updated from 2005 (London: Metropolitan Police Service).

(2007b), *Analysis of Murders in the Name of So-Called 'Honour' within the MPS between 1996 and 2006* (London: Metropolitan Police Service).

(2007), *Honour Based Violence Resource Document for Police Officers* (London: ACPO).

Richards, L and Hyatt, B (2007), Honour Based Violence Advice Leaflet (London: ACPO).

Robinson, AL (2003), *The Cardiff Women's Safety Unit: A multi-agency approach to domestic violence* (School of Social Sciences, Cardiff University).

(2004), *Domestic Violence MARACs (Multi-Agency Risk Assessment Conferences) for Very High-Risk Victims in Cardiff: A process and outcome evaluation* (School of Social Sciences, Cardiff University).

(2006a), *Advice, Support, Safety & Information Services Together (ASSIST): The benefits of providing assistance to victims of domestic abuse in Glasgow* (School of Social Sciences, Cardiff University).

(2006b), 'Reducing repeat victimisation among high-risk victims of domestic vio-lence: The benefits of a coordinated community response in Cardiff, Wales', *Violence Against Women: An International and Interdisciplinary Journal*, 12(8), 761–88.

Rosenfeld, B (2004), 'When stalking turns violent: Developments in the assessment of stalking risks', in M Brewster (ed), *Stalking Victims and Offenders: Treatment, interven-tion and research* (Kingston, NJ: Civic Research Institute), 98–114.

Royal College of Psychiatrists (2004), 'Mental health and growing up: Domestic violence—Its effects on children' (London: Royal College of Psychiatrists). Available at <http://www.rcpsych.ac.uk/mentalhealthinformation/ mentalhealthandgrowingup/17domesticviolence.aspx>.

Saunders, DG (1995), 'Prediction of wife assault', in JC Campbell (ed), *Assessing Dangerousness: Violence by sexual offenders, batterers and child abusers* (Thousand Oaks, CA: Sage), 68–95.

Saunders, H (2004), *Twenty-Nine Child Homicides. Lessons still to learn on domestic vio-lence and child protection* (London: Women's Aid).

Sheridan, L (2001), 'The course and nature of stalking: An in-depth victim survey', *Journal of Threat Assessment*, 1, 61–79.

Sheridan, L and Boon, J (2002), 'Stalker typologies: Implications for law enforcement', in J Boon and L Sheridan (eds), *Stalking and Psychosexual Obsession: Psychological perspectives for prevention, policing and treatment* (Chichester: Wiley), 63–82.

Sheridan, L, and Davies, GM (2001), 'Violence and the prior victim-stalker relation-ship', *Criminal Behaviour and Mental Health*, 11, 102–16.

Sheridan, L, Gillett, R and Davies, GM (2002), 'Perceptions and prevalence of stalking in a male sample', Psychology, Crime and Law, 8, 289–310.

Sheridan, L and Grant, T (2007), 'Is cyberstalking different?', *Psychology, Crime and Law*, 13, 627–40.

Sidebottom, P, and Heron J, (2006), 'Child maltreatment in the "children of the nine-ties": A cohort study of risk factors', *Child Abuse and Neglect*, 30, 497–522.

Sonkin, DJ (1987), 'The assessment of court-mandated male batterers', in DJ Sonkin (ed), *Domestic Violence on Trial: Psychological and legal dimensions of family violence* (New York: Springer), 174–96.

Sonkin, DJ, Martin, D, and Walker, L (1985), *The Male Batterer: A treatment approach* (New York: Springer).

Stanko, E (1990), *Everyday Violence,* (London: Pandora Press).

(2000), 'The day to count: A snapshot of the impact of domestic violence in the UK', *Criminal Justice*, 1(2).

Stanko, EA, Kielinger, V, Paterson, S, Richards, L, Crisp, D, and Marsland, L (2003), 'Grounded crime prevention: Responding to and understanding hate crime', in H Kury and J Obergell-Fuchs (eds), *Crime Prevention: New approaches* (Germany: Weiser Ring), 123–53.

Steadman, HJ, Mulvey, EP, Monahan, J, Robbins, PC, Appelbaum, PS, Grisso, T, et al (1998), 'Violence by people discharged from acute psychiatric inpatient facilities and by others in the same neighborhoods', *Archives of General Psychiatry*, 55, 393–401.

Straus, MA (1990), 'The national family violence surveys', in MA Straus and RJ Gelles (eds), *Physical Violence in American Families: Risk factors and adaptation to violence in 8,145 families* (New Brunswick, NJ: Transaction Publishing), 3–16.

Stuart, EP and Campbell, JC (1989), 'Assessment of patterns of dangerousness with battered women', *Issues in Mental Health Nursing*, 10, 245–60.

Thompson, M, Saltzman, L, and Johnson, H (2001), 'Risk factors for physical injury among women assaulted by current or former spouses', *Violence Against Women*, 7(8), 886–99.

Toch, H (1969), *Violent Men: An inquiry into the psychology of violence* (Chicago: Aldine).

Walby, S (2004), *The Cost of Domestic Violence* (London: DTI). Available at <http://www.womenandequalityunit.gov.uk>.

Walby, S and Allen, J (2004), *Domestic Violence, Sexual Assault and Stalking: Findings from the British Crime Survey*, Home Office Research Study No 276 (London: Home Office).

Walby, S and Myhill, A (2000a), *Assessing and Managing the Risk of Domestic Violence* (London: Crime Reduction Research Series).

(2000b), *Reducing Domestic Violence...What Works? Assessing and managing the risk of domestic violence*, Policing and Reducing Crime Unit Briefing Notes (London: Home Office).

Walker, LE (1979), *The Battered Woman* (New York: Harper and Row).

Walker, A, Kershaw, C, and Nicholas, S (2006), *Crime in England and Wales 2005/06*, Home Office Statistical Bulletin 12/06 (London: Home Office).

Websdale, N (1999), *Understanding Domestic Homicide* (Boston: Northeastern University Press).

Websdale, N (2000), *Lethality Assessment Tools: A critical analysis* (VAWnet, National Resource Centre on Domestic Violence).

Weisz, AN, Tolman, RM, and Saunders, D (2000), 'Assessing the risk of severe domestic violence: The importance of survivor's predictions', *Journal of Interpersonal Violence*, 15(1), 75–90.

Wilding, S (2006), 'TVCP—Domestic Violence Enforcement Campaign', presented at the ESRC/Royal Statistical Society Seminar on 'Developing indicators and statistics on gender based violence', London, May 2006.

Williamson, E (2001), 'Domestic matters', *Community Care*, 20–26 September: pp 22–3.

Wilson, M, and Daly, M (1993), 'Spousal homicide risk and estrangement', *Violence and Victims*, 8, 3–16.

Women's National Commission (2003), *Unlocking the Secret: Women open the door on domestic violence. Findings from consultations with survivors* (Women's National Commission).

World Health Organisation (2002), *Elder Abuse: A guide for primary health care workers* (Geneva: WHO).

Wright, A (2002), *Policing: An introduction to concepts and practice* (Devon: Willan).

Yllo, K (1999), 'The silence surrounding sexual violence: The issue of marital rape and the challenges it poses for the Duluth model', in MF Shepard and EL Pence (eds), *Co-ordinating Community Responses to Domestic Violence: Lessons from Duluth and Beyond* (Thousand Oaks, CA: Sage).

Young, H, Richards, L, and McCusker, S (2006), 'Profiling mentally disordered homicide offenders to inform investigative decision making and intervention strategies', *The Journal of Homicide and Major Incident Investigation*, 2(1).

Index